T0399862

Debating Relational Psychoanalysis

In *Debating Relational Psychoanalysis*, Jon Mills provides an historical record of the debates that had taken place for nearly two decades on his critique of the relational school, including responses from his critics.

Since he initiated his critique, relational psychoanalysis has become an international phenomenon with proponents worldwide. This book hopes that further dialogue may not only lead to conciliation, but more optimistically, that relational theory may be inspired to improve upon its theoretical edifice, both conceptually and clinically, as well as develop technical parameters to praxis that help guide and train new clinicians to sharpen their own theoretical orientation and therapeutic efficacy. Because of the public exchanges in writing and at professional symposiums, these debates have historical significance in the development of the psychoanalytic movement as a whole simply due to their contentiousness and proclivity to question cherished assumptions, both old and new. In presenting this collection of his work, and those responses of his critics, Mills argues that psychoanalysis may only advance through critique and creative refinement, and this requires a deconstructive praxis within the relational school itself.

Debating Relational Psychoanalysis will be of interest to psychoanalysts of all orientations, psychotherapists, mental health workers, psychoanalytic historians, philosophical psychologists, and the broad disciplines of humanistic, phenomenological, existential, and analytical psychology.

Jon Mills, PsyD, PhD, ABPP is a philosopher, psychoanalyst, and clinical psychologist. He is a faculty member in the postgraduate programs in psychoanalysis and psychotherapy, Gordon F. Derner School of Psychology, Adelphi University, emeritus professor of psychology and psychoanalysis, Adler Graduate Professional School, and runs a mental health corporation in Ontario, Canada. Recipient of numerous awards for his scholarship, he is the author and editor of over 20 books in psychoanalysis, philosophy, psychology, and cultural studies.

"Imagine a book on psychoanalysis that gets your heart racing and your own critical mind aroused into action! Jon Mills and his critics hold nothing back in their critique of the relational model and of each other. The reader has a front seat to a theoretical and practical boxing match that vitalizes the conversation, sharpens our theories and practices, prompting further debate and dialogue. In this provocative, deeply stirring and academically rigorous collection, we are challenged to be as thoughtful and thorough in our own theorizing and practices, as is Jon Mills and his contributors. This is a text that clarifies, informs, and ultimately inspires."

Roy Barsness, PhD, Professor, The Seattle School of Theology & Psychology and the Brookhaven Institute of Psychoanalysis—author of *Core Competencies in Relational Psychoanalysis*

"This is an exhilarating, refreshing, and brave volume. Why? Because Jon Mills is not afraid to challenge dogma and theoretical hegemony, to ask the reader to think with (or for that matter, against) him. Mills' commanding and passionate rhetorical and intellectual skills shine through as he engages both his sophisticated interlocutors, and the vexing conundrums and aporias at the heart of contemporary psychoanalytic relational theorizing. The best kind of psychoanalytic journey, *Debating Relational Psychoanalysis*, offers a vigorous, rigorous, and ultimately compassionate and redemptive conversation between Mills, the critic, and Mills' critics, in which familiar thought is tested, and one's truths are turned over, maybe tossed aside, maybe reaffirmed with renewed (and newly philosophically grounded) conviction."

Jill Gentile, PhD, NYU Postdoctoral Program in Psychotherapy and Psychoanalysis—author of *Feminine Law*

"Jon Mills tells us "There is nothing more exciting than a clash of ideas, except for, perhaps, sex." I think that says it all. His controversial critique of Relational Psychoanalysis is provocative on many grounds. And the often-heated responses by his critics reveal both intellectual differences and personal affronts. In the end, it is the reader who benefits from this unique dialogue between intellectuals nimbly defending their own ideas. It will force you to think harder, and feel more deeply, not only about what you believe, but also how you practice."

Karen J. Maroda, PhD, ABPP—author of *Psychodynamic Techniques*

Debating Relational Psychoanalysis

Jon Mills and his Critics

Jon Mills

Routledge
Taylor & Francis Group
LONDON AND NEW YORK

First published 2020
by Routledge
2 Park Square, Milton Park, Abingdon, Oxon OX14 4RN

and by Routledge
52 Vanderbilt Avenue, New York, NY 10017

Routledge is an imprint of the Taylor & Francis Group, an informa business

© 2020 Jon Mills

The right of Jon Mills to be identified as author of this work has been asserted by him in accordance with sections 77 and 78 of the Copyright, Designs and Patents Act 1988.

All rights reserved. No part of this book may be reprinted or reproduced or utilized in any form or by any electronic, mechanical, or other means, now known or hereafter invented, including photocopying and recording, or in any information storage or retrieval system, without permission in writing from the publishers.

Trademark notice: Product or corporate names may be trademarks or registered trademarks, and are used only for identification and explanation without intent to infringe.

British Library Cataloguing-in-Publication Data
A catalogue record for this book is available from the British Library

Library of Congress Cataloging-in-Publication Data
Names: Mills, Jon, 1964- author.
Title: Debating relational psychoanalysis : Jon Mills and his critics / Jon Mills.
Identifiers: LCCN 2020001325 (print) | LCCN 2020001326 (ebook) | ISBN 9780367902070 (paperback) | ISBN 9780367902063 (hardback) | ISBN 9781003023104 (ebook)
Subjects: LCSH: Psychoanalysis. | Interpersonal relations--Psychological aspects.
Classification: LCC BF173 .M52725 2020 (print) | LCC BF173 (ebook) | DDC 150.19/5--dc23
LC record available at https://lccn.loc.gov/2020001325
LC ebook record available at https://lccn.loc.gov/2020001326

ISBN: 978-0-367-90206-3 (hbk)
ISBN: 978-0-367-90207-0 (pbk)
ISBN: 978-1-003-02310-4 (ebk)

Typeset in Times New Roman
by Nova Techset Private Limited, Bengaluru & Chennai, India

Contents

Foreword

Arnold D. Richards

Most would agree that *Object Relations in Psychoanalytic Theory*, a book published in 1983, marked the beginning of relational psychoanalysis. It was written by two young psychologists, Stephen Mitchell and Jay Greenberg. They both had been trained at the William Alanson White Institute and were excluded from membership in the American Psychoanalytic Association, the dominant psychoanalytic association in the United States.

Greenberg believed their approach had prevailed and become part of the American psychoanalytic mainstream. He did not believe that relational psychoanalysis should become a movement. In contrast, Mitchell (1988) contends that drive and relational thinking cannot work together "in a smooth and consistent manner which is mutually enhancing" (p. 53).

Mills is not alone in criticizing Mitchell's portrayal of contemporary psychoanalysis as divided between perspectives that are based in Freud's drive theory and those more relationally based. This dichotomy Mitchell presents us with is, I think, misleading (Bachant & Richards, 1993; Bachant, Lynch, & Richards, 1995). Mills agrees that the dichotomy between inherent meaning and meaning negotiated through interaction is false.

I believe, and Mills would concur, that a close reading of Freud, especially the case studies written at the height of his drive-id psychical phase, persuades us there has not been a radical shift from a drive to a relational model: what we see then and now in contemporary psychoanalysis are different ways of integrating drive and relational considerations. Two common problems with Mitchell and the approach of other relationalists is that they are responding to a misrepresentation of Freudian practice and an oversimplified view of Freud's theoretical system—offering Freud's tension reduction drive-discharge model as the essential Freudian theory.

Why would Mitchell go out on a theoretical limb with his understanding of the relational model as a radical shift? I would argue that his purpose was political, to establish a movement with a set of principles disjunctive from contemporary Freudian psychoanalysis; his aim was to be, in Martin Bergmann's terms, a modifier rather than an extender, or, perhaps closer, to be a heretic. Greenberg, in contrast, felt that relational ideas were helpful in our effort to refine psychoanalytic process and psychoanalytic interaction—the role of the analyst in the dyad, but that relational psychoanalysis is evolutionary, not revolutionary.

Another context for reading the contributions in this book is to consider Irwin Hoffman's (1991) view that the "fundamental and still germinal model in psychoanalytic theory and practice" is not a shift from the drive model to the relational model but "from a positivist model of understanding the psychoanalytic situation to a constructivist model" (p. 135). Hoffman likes Mitchell's hearty investment in the notion of a paradigm shift, and tends to exaggerate the novelty of his own views. He asserts that in the constructivist approach, "the personal participation of the analyst in the process is considered to have a continuous effect on what he or she understands about himself or herself and about the patient in the interaction" (p. 136). I do not dispute the fact that the relational orientation has made a contribution in enlarging horizons and redirecting the aims of psychoanalytic inquiry, but Hoffman's description of relational process is not so different from what most of us do and what most psychoanalysts have been doing all along.

Another context for this publication is provided by three myths: The myth of the drive-based, nonrelational Freudian analyst (Mitchell & Greenberg), the myth of the isolated mind (Stolorow & Atwood), and the myth of the silent Freudian analyst (many relationalists' points of view). I first discussed and debunked some of these myths in a review of Mitchell's *Relational Concepts in Psychoanalysis* written with Janet Bachant.

The myth of the silent analyst is pervasive among many relationalists. In an issue of the *Round Robin*, there was an exchange between Mitchell and me about the silent analyst. The title of my contribution was "Squeaky Chairs & Straw Persons." It was in response to the paper by Mitchell in which he told about a patient who had an analyst who was silent but the patient would infer what his analyst might be thinking by listening to squeaks made by his chair. Mitchell, Ghent, Brecht, and Summers et al. also participated in the exchange. We discussed whether Freudian analysts talk less than relational analysts, and whether the differences between the two are a matter of theory, styles, or something else. Someone offered that the Freudian analysts who came from Europe before the war said little because they were concerned about their accents and fluency in English. There is an anecdote, apocryphal perhaps, about Otto Isakower, who came from Berlin, whose analysand asserted that he did not say anything for two years. Finally, the analysand summoned up his courage, and asked Dr. Isakower, "How am I doing?" Isakower responded, "Average."

Wilson (1995) writes about the finality with which Mitchell invoked the Kuhnian concept of a scientific revolution to support his argument for "a dichotomized world of relational theories in opposition to drive theories" (p. 13). According to Wilson, Kuhn specified the conditions for the abandonment of a paradigm: "(a) A new hypothesis emerges so that the old paradigm no longer has a special status. (b) The new hypotheses are more aesthetic and promise to solve more problems economically. (c) The proponents of a new paradigm formulate new techniques and arguments that win general acceptance in the scientific community" (p. 13). Wilson argues the Mitchell's version of relational psychoanalysis failed to meet these criteria. I would agree in regard to A and B, but it could be argued that in the United States, and perhaps in Israel, relational psychoanalysis has gained acceptance in the scientific community. Wilson (1995) writes, "When psychoanalysis is dichotomized and relational analysts identify as 'orthodoxy' anything that is not explicitly relational in nature, strains can be recognized not as a Kuhnian paradigm shift but rather as a regression away from progress by a principled critique among a plurality of voices and positions" (p. 15).

What works best in the end is an empirical question. I think that deepening our understanding of how problematic these divisions are relates to the effort represented by this book. I would suggest that we look for instances of collegial interactions when we read the exchanges between Mills and his critics in this volume. Mills' critiques should be welcomed and considered.

References

Bachant, J. L., Lynch, A. A., & Richards, A. D. (1995). Relational models in psychoanalytic theory. *Psychoanalytic Psychology*, 12(1): 71–87.

Bachant, J.L., & Richards, A.D. (1993). Relational concepts in psychoanalysis: An integration by Stephen A. Mitchell. *Psychoanalytic Dialogues*, 3(3), 431–460.

Hoffman. (1991). *Ritual and Spontaneity in the Psychoanalytic Process*. Hillsdale, NJ: Analytic Press.

Mitchell, S.A. (1988). *Relational Concepts in Psychoanalysis: An Integration*. Cambridge, MA: Harvard University Press.

Wilson, A. (1995). Mapping the mind in relational psychoanalysis. *Psychoanalytic Psychology*, 12(1): 9–29.

Acknowledgments

The publisher, Kate Hawes, has been a long supporter of my scholarship and I wish to thank her immensely for all she has done and for advancing psychoanalytic publishing through the Routledge imprint. I want to also thank her impressive array of staff who have helped me over the years in various production and administrative duties including Kristopher Spring, Charles Bath, Katherine McCarty, Susannah Frearson, and Heather Evans. I also wish to thank the American Psychological Association for granting permission to have the following articles reproduced in this volume:

Jon Mills (2005). A critique of relational psychoanalysis. *Psychoanalytic Psychology*, 22(2), 155–188.

Jon Mills (2006). A response to my critics. *Psychoanalytic Psychology*, 23(1), 197–209.

Marilyn S. Jacobs (2006). Assertions of therapeutic excess: A reply to Mills (2005). *Psychoanalytic Psychology*, 23(1), 189–192.

Robert D. Stolorow, George E. Atwood, & Donna M. Orange (2006). Contextualizing is not nullifying: Reply to Mills (2005). *Psychoanalytic Psychology*, 23(1), 184–188.

Stuart A. Pizer (2006). "Neither Fish nor Flesh": Commentary on Jon Mills (2005). *Psychoanalytic Psychology*, 23(1), 193–196.

Special thanks to Tracy Morgan and New Books in Psychoanalysis, from the New Books Network, for interviewing me on her podcast after my book *Conundrums* was published, which was aired on December 19, 2012: https://newbooksnetwork.com/jon-mills-conundrums-a-critique-of-contemporary-psychoanalysis-routledge-2011/ I also thank the Psychotherapy and Counselling Federation of Australia Inc. (PACFA) for publishing my 2016 article, "Fine-Tuning Problems in Relational Psychoanalysis: New Directions in Theory and Praxis," *Psychotherapy and Counselling Journal of Australia (PACJA)*, which was posted online on September 1, 2016: https://pacja.org.au/?p=2998

I am especially grateful to the co-editors of *Psychoanalytic Perspectives*, Steven Kuchuck and Rachel Sopher, who published the conference proceedings of *The Relational Approach and its Critics: A Conference with Dr. Jon Mills*, held on February 13, 2015 at Bar-Ilan University in Israel, and for permissions granted by the © National Institute for the Psychotherapies, www.nipinst.org, reprinted by permission of Taylor & Francis Ltd, http://www.tandfonline.com on behalf of the National Institute for the Psychotherapies, for reproducing the following articles:

Aner Govrin (2017). Introduction to the relational approach and its critics: A conference with Dr. Jon Mills. *Psychoanalytic Perspectives*, 14(3), 309–312.

Boaz Shalgi (2017). Relational psychoanalysis and the concepts of truth and meaning: Response to Jon Mills. *Psychoanalytic Perspectives*, 14(3), 346–349.

Chana Ullman (2017). Straw men, stereotypes, and constructive dialogue: A response to Mills's criticism of the relational approach. *Psychoanalytic Perspectives*, 14(3), 336–340.

Jon Mills (2017). Challenging relational psychoanalysis: A critique of postmodernism and analyst self-disclosure. *Psychoanalytic Perspectives*, 14(3), 313–335.

Jon Mills (2018). Challenging relational psychoanalysis: A reply to my critics. *Psychoanalytic Perspectives*, 15(1), 2–9.

Liran Razinsky (2017). Psychoanalysis and postmodernism: A response to Dr. Jon Mills's "Challenging Relational Psychoanalysis: A Critique of Postmodernism and Analyst Self-Disclosure." *Psychoanalytic Perspectives*, 14(3), 356–363.

Merav Roth (2017). Projective identification and relatedness: A Kleinian perspective. *Psychoanalytic Perspectives*, 14(3), 350–355.

Shlomit Yadlin-Gadot (2017). On multiple epistemologies in theory and practice: A response to Jon Mills's "Challenging Relational Psychoanalysis: A Critique of Postmodernism and Analyst Self-Disclosure." *Psychoanalytic Perspectives*, 14(3), 341–345.

Steven Kuchuck, & Rachel Sopher (2017). Relational psychoanalysis out of context: Response to Jon Mills. *Psychoanalytic Perspectives*, 14(3), 364–376.

Author

Jon Mills, PsyD, PhD, ABPP is a philosopher, psychoanalyst, and clinical psychologist. He is a faculty member of the postgraduate programs in psychoanalysis and psychotherapy, Gordon F. Derner School of Psychology, Adelphi University, emeritus professor of psychology and psychoanalysis at Adler Graduate Professional School in Toronto, and runs a mental health corporation in Ontario, Canada. Recipient of numerous awards for his scholarship, he is the author and/or editor of over twenty books in psychoanalysis, philosophy, psychology, and cultural studies including *Inventing God* (Routledge, 2017); *Underworlds* (Routledge, 2014); *Conundrums: A Critique of Contemporary Psychoanalysis* (Routledge, 2012); *Origins: On the Genesis of Psychic Reality* (McGill-Queens University Press, 2010); *Treating Attachment Pathology* (Rowman & Littlefield, 2005); *The Unconscious Abyss: Hegel's Anticipation of Psychoanalysis* (State University of New York Press, 2002); and *The Ontology of Prejudice* (Rodopi, 1997).

Introduction

(Re)visioning relational psychoanalysis

The specific intent of this book is twofold: (1) to provide an historical record in one volume of the debates that had taken place for nearly two decades on my critique of the relational movement, including all the responses from my critics; and (2) to extend an olive branch to relational practitioners in the hopes that further dialogue may not only lead to conciliation, but more optimistically, that relational theory may be inspired to improve upon its theoretical edifice, both conceptually and clinically, as well as develop technical parameters to praxis that help guide and train new clinicians to sharpen their own theoretical orientation and therapeutic efficacy.

Since I started my critique, relational psychoanalysis, in its contemporary reliance on the notions of intersubjectivity, attachment theory, phenomenology, systems and field theory, and postmodernism, has blossomed from being a homegrown, United States East coast club to an international phenomenon with chapters in North America, Central America, South America, Europe, the Middle East, and Australia. One cannot deny the appeal and impact this movement has had on practitioners worldwide, and in a multitude of cultures and languages, without living in bad faith. The sheer number of professionals attracted to this school and style of thought empirically speaks for itself. In short, it's the hottest thing since sliced bread. So we must ask, Why? Although I address this in a number of ways throughout my writings, in retrospect, the mass appeal is obvious: we all want and value relationships. So, it is not unsurprising that many mental health professionals from diverse educational backgrounds would gravitate toward this perspective, and without having to observe orthodoxy or be formally ordained a "psychoanalyst." This level of inclusivity is historically unparalleled in psychoanalytic studies.

The reader may not be aware of the extent to these debates on the critique and value of relational psychoanalysis, nor on their divisiveness and acrimony, simply because the literature is so diverse and sprawling; one cannot keep up on every detail or burgeoning controversy unless you are attuned to these group microdynamics, identified with the movement, and/or subscribe to the copious publications the relational literature has spawned. Also, like fads, historical memory has a tendency to bathe in Lethe, the river of forgetfulness. But it may not be inappropriate to say that because of the public exchanges in writing and at professional conferences, these debates have historical significance in the development of the psychoanalytic movement as a whole simply due to their contentiousness and proclivity to question cherished assumptions, both old and new. And not unlike the early political skirmishes that led to the classical split from Adler, Stekel, Tausk, Jung, Groddeck, Rank, Ferenczi, and other pioneering thinkers, not to mention the historic Controversial Discussions over the Melanie Klein/Anna Freud debates that led to the formation of the British Independents, later followed by the French school, self psychology, the re-emergence of attachment paradigms, and most recently, neuropsychoanalysis, it is not necessarily a bad thing to challenge the conventional wisdom of our ancestors and new paragons that boast better approaches to theory and practice. After all, any discipline may only advance through critique and creative refinement. Although I am no longer interested in critiquing the relational school, and offer this volume as a means of putting matters to rest, it is my expressed intent that a continuation of critique and dialogue may only lead to improvements in relational thinking, especially with the tradition's recent turn toward self-critique and de-idealization of theory.

Controversy surrounding my critique

I have been referred to as "the most important and profound spokesman to critique the relational psychoanalytic movement" (Govrin, 2017, p. 309). How I got this epitaph is likely based on my original 2005 article that turned into my 2012 book, *Conundrums: A Critique of Contemporary Psychoanalysis*, which one reviewer called "a stimulating work that will enrage and provoke its readers" (Ridenour, 2012, p. 9). I won a Gradiva Award for Best Article given by the National Association for the Advancement of Psychoanalysis (NAAP) in New York City, and later a Goethe Award for Best Book by the Canadian Psychological Association. The book received an outpouring of reviews, which led to a podcast interview on *New Books in Psychoanalysis*, and eventually an international conference held in Israel, the conference proceedings of which were later published in a relational journal. Let me tell you why I wrote that book.

After receiving my first doctorate in clinical psychology and initiating psychoanalytic training (having been supervised by Merton Gill), I was given a full fellowship at Vanderbilt University to complete my PhD in philosophy. Although I still read canonical texts in psychoanalysis, I was virtually learning a new discipline and had engrossed myself in classical readings in the history of philosophy, eventually specializing in late Modern philosophy, German Idealism, psychoanalysis, and the Continental tradition. During this time of study, I could not follow all the new developments in psychoanalysis due to my other commitments, but because I was introduced to Stephen Mitchell during my first graduate studies, and had read some of his early books, I decided to reach out to him. Through our correspondence, I was invited to write two book reviews for his then newly founded journal, *Psychoanalytic Dialogues*. When I began to read the books sent to me, I was a Fulbright scholar in the departments of philosophy at the University of Toronto and York University where I was completing research for my dissertation. Then Steve tragically died.

After I received my PhD, I began to immerse myself in the contemporary psychoanalytic literature I had neglected to read over the previous five years. This is when I grew increasingly aware of how various intersubjective and relational authors were borrowing concepts and terms from philosophy, often relying on secondary sources and annexing ideas out of context and without following protocols for traditional scholarship I was accustomed to expect from my formal training in philosophy. The broad summaries of key figures in the history of philosophy without bothering to consult the original textual sources was particularly an irritant, as I had been trained this was poor if not substandard scholarship. In graduate school, I had a very profound awakening and learned a most invaluable lesson—what it means to be a scholar is to always engage original texts. Unlike psychology, where the convention is to summarize what other commentators have said about key sources, the humanities, and particularly philosophy, requires that original texts be consulted, and often in their native language, in order to determine for oneself what a theorist really said rather than relying on hearsay from a secondary expositor who may be distorting the meaning of what was actually conveyed by the original author, hence portraying an *explanandum* as an *explanans*, inaccurately I may add. For this reason, I came to adopt a scholarly attitude that if original texts are not consulted and referenced directly, then we have no real epistemological means of knowing if one's interpretation of theory is plausible, let alone logical or empirically accurate or verifiable, hence of merit or is correct.

After digesting the contemporary literature, including the proliferation of studies on attachment and neuroscience, I started writing. I felt identified as a relational practitioner given that is how I saw myself practicing in the office (based on my training in Chicago where interpersonal and self psychological perspectives were dominant, not to mention the contemporary writings at that time), but not without maintaining the academic scholarly standards I had acquired in my formal philosophical training. After consuming a wide swath of works in the contemporary psychoanalytic literature, I published the 2005 controversial paper, "A Critique of Relational Psychoanalysis," published in the APA Division 39: Psychoanalysis journal, *Psychoanalytic Psychology*. Little did I know what landmine I was stepping into, not to mention the politics behind the scenes that had been brewing before publishing this first critique paper.

I was surprised at first how this essay had immediately launched a storm. Later, I realized how going after sacred cows was not appreciated by many political camps within Division 39 who identified themselves as relational: this paper was an unwelcome trespass—critique was off-limits. Now, it is taught in psychoanalytic training environments throughout the world.

After the deluge, the editor of the journal had contacted me requesting my reply to many prominent senior analysts' responses to my article which were quite critical, some even scathing if not scandalous, including being accused of ethics violations and committing illegal libelous acts. My response escalated matters and this led to a coup within the Division 39 governance where I was eventually censored by the Publications Committee from providing further written commentary to my critics (see Mills, 2012, pp. 141–158 for details). Although Neil Altman (2007), Jody Messler Davies (2007), and Irwin Hoffman (2007) were allowed to critique me in professional public space, I was not allowed a response. This provoked the editor, Joseph Reppen, to publish the following response to the censorship:

> The preceding Commentaries are published as a consequence of a condition demanded by Drs. Altman, Davies, and Hoffman, and agreed upon by the Publications Committee of the Division of Psychoanalysis, that there be no response by Dr. Mills to their Commentaries published in *Psychoanalytic Psychology*. This stricture may not be in keeping with the spirit of openness of this journal under my editorship. Nonetheless, readers are free to draw their own conclusions as to the appropriateness of this condition. (Reppen, 2007, p. 406)

So there you have it. Why did I write *Conundrums*? Out of moral principle. Because I was silenced and not allowed democratic free speech within an established professional and academic organization, I felt compelled to conduct further research and expand my critique of relational psychoanalysis at a more in-depth level. And the rest is history.

Without getting into all of the gossip or betraying professional confidences and personal secrets, suffice it to say that I was banished from the relational community. The alliances I had forged and the so-called authentic relationships I thought I had developed all but vanished. The line was drawn in the sand. The relational enclave would not see me as their own, but rather as an enemy. Fortunately, I have a thick skin as I have always viewed myself as an independent thinker. A groupie I could never be. But many respectable and highly influential people came out of the woodwork to support me and helped to advance my career, for which I will be forever grateful and deeply appreciative. This was my crash course in psychoanalytic politics. Ironically, if Steve Mitchell were alive today, we likely would be friends, because I sensed a genuine philosophical spirit in our brief correspondence that was open to critique and criticism, or he would not have gone on to spur new directions in psychoanalytic discourse.

I must report that Altman, Davies, and Hoffman did not give their permission to have their 2007 Commentaries on my critique reproduced in this volume. The reader must refer to these articles independently in the published issue of *Psychoanalytic Psychology* (Issue 2, April) in order to read what they actually said in print. It was only for wanting to cull together the complete historical record and in full transparency that I invited their inclusion in the first place. I hope any bad feelings they harbor will come to pass.

Similarly, another related controversy arose during the production of this book when it was decided by the press that certain portions of my original 2005 critique article and my 2006 reply to my critics needed to be modified and/or cut due to potential legal liability concerns despite the fact that the original papers underwent a blind peer review process and were published in a leading APA journal. Not only were substantial controversial discussions omitted here, but the tone of my critique has softened. Therefore, readers will have to consult the original articles in order to fully savor the extent of the controversy. It is comforting to know how a free exchange of ideas can become legalized. Perhaps this is a good example of why Dick the Butcher said: "The first thing we do, let's kill all the lawyers."[1]

After *Conundrums* was published, an international conference was organized and held in Israel in 2015 titled, *The Relational Approach and its Critics: A Conference with Dr. Jon Mills*, which was sponsored by the Israeli Forum of the International Association for Relational Psychoanalysis and Psychotherapy (IARPP) and the Department of Hermeneutics and Cultural Studies at Bar-Ilan University. The conference proceedings were then later published in 2017 in the journal, *Psychoanalytic Perspectives*. My article from that conference received yet another Gradiva Award from NAAP in 2018. As you will see in this book, the responses to my lectures at this conference by several panelists were quite sophisticated and challenging, hence providing their own critiques of my critique. As a result, there was genuine dialogue and new friendships emerged, which is what the true spirit of relationality is all about.

The relational turn toward self-critique

Before the Israeli conference and before I was aware of the turn toward self-critique in some quarters of the relational community, I was deemed a principle critic of relational theory and practice. I always viewed myself as offering a critique from *within* the relational community when in fact I am seen as an outsider, like some Freudian in the closet. Yet despite my penchant for classical theory, by today standards I practice as a relationalist, at least in the sense of what is now dubbed "small r" rather than "big R" relational practice (Kuchuck, 2018). It was not until I examined the two edited volumes by Lewis Aron, Sue Grand, and Joyce Slochower, *De-Idealizing Relational Theory: A Critique from Within* (2018a), and *Decentering Relational Theory: A Comparative Critique* (2018b), that I realized I was airbrushed out of relational self-critique. In these two volumes, I am mentioned only once by Donnel Stern (2018, p. 30) who alerts the reader that he will *not* be "considering the philosophical critiques of relational psychoanalysis that have been mounted in recent years by North Americans (e.g., Mills, 2005c, 2012)." It is also an inconvenient truth that I am barely mentioned in reviews that I self-identify as a relational practitioner despite my numerous pronouncements otherwise (Mills, 2005a, 2005b, 2005c, 2012, 2017b). Even most recently I am mischaracterized, set up for a gross misrepresentation of my actual views, and pilloried by a posterchild of the relational scene (Rozmarin, 2019), presumably due to political partisanship, to which I provide a corrective (Mills, 2020).

Despite the fact that I have been praised by some relational authors for vitalizing the ongoing conversation around critique in efforts to sharpen relational theory (Barsness, 2018, p. 321), and new postrelational critics have emerged since I initiated my earlier critiques (Govrin, 2016; Brown, 2017; Mills, 2017a; Axelrod, Naso, & Rosenberg, 2018), the relational community has largely sought to marginalize and displace me by simply ignoring my writings. I suppose this is not to be unexpected, as no one likes a gadfly. But this unfortunately draws into question the notions of integrity, honesty, and ethics (Naso, 2010).

For example, in the recent turn toward self-critique, arguments made by me years ago are presented as fresh ideas by relational authors, such as the need to engage in "self-reflection," "critical self-examination" (see Aron, Grand, & Slochower, 2018a, p. 1), and observe how idealization of theory is a trope based on group overidentification and transference to theory. The notion of "excess" and "exaggerating difference" between other schools is now offered as counterarguments to critics of relationality (Slochower, 2018, p. 8), not to mention the indebtedness the relational school has to earlier psychoanalytic ideas they have historically inherited. And what about the analyst's epistemology? "Might we overlook our patient's need for us to *know*, to comfortably hold our authority" (Slochower, 2018, p. 20)? Yes, a point I have made repeatedly (Cf. most recently Mills, 2017b, p. 318), as well as questioning the ideal of mutuality and a lack of "self-restraint" on "speaking freely" (Slochower, 2018, p. 22). Examining the notions of "radical equality" (Mark, 2018, p. 81), decentering the unconscious (S. Stern, 2018), criticisms of relational scholarship and theory (D.B. Stern, 2018), and a critique of dissociation, multiplicity, and self-state theory (Orange, 2018) are topics I have covered at length (Mills, 2005a, 2010, 2012). These omissions represent, at minimum, shoddy scholarship and could be viewed by some as bordering on plagiarism, even if unintended or unconsciously informed, although, in my mind, it speaks to how selective our group identifications can be. In the spirit of the Frankfurt School of Critical Theory, what Marx called "ruthless critique," has been replaced by friendly interviews and surveys of past narratives noting minor differences that are peppered with self-congratulatory, appreciative ceremonials among friends. That is not what I had in mind. What I had envisioned as radical reengagement via wrestling with many of the key assumptions and tenets of relational theory and praxis has still to materialize. But with this turn toward critical self-analysis opens certain clearings that were heavily occluded and resisted against in the past by earlier relational founders (as is typical of psychoanalytic history), and ushers in new possibilities for rigor and improvement. This new pronounced attitude of openness to self-critique should also include any critique, as critique should not be parochial or based on a political following due to the fact that criticism of ideas is open to universal opinion and worthy of analysis regardless of identification with a particular psychoanalytic school.

The future of relational psychoanalysis

Let us set aside the caricatures of the relational analyst, what I have admittedly raised in past writings to highlight differences, as I did with the caricatures of classical practitioners, hence emulating a style largely adopted by many relational authors. As Joyce Slochower (2018) currently observes is the popular opinion of relational critics:

> We've been depicted as clinically impulsive, self-referential, superficial, foreclosing, or sidestepping reflective space. These are caricatures that exaggerate and distort. But in the absence of clinical thoughtfulness, they're the doors we're vulnerable to walking through. (p. 20)

What is interesting for me to notice in my own self-reflections on my previous valuations is the fact that I have been more critical of the relational community's lack of its own theory versus clinical attitudes, sensibility, and technique. I have in fact praised the liberation of relational praxis to classical technique, at least how it has been presented (if not distorted) in the literature. The liberation of customizing an intersubjective fit in the analytic dyad between two subjects is essential in a successful treatment rather than the superimposition of a structural model of rules or mechanical expectations and events that both participants must conform to before professional work is commenced. This is not the real world of lived experience, conflict and desire, nor the needs of the masses. Relational treatment parameters have opened up a new and vital space for attracting and treating the contemporary public which classical models have failed to achieve. Having said this, and before offering caveats and concerns, I wish to reflect on the future (re)visioning of relational psychoanalysis and what it may potentially achieve if sufficient attention is paid to a refashioning of its core principles, values, and developmental trajectory as a new psychoanalytic school of thought.

I do not think traditional psychoanalysis has a prayer's chance in hell of surviving in the future in North America. It simply boils down to money and time (neither of which are forthcoming in today's world for social collectives), but we are also faced with a millennial and postmillennial mentality of quick-fix expectations, capitalistic impositions and greed, insurance and corporate directives and interferences, exploitation of consumer ignorance, political ideology, professional in-fighting, and every conceivable obstacle to entering into classical psychoanalytic treatment. The multiple-weekly patient attendance for analysis is now confined to those clinicians who are in training to become psychoanalysts in order to fulfill their institutional requirements, and/or for supervisory mandates, unless you are wealthy and have a proclivity for self-reflection, curiosity, and leisure. Psychoanalysis these days is weekly face-to-face psychoanalytic therapy with those who have appropriate clinical training, sensibility, and skill. Unlike other parts of the world, such as in Europe and South America, where the fee for service is marginally low in comparison to their North American counterparts, psychoanalytic clinical practice is destined to become a far less frequent face-to-face interaction, let alone to use the sacrosanct "couch." The "frequency and furniture wars" are dead and buried. It is the education and mindset of the clinician in relation to the personality and needs of the patient within the unique therapeutic dyad that will determine the scope and depth the treatment will manifest, develop, or otherwise have to offer, and these are subject to many contextual contingencies that are part of any individualized treatment.

Negation versus Innovation

One of the main goals that lie ahead for the stakeholders of relational psychoanalysis is the need to develop more of a cohesive theoretical paragon and systematic guidelines to praxis that take into account how relationality is differentiated from other psychoanalytic and psychotherapeutic models. In other words, What does relational psychoanalysis offer that other schools of psychoanalysis do not? Currently, it lacks formalization. It has made its claim to fame more about practice rather than theoretical orientation, explanation, or offering a philosophy of mind and culture. Relational theory is built on negation and anti-Freudianism: it seeks to replace drive theory but offers little novelty that has not already been offered by earlier psychoanalytic movements. Because of this, it suffers an image problem to psychoanalytic audiences worldwide who had already adopted relational principles in theory and practice. The exaggerations, distorted position statements, and manufactured misinterpretations attributed to classical authors hardly demonstrate scholarship. A most recent example is Stephen Seligman's (2018) sophomoric attempt to dismiss "instinct theory" (pp. 119–120), itself a misnomer, by reclaiming the primacy of the "two-person" approach that has "dislocated" the "centrality of the endogenous primitive instincts" (p. 4), when he exposes his profound mischaracterization of Freud's texts. When a so-called "new" paradigm is orchestrated based on the refutation of the old, when the old is not even accurately presented and articulated, let alone quoted, then original ideas lose their original radicality, significance, and understanding.

Another embarrassment is the insistence that relational psychoanalysis constitutes a "paradigm shift," oratory devised by Mitchell in order to fuel revolt against so-called classical dogma by practitioners who were more interpersonally trained, such as at the William Alanson White Institute. This is overinflated (if not grandiose) hype. The misattribution of paradigm shifts in science brought to bear on psychoanalysis betrays the historical and actual conditions inherent in the philosophy and institution of science proper. Paradigm shifts only apply to the natural sciences. According to Kuhn, theories and methodology in the social sciences are *preparadigmatic*.

In his Preface to the second edition of *The Structure of Scientific Revolutions*, Kuhn (1970) recounts how surprised he was to discover, during his time at the Center for Advanced Studies in the Behavioral Sciences, that "the practice of astronomy, physics, chemistry, or biology normally fails to evoke the controversies over fundamentals that today often seem endemic among, say, psychologists or sociologists" (p. viii). This is to say that the social sciences do not undergo paradigm shifts because they have no proper paradigm to begin with that meets the criteria of natural science, physics being the exemplar. Science can at least agree upon fundamental conjectures and laws, which must be refuted or overturned to create new paradigms. The social, and to a lesser extent, the human sciences, which psychoanalysis by definition is part of, is a failed emulation of natural science, not because it should not be attempted, as Kuhn argues, but because the social sciences simply do not presently meet the standards of natural science, not that they should not try or may not one day succeed in. This is why claims of paradigm shifts in the humanities and behavioral sciences have met with rancor among actual scientists who conduct experiments, test, and measure phenomena in the natural world, and who have adopted a customary view of what constitutes authentic science. Of course, psychoanalysis can claim to have its own theoretical and methodological paradigms which undergo evolution, devolution, revolution, and supersession, but they would not meet the strict criterion attributed to the hard sciences. Despite Freud's (1940) insistence that psychoanalysis is a "natural science" (p. 282), by today's standards, this would be a category mistake.

Psychoanalysis in general is guilty of speaking to its own coteries regardless of theoretical orientation, but when theory is built on negation it can suffer from its own lack of self-development, creativity, innovation, and progressive enrichment. A good example of this is the invented "myth of the isolated mind," wrongfully attributed to Freud, and the so-called absence of a two-person psychology classical psychoanalysis has purportedly omitted from its canon, when there is no textual evidence *at all* in Freud's *Gesammelte Werke* to substantiate this (false) accusation. Furthermore, there is no such thing as a "post-Cartesian" psychoanalysis, as if Freud's sophisticated theory of mind is boiled down to a freshman introductory textbook description of Descartes' philosophy (itself wholly inaccurate) and then conveniently retrofitted to repudiate Freud. Freud was no Cartesian (see Mills, 2012, pp. 90–94), and I bet most relationalists don't even know why. Springboarding off of the misinterpretation of classical theory to then erect a "new and improved" rendition of the human condition and its application to the consulting room is not the positive theory building that is needed to establish a more solid theoretical, philosophical, and methodological foundation the relational movement requires at this stage in its history. The revolution now needs evolution as the epigenesis of its modest beginnings.

Uniformity of theory?

How could relational theory become more novel and original to set it apart from its earlier ancestors? Of course, this is a question I cannot answer. Some attempt to establish a uniformity of theory may help, even among a sea of diversity, difference, and plurality of authors' voices. To get us started, we may ask, What is the essence of the relational platform? What unites like-minded practitioners? What does relational sensibility, theory, and praxis stand for that is:

1. Descriptive,
2. Coherent,
3. Expository,
4. Generalizable,

5. Meaningful, and
6. Pragmatic, namely, useful?

Steve Kuchuck and Rachel Sopher (2017) alert us to an attempt to reclaim the unconscious in relational theory, which I applaud. But how does a relational unconscious look like that is any different from previous incarnations of classical and postclassical iterations? Here, I imagine, the creative intellect could, in theory, fashion a logic of unconscious process that prioritizes relational dynamics in a systematic manner, but without having to appeal to the strong revolutionary language of jettisoning our archaic primacy on what psychoanalysis originally offered to humanity, namely, an encompassing interpretation and explanation of universal unconscious processes inherent in our embodied individuality and social collectives. I have attempted to show in a philosophical context how relationality is ontically prepared by an a priori presubjective unconscious ground that allows for the birth of conscious subjectivity and agency actualized through relational principles (Mills, 2010); but the full development and articulation of a theory of the relational unconscious is still to be actualized.

If no uniformity of relational theory is possible, even when attempting to allow for diversity by integrating difference and plurality, then fertility may be found in a radical rejection of uniformity. This is the postmodern position, which, as I will argue in this book, has its own endemic problems. But offering a theoretical groundwork for a "postmodern psychoanalysis" will at the very least be an attempt to organize a coherent framework of thought.

Relationality faces the same dilemma as do other psychological theories, methodologies, and systems of therapy as it attempts to embrace and incorporate the new "integrationist" pulse. We not only see this trend, if not academic requirement, in all droves of discourse in the history and systems of psychology, but contemporary predilections in theory and practice suffer various tensions and inadequacies of incorporation that have traditionally been seen as separate subdisciplines of the behavioral sciences: namely, insight-oriented, Gestalt, phenomenological, existential, humanistic, behavioral, cognitive, systems, interpersonal, emotion-focused, and the like. As the biological and neurosciences gain empirical ground in medicine and popularity, psychoanalysis must keep up with the times. Relational perspectives have enthusiastically embraced the broad diversity of many important scientific, philosophical, and political developments in culture and society including, but not limited to, offering a psychoanalytic theory of development based on attachment theory and infant observation research, cognitive science, affect regulation and mentalization, trauma studies, social-political activism, and distinct views on feminism, race, gender, sexuality, LGBTQ communities and the Trans movement, cultural differences, immigration, diasporas, sex-trade, the ethical turn, and ecopsychology, not to mention the disenfranchisement of identities and eroding national security in the globalization of technology, geopolitics, and economic disparities. As relational psychoanalysis flirts with political social philosophy, it may find new vistas in a marriage with philosophy, particularly Critical Theory (Mills, 2019a, 2019b, 2019c). As a human science, psychoanalysis will prosper in the future by engaging other disciplines and discourses in the sciences and humanities by bringing a critical dialogue, critique, and reformulation of its principle hypotheses and assumptions to bear on those ideas that lie outside of its traditional scope of reference and engagement. Whether interdisciplinary encounters will lead to further disciplinary and subdisciplinary refinement is an open possibility, but I doubt it will lead to transdisciplinarity simply because most specialists cannot absorb the scholarship of other disciplines due to many prohibitive factors, including a lack of time for new studies and academic and institutional politics that thwart transdisciplinary publications and scholarship.

Toward a theory of technique

Is it possible to have a consensus on common therapeutic assumptions, principles, technical procedures, instruction, delivery, and on the forms of therapeutic action that are uniquely relational? According to Kuchuck (2018), "each Relational analyst defines and practices the perspective in his/her own particular way" (pp. 343–344), making relational theory and praxis susceptible to radical subjectivity, particularization, idiosyncrasy, and/or relativism. If this is the case, what sets the relational practitioner apart from other leanings, technical approaches, and schools? Although every clinician comes to define concepts and practice in their own individualized way, this does not mean they are devoid of a solid grounding in certain preferred theoretical orientations and techniques adopted in the consulting room that follow particular methodologies introduced in training and refined throughout independent practice. Despite the fact that certain therapeutic sensibilities, attitudes, preferences, viewpoints, and susceptibilities saturate the clinical milieu with wide variation and overlap in training, the question remains, What is exclusively relational?

To my knowledge, Roy Barsness (2018) provides the first comprehensive text on core competencies in relational practice based on Grounded Theory Analysis of qualitative data obtained by interviewing fifteen (N=15) self-identified relational psychoanalysts. Although the sample size is small and limited in generalizability, it provides a wealth of in-depth coding and analysis of data around defining characteristics, organizing principles, delimiting theory, and integrating categories and their properties into a set of central explanatory concepts. What emerged from his qualitative analysis are three primary categories, namely, (1) *positioning*, (2) *reflecting*, and (3) *engaging*, which were further grouped into seven core competencies including (a) therapeutic intent or purpose of treatment, (b) nonauthoritarian, collaborative therapeutic stance or attitude, (c) deep listening and immersion in the analytic process, (d) relational dynamics between the past and present (the there and then and the here and now), (e) patterning and linking, (f) repetition and working through, and (f) courageous honest speech and disciplined spontaneity. In fact, the study did arrive at one broad core category: *love*. I will let the reader reflect upon whether these clinical factors are transdisciplinary values shared by most if not all psychoanalytic schools of thought by adopting at least some of these identified core competencies, hence begging the question of what is uniquely relational; yet the focus on the interpersonal field and the therapy relationship between the clinician and patient may be decisive features that differentiate relational practitioners from other forms of psychoanalytic treatment. With the centrality of "love" associated with the kind of relationship the analyst engenders, it is appropriate to remind the reader that several early analysts, such as Otto Gross, Jung, Ferenczi, and Ian Suttie, to name a few, focused on love and tenderness between patient and analyst, and this was also a core feature of Binswanger's (1962) Daseinsanalysis where he re-appropriates Heidegger's notion of care or concernful solicitude as an extension of love in the therapeutic encounter.

Barsness has done a great service by attempting to categorize and systematize fundamental relational practices that may inspire further research, progress, innovation, and development in clinical theory and technique. Perhaps the direct and mutual sharing of emotion, feelings, thoughts, desires, and sometimes fantasies for each other in the treatment is the most controversial yet liberating dimension to relational practice. While classical perspectives are quick to curb the use and proclivity of self-disclosure of this type, specifically analyst self-disclosure or self-revelation, as it willows the traditional frame, if not seen as taboo, these factors are inherently risky and can lead to unpredictable outcomes at best. Although the use, scope, parameters, and limits of analyst self-disclosure are hotly contested, this is not a new phenomenon and has a prehistory in experimental technique dating back to Freud.

Karen Maroda (1991, 2010), a relational practitioner who has offered extensive guidelines for when and when not to make personal disclosures, is very sensitive to this issue as am I. The future of relational psychoanalysis would profit from debates and a more nuanced critique of analyst self-disclosure and revelation as this seems to be where the meat and contention lies, if not the Achilles' heel. As with all clinical judgement, context is everything, but examining the conditions within therapeutic encounters, clinical phenomena, and demarcations to therapist self-disclosure will help us consider best practice approaches grounded in solid rationale apprising when disclosure or revelation is warranted, ambiguous, excessive, and/or prohibited. The same caveat may be said for when and when not to make an interpretation. This issue also interweaves with professional ethics and jurisdictional legislation based upon where one practices. These are the types of controversial discussions the relational community should welcome and tussle with (from critics and adherents alike), as justification for clinical practices and orienting principles to method and technique are what is relevant to all psychoanalytic schools.

On clinical theory

Because therapeutic praxis and technique rest on certain theoretical, philosophical, and empirical assumptions about human nature, the analytic process, and therapeutic action, they necessarily derive from and inform clinical theory. Because the assumptions we make, assert, or take for granted guide our approach in the clinic, interventions can either substantiate, reinforce, nullify, or refute our assumptions and conjectures. Therefore, clinical theory is intimately associated with the types of interventions we employ, experiment with, avoid, or suspend based upon treatment effects and utility.

Let us examine a recent example of clinical theory operative in erotic revelations and in the transference-countertransference dynamic. Andrea Celenza (2007) tells us that "all therapy revolves around one basic question, 'Why can't we be lovers?'" (p. 3). Elsewhere she adds: "This question must be reckoned with and will involve the use of erotic arousal in the dyad" (Celenza, 2010, p. 66). Continuing this theme, she further asks us "to wonder why there might be an absence of sexual desire with a particular patient. Why does this patient fail to erotically arouse, and might this be related to the issues of the treatment?" (Celenza, 2014, p. 20), something she calls a "universal longing" (p. 23). Taken at face value, this clinical assumption is not only naïvely reductive, it is palpably absurd because it simply is not true. This is not a theoretical speculation that libidinal forces and fantasies are innate in all people and are mobilized in the therapy, at least on some unconscious level, but that "all therapy revolves around" this "one basic" premise.

How is it possible to make such universal statements? Perhaps these propositions are designed to be cute or clever, theatrical, even amusing, playing on the trope and specter of the unconscious. Granted that erotic transferences and countertransferences are common, especially in formal analyses that entail multiple-weekly sessions (where fantasies are magnified and nurtured through the artificial social arrangement that does not reflect one's real life with others outside of analysis), these are exceptions to the norm. When we are told that an absence of sexual desire in the analyst for the patient suggests that something is wrong with the treatment, hence insinuating the therapist's deficits or incompetence, then this makes dogmatic ontic assertions that are simply indefensible—a transference to theory. And when we are asked to ponder why a patient "fail[s] to erotically arouse" the therapist, as if there is something wrong either with the analyst or patient, and that the treatment has suffered, then this begs the question and fails to demonstrate why this is so. When this pronouncement is placed in the context of why my appallingly homely male patient fails to "erotically arouse" me in session, the answer is obvious. This question would never enter my mind if it were the last thing in the world.

One cannot draw a generalized universal statement of this magnitude unless it is experienced by the therapist for every patient. And how could this be possible? Where is there such salience in clinical work, let alone empirical evidence to validate such a blanket statement? But if an analyst holds this clinical theory that every therapeutic relationship will have to reckon with *a fortiori*, by necessity, then it is easier to imagine how we would project our own theories and psychic energies in this belief and quest to find it universally true. Perhaps Celenza has this issue more often than others, especially if she is looking to support her clinical theory, or finds herself in many eroticized treatment milieus due to the people she takes into her practice, but I highly doubt this could be the case for all her patients. But to her credit, she at least gives guidelines for when and when not to address erotic revelations and offer countertransference disclosures by the analyst.

Clinical theory is the most plastic and fluid of our professional constructions, open to conceptual analysis, experimentation, experiential muse, critique, and play, and to this end is perennially open to revision and reformulation. Relational thought has much to contribute to this burgeoning area in how theory guides technique.

Moving forward

I hope these debates do not take a backseat in psychoanalytic history, let alone become displaced or suppressed by the relational school, as nobody likes to be criticized and hence resists change or engagement with antagonists. There are many contemporary authors who I admire for their courageous writings, honesty, integrity, leadership, and vision for the future of the profession that anticipates and adapts well to the current climate of mental healthcare service delivery, that is, what people are genuinely looking for and are in need of when they seek out therapeutic help, and relationalists portend social realities that are likely to come to fruition in our tempestuous and often unpredictable times. It is my hope that the relational movement will improve upon its theoretical, clinical, and applied edifice as it faces and embraces critique, as there can be no progress without self-examination, reflection, and reevaluation.

Endnote

1. William Shakespeare, *Henry VI*, Part 2, Act IV, Scene 2.

References

Altman, N. (2007). A lapse in constructive dialogue: The Journal's Responsibility. *Psychoanalytic Psychology*, 2, 395–396.

Aron, L., Grand, S., & Slochower, J. (Eds.) (2018a). *Decentering Relational Theory: A Comparative Critique*. London: Routledge.

Aron, L., Grand, S., & Slochower, J. (Eds.) (2018b). *De-Idealizing Relational Theory: A Critique from Within*. London: Routledge.

Axelrod, S.D., Naso, R.C., & Rosenberg, L.M. (2018). *Progress in Psychoanalysis: Envisioning the Future of the Profession*. London: Routledge.

Barsness, R.E. (Ed.) (2018). *Core Competencies in Relational Psychoanalysis: A Guide to Practice, Study and Research*. London: Routledge.

Binswanger, L. (1962). Ausgewählte Werke Band 2: Grundformen und Erkenntnis menschlichen Daseins. In M. Herog, & Has-Jürgen Braun (Eds). Heidelberg: Asanger, 1993.

Brown, R.S. (2017). *Psychoanalysis Beyond the End of Metaphysics: Thinking Towards the Post-Relational*. London: Routledge.

Celenza, A. (2007). *Sexual Boundary Violations*. Lantham, MD: Rowman & Littlefield.

Celenza, A. (2010). The analyst's need and desire. *Psychoanalytic Dialogues*, 20, 60–69.

Celenza, A. (2014). *Erotic Revelations*. New York: Routledge.
Davies, J.M. (2007). Response to Jon Mills: An open letter to the members of division 39. *Psychoanalytic Psychology*, 2, 397–400.
Freud, S. (1940). *Some Elementary Lessons in Psycho-Analysis*. Standard Edition, Vol. 23. London: Hogarth Press.
Govrin, A. (2016). *Conservative and Radical Perspectives on Psychoanalytic Knowledge: The Fascinated and the Disenchanted*. London: Routledge.
Govrin, A. (2017). Introduction to the relational approach and its critics: A conference with Dr. Jon Mills. *Psychoanalytic Perspectives*, 14(3), 309–312.
Hoffman, I. (2007). Reply to Jon Mills (2006): An open letter to the members of division 39. *Psychoanalytic Psychology*, 2, 401–405.
Kuchuck, S. (2018). Postscript to Chapter 17. In R.E. Barsness (Ed.), *Core Competencies in Relational Psychoanalysis: A Guide to Practice, Study and Research*. London: Routledge, pp. 342–352.
Kuchuck, S., & Sopher, R. (2017). Relational psychoanalysis out of context: Response to Jon Mills. *Psychoanalytic Perspectives*, 14(3), 364–376.
Kuhn, T.S. (1970). *The Structure of Scientific Revolutions*. 2nd ed. Chicago: University of Chicago Press.
Mark, D. (2018). Forms of equality in relational psychoanalysis. In Aron, L., Grand, S., & Slochower, J. (Eds.), *De-Idealizing Relational Theory: A Critique from Within*. London: Routledge, pp. 80–101.
Maroda, K. J. (1991). *The Power of Countertransference*. Chichester, UK: Wiley.
Maroda, K. J. (2010). *Psychodynamic Techniques: Working with Emotion in the Therapeutic Relationship*. New York: Guilford Press.
Mills, J. (2005a). A critique of relational psychoanalysis. *Psychoanalytic Psychology*, 22(2), 155–188.
Mills, J. (2005b). *Treating Attachment Pathology*. Lanham, MD: Aronson/Rowman & Littlefield.
Mills, J. (2005c). *Relational and Intersubjective Perspectives in Psychoanalysis: A Critique*. Lanham, MD: Aronson/Rowman & Littlefield.
Mills, J. (2010). *Origins: On the Genesis of Psychic Reality*. Montreal: McGill-Queens University Press.
Mills, J. (2012). *Conundrums: A Critique of Contemporary Psychoanalysis*. New York: Routledge.
Mills, J. (2017a). Psychoanalysis and the philosophical turn. *Psychoanalytic Psychology*, 35(1), 3–7. DOI: 10.1037/pap0000147
Mills, J. (2017b). Challenging relational psychoanalysis: A critique of postmodernism and analyst self-disclosure. *Psychoanalytic Perspectives*, 14, 313–335.
Mills, J. (2019a). Dysrecognition and social pathology: New directions in critical theory. *Psychoanalysis, Culture & Society*, 24(1), 15–30. DOI: 10.1057/s41282–018-0113-0
Mills, J. (2019b). Recognition and pathos. *International Journal of Jungian Studies*, 11(1), 1–22. DOI: 10.1163/19409060-01101001
Mills, J. (2019c). Contemporary psychoanalysis and critical theory: A new synthesis. *Critical Horizons: A Journal of Philosophy and Social Theory*, 20(3), 233–245. DOI: 10.1080/14409917.2019.1616484
Mills, J. (2020). Relational polemics. *The International Journal of Psychoanalysis*, 101. DOI: 10.1080/00207578.2019.1689791100(4).
Naso, R.C. (2010). *Hypocrisy Unmasked: Dissociation, Shame, and the Ethics of Inauthenticity*. Lanham, MD: Rowman & Littlefield/Aronson.

Orange, D. M. (2018). Multiplicity and integrity: Does an anti-developmental tilt still exist in relational psychoanalysis? In L. Aron, S. Grand, & J. Slochower (Eds.), *Decentering Relational Theory: A Comparative Critique*. London: Routledge, pp. 148–172.

Reppen, J. (2007). Editor's note. *Psychoanalytic Psychology*, 2, 406.

Ridenour, J. (2012). Critique and reason. *Conundrums: A Critique of Contemporary Psychoanalysis (Book Review). DIVISION Review*, Vol. 5, Summer, pp. 9–11.

Rozmarin, Eyal (2019). Relational conundrums: A critique of contemporary psychoanalysis by Jon Mills. *The International Journal of Psychoanalysis*, 100, 166–169.

Seligman, S. (2018). *Relationships in Development: Infancy, Intersubjectivity, and Attachment*. London: Routledge.

Shakespeare, W. Henry VI. Entire Play. shakespeare.mit.edu. Retrieved 2019-11-10.

Slochower, J. (2018). Going too far: Relational heroines and relational excess. In Aron, L., Grand, S., & Slochower, J. (Eds.), *De-Idealizing Relational Theory: A Critique from Within*. London: Routledge, pp. 8–34.

Stern, D.B. (2018). Otherness within psychoanalysis: On recognizing the critics of relational psychoanalysis. In L. Aron, S. Grand, & J. Slochower (Eds.), *Decentering Relational Theory: A Comparative Critique*. London: Routledge, pp. 27–48.

Stern, S. (2018). Needed analytic relationships and the disproportionate relational focus on enactments. In Aron, L., Grand, S., & Slochower, J. (Eds.), *De-Idealizing Relational Theory: A Critique from Within*. London: Routledge, pp. 102–131.

1 A critique of relational psychoanalysis

Jon Mills

Abstract: Psychoanalysis today is largely a psychology of consciousness: post- and neo-Freudians form a marginalized community within North America in comparison to contemporary relational and intersubjective theorists who emphasize the phenomenology of lived conscious experience, dyadic attachments, affective attunement, social construction, and mutual recognition over the role of insight and interpretation. Despite the rich historical terrain of theoretical variation and advance, many contemporary approaches have displaced the primacy of the unconscious. Notwithstanding the theoretical hairsplitting that historically occurs across the psychoanalytic domain, we are beginning to see with increasing force and clarity what Mitchell and Aron (1999) refer to as the emergence of a new tradition, namely, relational psychoanalysis. Having its edifice in early object relations theory, the British middle school and American interpersonal traditions, and self psychology, relationality is billed as "a distinctly new tradition" (Mitchell & Aron, 1999, p. x). What is being labeled as the American middle group of psychoanalysis (Spezzano, 1997), relational and intersubjective theory have taken center stage. It may be argued, however, that contemporary relational and intersubjective perspectives have failed to be properly critiqued from within their own school of discourse. The scope of this article is largely preoccupied with tracing the (a) philosophical underpinnings of contemporary relational theory, (b) its theoretical relation to traditional psychoanalytic thought, (c) clinical implications for therapeutic practice, and (d) its intersection with points of consilience that emerge from these traditions.

Relational psychoanalysis is an American phenomenon, with a politically powerful and advantageous group of members advocating for conceptual and technical reform. Relational trends are not so prevalent in other parts of the world where one can readily observe the strong presence of Freud throughout Europe and abroad, Klein in England and South America, Lacan in France and Argentina, Jung in Switzerland, the Independents in Britain, Kohut in the Midwestern United States, and the Interpersonalists in the East, among others. Despite such secularity and pluralism, relational thinking is slowly gaining mainstream ascendency.

Perhaps this is due in part to the following factors: (a) In the United States there is an increasing volume of psychoanalytically trained psychologists who graduate from and teach at many progressive contemporary training institutes and postdoctoral programs, thus exerting a powerful conceptual influence on the next generation of analysts who are psychologically rather than medically trained;[1] (b) There has been a magnitude of books that have embraced the relational turn and are financially supported by independent publishing houses that lie beyond the confines of academe, thus wielding strong political identifications; (c) There has been a proliferation of articles and periodicals that have emerged from the relational tradition and hence favor relational concepts in theory and practice; and (d) Several identified relational analysts or those friendly to relational concepts are on the editorial boards of practically every respectable peer refereed psychoanalytic journal in the world, thus insuring a presence and a voice. Politics aside, it becomes easy to appreciate the force, value, and loci of the relational turn:

1. Relational psychoanalysis has opened a permissible space for comparative psychoanalysis by challenging fortified traditions ossified in dogma, such as orthodox conceptions of the classical frame, neutrality, abstinence, resistance, transference, and the admonition against analyst self-disclosure.
2. Relational perspectives have had a profound impact on the way we have come to conceptualize the therapeutic encounter, and specifically the role of the analyst in technique and practice. The relational turn has forged a clearing for honest discourse on what we actually do, think, and feel in our analytic work, thus breaking the silence and secrecy of what actually transpires in the consulting room. Relational approaches advocate for a more natural, humane, and genuine manner of how the analyst engages the patient rather than cultivating a distant intellectual attitude or clinical methodology whereby the analyst is sometimes reputed to appear as a cold, staid, antiseptic or emotionless machine. Relational analysts are more revelatory, interactive, and inclined to disclose accounts of their own experience in professional space (e.g., in session, publications, and conference presentations), enlist and solicit perceptions from the patient about their own subjective comportment, and generally acknowledge how a patient's responsiveness and demeanor is triggered by the purported attitudes, sensibility, and behavior of the analyst. The direct and candid reflections on countertransference reactions, therapeutic impasse, the role of affect, intimacy, and the patient's experience of the analyst are revolutionary ideas that have redirected the compass of therapeutic progress away from the uniform goals of interpretation and insight to a proper holistic focus on psychoanalysis as process.
3. The relational turn has displaced traditional epistemological views of the analyst's authority and unadulterated access to knowledge, as well as the objectivist principles they rest upon. By closely examining the dialogic interactions and meaning constructions that emerge within the consulting room, relational psychoanalysis has largely embraced the hermeneutic postmodern tradition of questioning the validity of absolute truth claims to knowledge,

> objective certainty, and positivist science. Meaning, insight, and conventions of interpretation are largely seen as materializing from within the unique contexts and contingencies of interpersonal participation in social events, dialogical discourse, dialectical interaction, mutual negotiation, dyadic creativity, and reciprocally generated co-constructions anchored in an intersubjective process. This redirective shift from uncritically accepting metaphysical realism and independent, objective truth claims to reclaiming the centrality of subjectivity within the parameters of relational exchange has allowed for a reconceptualization of psychoanalytic doctrine and the therapeutic encounter.

No small feat indeed. But with so many relational publications largely dominating the American psychoanalytic scene, we have yet to see relational psychoanalysis undergo a proper conceptual critique from within its own frame of reference. With the exception of Jay Greenberg (2001) who has recently turned a critical eye toward some of the technical practices conducted within the relational community today, most of the criticism comes from those outside the relational movement (Frank, 1998a, b; Silverman, 2000; Eagle, Wolitzky, & Wakefield, 2001; Josephs, 2001; Eagle, 2003; Lothane, 2003; Masling, 2003). In order to prosper and advance, it becomes important for any discipline to evaluate its theoretical and methodological propositions from within its own evolving framework rather than insulate itself from criticism due to threat or cherished group loyalties. It is in the spirit of advance that I offer this critique as a psychoanalyst and academically trained philosopher who works clinically as a relational analyst. Because the relational movement has become such a progressive and indispensable presence within the history of the psychoanalytic terrain, it deserves our serious attention, along with a rigorous evaluation of the philosophical foundations on which it stands. I do not intend to polemically abrogate nor undermine the value of relationality in theory and practice, but only to draw increasing concern to specific theoretical conundrums that may be ameliorated without abandoning the spirit of critical, constructive dialogue necessary for psychoanalysis to continue to thrive and sophisticate its conceptual practices. Admittedly, I will ruffle some feathers of those overly-identified with the relational movement. But it is my hope that through such crucial dialogue psychoanalysis can avail itself to further understanding.

Key tenets of the relational model

I should warn the reader up front that I am not attempting to critique every theorist who is identified with the relational turn, which is neither desirable nor practical for our purposes, a subject matter that could easily fill entire volumes. Instead I hope to approximate many key tenets of relational thinking that could be reasonably said to represent many analysts' views on what relationality represents to the field. To prepare our discussion, we need to form a working definition of precisely what constitutes the relational platform. This potentially becomes problematic given that each analyst identified with this movement privileges certain conceptual and technical assumptions over those of others, a phenomenon all analysts are not likely to dispute. However, despite specific contentions or divergences, relational analysts maintain a shared overarching emphasis on the centrality of relatedness. This shared emphasis on therapeutic relatedness has become the centerpiece of contemporary psychoanalysis to the point that some relationalists boast to have achieved a "paradigm shift" in the field.[2] On the face of things, this claim may sound palpably absurd to some analysts because the relational tradition hardly has a unified theory let alone a consensual body of knowledge properly attributed to a paradigm. Nevertheless, for our purposes, it becomes important to delineate and clarify what most relational analysts typically agree upon. Where points of difference, disagreement, and controversy exist, they tend not to cancel out certain fundamental theoretical assumptions governing relational discourse. Let us examine three main philosophical tenets of the relational school.

The primacy of relatedness

When Greenberg and Mitchell (1983) inaugurated the relational turn by privileging relatedness with other human beings as the central motive behind mental life, they displaced Freud's drive model in one stroke of the pen. Although Greenberg (1991) later tried to fashion a theoretical bridge between drive theory and a relational model, he still remained largely critical. Mitchell (1988, 2000), however, had continued to steadfastly position relationality in antithetical juxtaposition to Freud's metapsychology until his untimely death. From his early work, Mitchell (1988) states that the relational model is "an alternative perspective which considers relations with others, *not drives*, as the basic stuff of mental life" (p. 2, italics added), thus declaring the cardinal premise of all relational theorists. Greenberg (1991) makes this point more forcefully: the relational model is "based on the *radical rejection of drive* in favor of a view that all motivation unfolds from our personal experience of exchanges with others" (p. vii, italics added). The centrality of interactions with others, forming relationships, interpersonally mediated experience, human attachment, the impact of others on psychic development, reciprocal dyadic communication, contextually based social influence, and the recognition of competing subjectivities seem to be universal theoretical postulates underscoring the relational perspective. These are very reasonable and sound assertions, and we would be hard pressed to find anyone prepared to discredit these elemental facts. The main issue here is these propositions are nothing new: relational theory is merely stating the obvious. These are simple reflections on the inherent needs, strivings, developmental trajectories, and behavioral tendencies propelling human motivation, a point Freud made explicit throughout his theoretical corpus, which became further emphasized more significantly by early object relations theorists through to contemporary self psychologists. Every aspect of conscious life is predicated on human relatedness by the simple fact that we are thrown into a social ontology as evinced by our participation in family interaction, communal living, social custom, ethnic affiliation, local and state politics, national governance, and common linguistic practices that by definition cannot be refuted nor annulled by virtue of our embodied and cultural facticity, a thesis thoroughly advanced by Heidegger (1927), originally dating back to antiquity. But what is unique to the relational turn is a philosophy based on antithesis and refutation: namely, the abnegation of the drives.

Intersubjective ontology

Relational psychoanalysis privileges intersubjectivity over subjectivity and objectivity, although most theorists would generally concede that their position does not refute the existence of individual subjects nor the external objective world. Yet this is still a topic of considerable debate among philosophy let alone the field of psychoanalysis which remains relatively naive to formal metaphysics. It is unclear at best what "intersubjectivity" may mean to general psychoanalytic audiences due to the broad usage of the term, and despite it having very specific and diversified meanings. Among many contemporaneous thinkers, intersubjectivity is used anywhere from denoting a specific interpersonal process of recognizing the individual needs and subjective experiences of others, to referring to a very generic condition of interpersonal interaction.

It may be helpful to identify two forms of intersubjectivity in the analytic literature: a *developmental* view, and a *systems* view, each of which may be operative at different parallel process levels. Both Robert Stolorow and his colleagues, as well as Jessica Benjamin, are often identified as introducing intersubjective thinking to psychoanalysis, although this concept has a two-hundred year history dating back to German Idealism. Intersubjectivity was most prominently elaborated by Hegel (1807) as the laborious developmental attainment of ethical self-consciousness through the rational emergence of *Geist* in the history of the human race. This emergent process describes the unequal power distributions between servitude and lordship culminating in a developmental, historical, and ethical transformation of recognizing the subjectivity of the other, a complex concept Benjamin (1988) has reappropriated within the context of the psychoanalytic situation as the ideal striving for mutual recognition.

Like Hegel, Stern (1985), Benjamin (1988), and Mitchell (2000) view intersubjectivity as a developmental achievement of coming to acknowledge the existence and value of the internalized other, a dynamic that readily applies to the maternal–infant dyad and the therapeutic encounter. Daniel Stern (1985) has focused repeatedly on the internal experience of the infant's burgeoning sense of self as an agentic organization of somatic, perceptual, affective, and linguistic processes that unfold within the interpersonal presence of dyadic interactions with the mother. In his view, intersubjectivity is like Hegel's: there is a gradual recognition of the subjectivity of the m/other as an independent entity with similar and competing needs of her own. In Fonagy's (2000, 2001) and his colleagues (Fonagy, Gergely, Jurist, & Target, 2002) more recent contributions, he describes this process as the development of "mentalization," or the capacity to form reflective judgments on recognizing and anticipating the mental states of self and others. Stern's work dovetails nicely with the recent developments in attachment theory (Cassidy & Shaver, 1999; Solomon & George, 1999; Hesse & Main, 2000;

Main, 2000; Mills, 2005) and reciprocal dyadic systems theories derived from infant observation research.

Following Stern's developmental observation research, Beebe, Lachmann, and their colleagues (Beebe, Jaffe, & Lachmann, 1992; Beebe & Lachmann, 1998) have also focused on the primacy of maternal–infant interactions, and thus following the relational turn, have shifted away from the locus of inner processes to relational ones (Beebe & Lachmann, 2003). Beebe and Lachmann's dyadic systems theory is predicated on intersubjectivity and the mutuality of dyadic interactions whereby each partner within the relational matrix affects each other, thus giving rise to a dynamic systems view of self-regulation based on bidirectional, coordinated interactional attunement and cybernetic interpersonal assimilations resulting in mutual modifications made from within the system.

Stolorow, Atwood, and their colleagues (Stolorow, Brandchaft, & Atwood, 1987; Stolorow & Atwood, 1992; Orange, Atwood, & Stolorow, 1997) cast intersubjectivity as a more basic, ontological category of interdependent, intertwining subjectivities that give rise to a "field" or "world," similar to general references to an intersubjective "system" or an "analytic third" (Ogden, 1994). Stolorow and his collaborators are often misunderstood as saying that intersubjective constellations annul intrapsychic life and a patient's developmental history prior to therapeutic engagement (see Frank, 1998b), but Stolorow et al. specifically contextualize intrapsychic experience within the greater parameters of the intersubjective process (Orange, Atwood, & Stolorow, 1997, pp. 67–68). Yet it becomes easy to see why Stolorow invites misinterpretation. Intersubjectivity is ontologically constituted: "experience is *always* embedded in a constitutive intersubjective context" (Stolorow & Atwood, 1992, p. 24, italics added). Elsewhere he states that the intersubjective system is the "constitutive role of relatedness in the making of *all* experience" (Stolorow, 2001, p. xiii, italics added). These absolutist overstatements lend themselves to decentering intrapsychic activity over relational interaction, draws into question the separateness of the self, the preexistent developmental history of the patient prior to treatment, the prehistory of unconscious processes independent of one's relatedness to others, and *a priori* mental organization that precedes engagement with the social world.[3] These statements irrefutably replace psychoanalysis as a science of the unconscious with an intersubjective ontology that gives priority to conscious experience.[4] To privilege consciousness over unconsciousness to me appears to subordinate the value of psychoanalysis as an original contribution to understanding human experience. Even if we as analysts are divided by competing theoretical identifications, it seems difficult at best to relegate the primordial nature of unconscious dynamics to a trivialized backseat position that is implicit in much of the relational literature. For Freud (1900), the "unconscious is the true psychical reality" (p. 613), which by definition is the necessary condition for intersubjectivity to materialize and thrive.

Although there are many relational analysts who are still sensitive to unconscious processes in their writings and clinical work, including Donnel Stern, Phillip Bromberg, Thomas Ogden, and Jody Messler Davies among others, hence making broad generalizations unwarranted, it nevertheless appears that on the surface, for many relational analysts, the unconscious has become an antiquated category. And Stolorow (2001) specifically tells us so: "In place of the Freudian unconscious … we envision a multiply contextualized experimental world, an organized totality of lived personal experience, *more or less conscious* … In this view, psychoanalytic therapy is no longer an archeological excavation of deeper layers of an isolated unconscious mind" (p. xii–xiii, italics added). For Stolorow and many other relational thinkers, psychoanalysis has tacitly become a theory of consciousness. But regardless of the multiple contradictions that pervade his early work, a ghost that continues to problematize his theoretical positions, in all fairness to Stolorow, he and his colleagues have cogently embraced the primacy of contextual complexity situated within intersubjective relations, an observation most would find difficult to refute.

What is clearly privileged in the relational platform over above the unique internal experiences and contingencies of the individual's intrapsychic configurations is the intersubjective field or dyadic system that interlocks, emerges, and becomes contextually organized as a distinct entity of its own. The primary focus here is not on the object, as in relatedness to others (object relations) or the objective (natural) world, nor on the subject, as in the individual's lived phenomenal experience, rather the emphasis is on the system itself. The intersubjective system, field, territory, domain, realm, world, network, matrix—or whatever words we wish to use to characterize the indissoluble intersection and interactional enactment between two or more human beings—these terms evoke a spatial metaphor; hence, they imply presence or being, the traditional subject matter of metaphysical inquiry. Following key propositions from the relational literature, the intersubjective system must *exist* for it is predicated on being, hence on actuality; therefore, we may assume it encompasses its own attributes, properties, and spatiotemporal dialectical processes. This can certainly be inferred from the way in which relational analysts use these terms even if they don't intend to imply this as such, thus making the system into an actively organized (not static or fixed) entity of its own. Ogden (1994) makes this point most explicitly: "The analytic process reflects the interplay of three subjectivities: that of the analyst, of the analysand, and of the analytic third" (p. 483). In fact, the intersubjective system is a process-oriented entity that derives from the interactional union of two concretely existing subjective entities, thus making it an *emergent property* of the multiple (often bidirectional) interactions that form the intersubjective field. This ontological commitment immediately introduces the problem of agency, a topic I will repeatedly address throughout this critique.

How can a system acquire an agency of its own? How can the interpersonal field become its own autonomous agent? What happens to the agency of the individual subjects that constitute the system? How can a "third" agency materialize and have determinate choice and action over the separately existing human beings that constitute the field to begin with? What becomes of individual freedom, independence, and personal identity with competing needs, intentions, wishes, and agendas that define individuality if the "system" regulates individual thought, affect, and behavior? What happens to the system if one participant decides to no longer participate? Does the system die, is it suspended, does it reconstitute later? What becomes of the system if one participant exerts more will or power over that of the other subject? Is not the system merely a temporal play of events rather than an entity? And if these experiences were possible, it would render the system impotent, acausal, and nonregulatory, which directly opposes the relational view that the intersubjective field, dyadic system, relational matrix, or analytic third has causal influence and supremacy over the individual autonomy of its constituents. The system would merely be an epiphenomenon,[5] thus completely lacking determinate freedom or influence, hence merely relegated and deferred to the individual subjects that constitute the field. So how can the intersubjective system be granted such an exalted status by the relational movement? What becomes of the individually constituted and constitutive self? These questions are indeed difficult to sustain because they imply the intersubjective system has no causal power, autonomy, nor deference to individually mediated events that comprise the system to begin with. These conundrums have led Peter Giovacchini (2005) to conclude that for the intersubjectivists the individual mind becomes this ephemeral ether that evaporates the moment one enters into dialogue or social relations with anyone. While intersubjectivists do not claim the individual mind vanishes, they do unequivocally concede that it becomes subordinated to the intersubjective system or relational matrix that regulates it.

Psychoanalytic hermeneutics

The relational turn has largely embraced a constructivist epistemology and method of interpretation, what Hoffman (1998) refers to as "critical" or "dialectical" constructivism based on "mutual influence and constructed meaning" (p. xii) in the analytic encounter. Many relational authors generically refer to "co-constructed" experience that is sensitive to the contextually derived elements of the interpersonal encounter subject to each person's unique perspective and interpretation, but ultimately shaped by mutually negotiated meaning that is always susceptible to a fallibilistic epistemology (Orange, 1995). As Stolorow (1998) puts it, "the analyst has no privileged access" to the patient's mind or what truly transpires between the analyst and analysand, for "objective reality is unknowable by the psychoanalytic method" (p. 425). Drawing on Kant's Idealism, whereby claiming that we cannot have true knowledge of things in themselves, these epistemological positions are largely gathered from postmodern sensibilities that loosely fall under the umbrella of what may not be inappropriately called psychoanalytic hermeneutics: namely, methods of interpretation derived from subjective experience and participation in social relations that constitute meaning and knowledge.

Constructivist positions, and there are many kinds—social, ethical, feminist, empirical, mathematical—hold a variety of views with points of similarity and divergence depending upon their agenda or mode of inquiry. Generally, we may say that many relational analysts have adopted a variant of social constructivism by claiming that knowledge is the product of our linguistic practices and social institutions that are specifically instantiated in the interactions and negotiations between others. This readily applies to the consulting room where knowledge emerges from dialogic relational involvement wedded to context. This is why Hoffman and others rightfully state that meaning is not only discovered but also created, including the therapeutic encounter and the way we come to understand and view our lives. In fact, analysis is a creative self-discovery and process of becoming. Mild versions of constructivism hold that social participation and semantic factors lend interpretation to the world while extreme forms go so far to claim that the world, or some significant portion of it, is constituted via our linguistic, political, and institutional practices. Despite the generic use of the terms construction and co-construction, relational analysts have largely avoided specifically delineating their methodology. With the exception of Donnel Stern (1997) who largely aligns with Gadamer's hermeneutic displacement of scientific conceptions of truth and method,[6] Donna Orange's (1995) perspectival epistemology, which is a version of James' and Peirce's pragmatic theories of truth, and Hoffman's brand of dialectical constructivism—the term "dialectic" lacking any clear definition or methodological employment—relational psychoanalysis lacks a solid philosophical foundation, one it claims to use to justify its theories and practices. Perhaps with the exception of Stolorow and his collaborators' numerous attempts, none of the relational analysts I've mentioned provide their own detailed theoretical system that guides analytic method, hence falling short of offering a formal framework based on systematically elaborated, logical rigor we would properly expect from philosophical paradigms. Of course, psychoanalysis can claim that it is not philosophy, so placing such demands on the field is illegitimate; but contemporary frameworks are basing their purported innovations on justifications that derive from established philosophical traditions. Therefore, it is incumbent upon these "new view" theorists (Eagle et al., 2001) to precisely define their positions. Without doing so, relational analysts will continue to invite misinterpretation. Moreover, the psychoanalytic community may continue to misinterpret their frequent use of employing arcane and abstruse philosophical language culled from a very specific body of demarcated vocabulary that is reappropriated within the analytic context, to such a degree that the reader is either confused or sufficiently impressed because on the face of things it may seem profound. The obfuscating use of philosophical buzzwords may give the appearance of profundity, but they may be quite inaccurate when they are dislocated from the tradition in which they originally emerged.

Take for example Hoffman's use of the term "dialectical." This word imports a whole host of different meanings in the history of Western philosophy. Is he merely invoking the interplay of opposition? Does this imply difference only or also similarity? How about the role of symmetry, continuity, measure, force, unity, and/or synthesis? Is there a certain function to the dialectic, a movement, a process, or an emergence? If so, how does it transpire? Does it follow formal causal laws or logical operations, or is it merely acausal, amorphous, accidental, invariant, undecidable, spontaneous? Is it universal or merely contingent? Is it a necessary and/or sufficient condition of interaction, or perhaps just superfluous? Is his approach Socratic? Does he engage the impact of Kant, Fichte, Schelling, Hegel, or Marx on his view of the dialectic? He does not say. Hoffman (1998) emphasizes "ambiguity and construction of meaning." While I do not dispute this aspect to the dialectic, I am left pining for more explanation. Is there a teleology to the dialectic, or is everything "unspecified and indeterminate" (p. xvii), what he tends to emphasize in a move from "symbolically" well-defined experience, to "underdeveloped, ambiguous" features of mental activity or the lived encounter, to "totally untapped potentials" (p. 22)? Here Hoffman seems to be equating dialectics with construction *qua* construction. We might ask: Constructed from what? Are we to assume the intersubjective system is the culprit? Cursory definitions are given, such as the implication of "an interactive dynamic between opposites" (p. 200, fn2), but he ultimately defers to Ogden (1986): "A dialectic is a process in which each of two opposing concepts creates, informs, preserves, and negates the other, each standing in a dynamic (ever changing) relationship with the other" (p. 208). This definition emphasizes dichotomy, polarity, and change, but lacks articulation on how opposition brings about change, let alone what kind, for example, progressive or regressive, (given that change annuls the concept of stasis); or whether this process is subject to any formal laws, pressures, trajectories, or developmental hierarchies; nor does he explain how opposition emerges to begin with. Is the dialectic presumed to be the force behind all construction? And if so why? In all fairness to Hoffman, he does concede to the "givens" of reality and appreciates the historicity, causal efficacy, and presence of the past on influencing the present, including all modes of relatedness, and in shaping future possibilities. While I am admittedly using Hoffman here in a somewhat caviling manner, my point is to show how omission and theoretical obscurity in progressive psychoanalytic writing leaves the attentive reader with unabated questions.

A coherent framework of psychoanalytic hermeneutics has not been attempted since Ricoeur's (1970) critique of Freud's metapsychology, and there has been nothing written to my knowledge that hermeneutically critiques contemporary theory. What appears is a pluralistic mosaic—perhaps even a cacophony—of different amalgamated postmodern, hermeneutic traditions derived from constructivism, critical theory, post-structuralism, feminist philosophy, sociology, linguistics, narrative literary criticism, deconstructionism, and—believe it or not—analytic philosophy that have shared visions and collective identifications, but with misaligned projects and competing agendas. For these reasons alone, I doubt we will ever see one coherent comparative-integrative contemporary psychoanalytic paradigm. These disparate groups of theories exist because human knowledge and explanation radically resist being reduced to a common denominator, and here the relationalist position is well taken. There is too much diversity, complexity, difference, particularity, and plurality to warrant such an onerous undertaking. While I have emphasized the recent upsurge of attention on constructivist epistemology in relational circles, it may be said that a general consensus exists for most practicing analysts that absolute truth, knowledge, and certainty does not rest on the crown of the analyst's epistemic authority, and that insight, meaning, and explanation are an ongoing, emerging developmental aspect of any analytic work subject to the unique intersubjective contingencies of the analytic dyad.

Having sufficiently prepared our discussion, I now wish to turn our attention to what may perhaps be the most controversial theoretical debate between the relational traditions and previous analytic schools: namely, the subject–object divide. Contemporary relational psychoanalysis claims to have transcended the theoretical ailments that plague classical analysis by emphasizing the irreducible subjectivity of the analyst (Renik, 1993) over objective certainty, the fallacy of the analyst's epistemological authority, the primacy of context and perspective over universality and essentialism, and the adoption of a "two-person psychology" that is thoroughly intersubjective. But these premises are not without problems. Does the analyst's subjectivity foreclose the question of objectivity? Does epistemically limited access to knowledge necessarily delimit our understanding of truth and reality? Does particularity and pluralism negate the notion of universals and collectivity? Does a nominalist view of subjectivity necessarily annul the notion of essence?[7] And does a two-person model of intersubjectivity minimize or cancel the force and value of intrapsychic reality and lived individual experience? These are but some of the philosophical quandaries that arise from the relational literature. But with a few exceptions, it may be said that contemporary psychoanalytic theory is premised on reappropriating old paradigms under the veil of popular garb. Here enters postmodernism.

The lure and ambiguity of postmodernism

What do we mean by the term postmodernism? And what is its burgeoning role in psychoanalytic discourse? Within the past two decades we have seen a resurgence of interest in philosophy among contemporary relational and intersubjective theorists whom have gravitated toward key postmodern tenets that draw into question the notion of universals, absolute standards of truth and objectivity, and the problem of essence within clinical theory and practice. The lure of postmodernism is widely attractive because it explains the hitherto unacknowledged importance of the analyst's interjected experience within the analytic encounter, displaces the notion of the analyst's epistemic authority as an objective certainty, highlights contextuality and perspective over universal proclamations that apply to all situations regardless of historical contingency, culture, gender, or time, and largely embraces the linguistic, narrative turn in philosophy. Although postmodern thought has propitiously criticized the pervasive historical, gendered, and ethnocentric character of our understanding of the world, contemporary trends in psychoanalysis seem to be largely unaware of the *aporiai* postmodern propositions introduce into a coherent and justifiable theoretical system.

Although postmodernism has no unified body of theory, thus making it unsystematized, one unanimous implication is the demise of the individual subject. Postmodernism may be generally said to be a cross-disciplinary movement largely comprising linguistic, poststructural, constructivist, historical, narrative, deconstructivist, and feminist social critiques that oppose most Western philosophical traditions. As a result, postmodern doctrines are antimetaphysical, antiepistemological, and anticolonial, thus opposing realism, foundationalism, essentialism, neutrality, and the ideal sovereignty of reason. In this respect, they may be most simply characterized by negation—No! Moreover, erasure—~~Know~~.

Although postmodern sensibility has rightfully challenged the omnipresence of historically biased androcentric and logocentric interpretations of human nature and culture, it has done so at the expense of dislocating several key modern philosophical tenets that celebrate the nature of subjectivity, consciousness, and the teleology of the will. Consequently, the transcendental notions of freedom, liberation, individuality, personal independence, authenticity, and reflective deliberate choice that comprise the essential activities of personal agency are altogether disassembled. What all this boils down to is the dissolution of the autonomous, rational subject. In other words, the self is anaesthetized.

Postmodernism has become very fashionable with some relationalists because it may be used selectively to advocate for certain contemporary positions, such as the co-construction of meaning and the disenfranchisement of epistemic analytic authority, but it does so at the expense of introducing antimetaphysical propositions into psychoanalytic theory that are replete with massive contradictions and inconsistencies. For example, if meaning is merely a social construction, and all analytic discourse that transpires within the consulting room is dialogical, then meaning and interpretation are conditioned on linguistic social factors that determine such meaning, hence we are the product of language instantiated within our cultural ontology. This means language and culture are causally *determinative*. And since therapeutic action is necessarily conditioned by verbal exchange, language causally structures the analytic dyad; and even more to the extreme, as Mitchell (1988) proposes, "interpretively constructs" another's mind (p. 16), to which Morris Eagle (2003) argues is absurd. The implications of these positions immediately annul metaphysical assertions to truth, objectivity, freewill, and agency, just to name a few. For instance, if everything boils down to language and culture, then by definition we cannot make legitimate assertions about truth claims or objective knowledge because these claims are merely constructions based upon our linguistic practices to begin with rather than universals that exist independent of language and socialization. So by definition, the whole concept of epistemology is merely determined by social discourse, so one cannot conclude that truth or objectivity exists. These become mythologies, fictions, narratives, and illusions regardless of whether we find social consensus or not. Therefore, natural science, mathematics, and formal logic are merely social inventions based on semantic construction that by definition annul any claims to objective observations or mind-independent reality. In other words, metaphysics is dead and buried—nothing exists independent of language.

These propositions problematize the whole contemporary psychoanalytic edifice. If nothing exists independent of language and the social matrix that sustains it (in essence, the relational platform), then not only is subjectivity causally determined by culture, subjectivity is dismantled altogether. When analysts use terms such as "construction," hence invoking Foucault—whose entire philosophical project was to get rid of the subject and subjectivity, or even worse, "deconstruction," thus exalting Derrida, the king of postmodernism, whose entire corpus is devoted to annihilating any metaphysical claims whatsoever, thus collapsing everything into undecidability, ambiguity, and chaos, analysts open themselves up to misunderstanding and controversy, subsequently inviting criticism.

What perhaps appears to be the most widely shared claim in the relational tradition is the assault on the analyst's epistemological authority to objective knowledge. Stolorow (1998) tells us that "objective reality is unknowable by the psychoanalytic method, which investigates only subjective reality … there are no neutral or objective analysts, no immaculate perceptions, no God's-eye views of anything" (p. 425). What exactly does this mean? If my patient is suicidal and he communicates this to me, providing he is not malingering, lying, or manipulating me for some reason, does this not constitute some form of objective judgment independent of his subjective verbalizations? Do we not have some capacities to form objective appraisals, here the term "objective" being used to denote making reasonably correct judgments about objects or events outside of our unique subjective experience? Is not Stolorow making an absolute claim despite arguing against absolutism when he says that "reality is unknowable?" Why not say that knowledge is proportional or incremental rather than totalistic, thus subject to modification, alteration, and interpretation rather than categorically negate the category of an objective epistemology?

Although Stolorow is not trying to deny the existence of the external world, he is privileging a subjective epistemology, and this is no different from Kant's (1781) view expounded in his *Critique of Pure Reason*. Ironically, this was also Freud's (1900) position in the dream book: "The unconscious is the true psychical reality; *in its innermost nature, it is as much unknown to us as the reality of the external world, and it is as incompletely presented by the data of consciousness as is the external world by the communications of our sense organs*" (p. 613). Following Kant, both Stolorow and Freud are critical realists: they accept the existence of objective reality because there must be something beyond the veil of appearance, but they can never know it directly. There is always a limit to pure knowing, a noumena—the *Ding an sich*, or the Fichtean (1794) *Anstoss*—a firm boundary, obstacle, or check. This is the hallmark of early German Idealism, which seems plausible and is defensible. But Stolorow, in collaboration with his colleagues, makes other claims that implicitly overturn his previous philosophical commitments. He reifies intersubjectivity at the expense of subjective life, subordinates the role, scope, and influence of the unconscious, and favors a relational focus in treatment rather than on the intrapsychic dynamics of the analysand. For example, take Donna Orange's extreme claim: "There is No Outside." For someone who rejects solipsism, this seems outlandish.

Because postmodern perspectives are firmly established in antithesis to the entire history of Greek and European ontology, perspectives widely adopted by many contemporary analysts today, relational psychoanalysis has no tenable metaphysics. This begs the question of an intelligible discourse on method for the simple fact that postmodern sensibilities ultimately collapse into relativism.[8] Since there are no independent standards, methods, or principles subject to uniform procedures for evaluating conceptual schemas, postmodern perspectives naturally lead to relativism. Categories of knowledge, truth, objectivity, and reality are merely based on *contingencies* fashioned by language, personal experience or opinion, preference and prejudice, parallel perspectives, social agreement, negotiated meaning, collective value practices that oppose other collective practices, and/or subjectively capricious conclusions. Contingency always changes and disrupts established order or causal laws, therefore there are no universals, only particulars. The relational focus on context, construction, and perspective is clearly a contingency claim. We can't know anything, but we can invent something to agree upon. This hardly should be toted under the banner of "truth," because for the postmoderns there is no truth, only truths—multiple, pluralistic, nominalistic, hence *relative* to person, place, and time. While we may all agree that subjectivity is infused in all human experience by virtue of the fact that we can never abrogate our facticity as embodied, sentient, desirous conscious beings—hence a universal proposition that transcends history, gender, cultural specificity, and time—this does not *ipso facto* rule out the notion of objectivity or realism.

For all practical purposes, the epistemic emphasis on subjectivity that opposes objectivity is a bankrupt claim because this devolves into untenability where everything potentially becomes relative. From the epistemic (perspectival) standpoint of a floridly psychotic schizophrenic, flying apparitions really *do* exist, but this does not make it so. Relativism is incoherent and is an internally inconsistent position at best, to simply being an unsophisticated form of sophistry based on crass opinion. I once had a student who was an ardent champion of relativism until I asked him to stand up and turn around. When he did I lifted his wallet from his back pocket and said: "If everything is relative, then I think I am entitled to your wallet because the university does not pay me enough." Needless to say, he wanted it back. Relativism collapses into contradiction, inexactitude, nihilism, and ultimately absurdity because no one person's opinion is anymore valid than another's, especially including value judgments and ethical behavior, despite qualifications that some opinions are superior to others. A further danger of embracing a "relativistic science" is that psychoanalysis really has nothing to offer over other disciplines who may negate the value of psychoanalysis to begin with, for example, empirical academic psychology, let alone patients themselves whose own opinions may or may not carry any more weight than the analysts with whom they seek out for expert professional help. When one takes relativism to the extreme, constructivism becomes creationism, which is simply a grandiose fantasy of omnipotence.

I suppose this debate ultimately hinges on how psychoanalysts come to define "objectivity," once again, a semantic determination. Words clarify yet they obfuscate. So do their omissions. Is this merely paradox, perhaps overdetermination, or is this a Derridean trope? One thing is for sure (in my humble opinion!), relational and intersubjective theorists seem to have a penchant for creating false dichotomies between inner/outer, self/other, universal/particular, absolute/relative, truth/fallacy, and subject/object. For those familiar with the late modern Kantian turn through to German Idealism, phenomenology, and early continental philosophy, contemporary psychoanalysis seems to be behind the times. The subject–object divide has already been closed.[9]

Although postmodern psychoanalytic thought is attractive for its emphasis on contextuality, linguistic, gender, and cultural specificity, political reform, postcolonial antipatriarchy, the displacement of pure reason and phallocentrism, and the epistemic refutation of positivistic science, is does so at the expense of eclipsing metaphysical inquiry, which was the basis of Freud's foray into understanding the ontology of the unconscious and establishing psychoanalysis as a science of subjectivity.

The separateness of the self?

One persistent criticism of relational theorizing is that it does not do justice to the notion of personal agency and the separateness of the self (Frie, 2003). Relationalists and intersubjectivists fail to adequately account for the problem of agency, freedom, contextualism, the notion of an enduring subject or self, and personal identity. It may be argued that relational thinking dissolves the centrality of the self, extracts and dislocates the subject from subjectivity, decomposes personal identity, and ignores the unique phenomenology and epistemological process of lived experience by collapsing every psychic event into a relational ontology, thus usurping the concretely existing human being while devolving the notion of contextualism into the abyss of abstraction.

Most relational analysts would not deny the existence of an independent, separate subject or self, and in fact have gone to great lengths to account for individuality and authenticity within intersubjective space. A problematic is introduced, however, when a relational or intersubjective ontology is defined in opposition to separateness, singularity, distinction, and individual identity. For example, Seligman (2003) represents the relational tradition when he specifically tells us that "the analyst and patient are co-constructing a relationship in which neither of them can be seen as *distinct* from the other" (pp. 484–485, italics added). At face value, this is an absurd ontological assertion. Following from these premises, there is no such thing as separate human beings, which is tantamount to the claim that we are all identical because we are ontologically indistinguishable. If there is no distinction between two subjects that form the relational encounter, then only the dyadic intersubjective system can claim to have any proper identity. Relational analysts are not fully considering the impact of statements such as these when they propound that "everything is intersubjective" because by doing so annuls individuality, distinctiveness, and otherness, which is what dialectically constitutes the intersubjective system to begin with. Clearly, we are not the same when we engage in social discourse or form relationships with others, which simply defies reason and empirical observation: individuals always remain unique, even in social discourse. We retain a sense of self independent from the intersubjective system while participating in it. Of course, contemporary psychoanalysis uses the term "self" as if it is an autonomous, separate entity while engaging in social relations, but when it imports an undisciplined use of postmodern theory, it unwittingly nullifies its previous commitments. Jon Frederickson (2005) perspicaciously argues that despite the relational emphasis on subjectivity over objectivity, relational analysis inadvertently removes the subject from the subjective processes that constitute relational exchange to begin with, hence contradicting the very premise it seeks to uphold.

Further statements such as this: "There is *no* experience that is not interpersonally mediated" (Mitchell, 1992, p. 2, italics added), lend themselves to the social-linguistic platform and thereby deplete the notion of individuation, autonomy, choice, freedom, and teleological (purposeful) action because we are constituted, hence caused, by extrinsic forces that determine who we are. Not only does this displace the centrality of subjectivity—the very thing relationality wants to account for, it does not take into account other nonlinguistic or extralinguistic factors that transpire within personal lived experience such as the phenomenology of embodiment, somatic resonance states, nonconceptual perceptive consciousness, affective life, aesthetic experience, *a priori* mental processes organized prior to the formal acquisition of language, and most importantly, the unconscious. The confusional aspects to relational thinking are only magnified when theorists use terminology that align them with postmodernism on the one hand, thus eclipsing the self and extracting the subject from subjectivity, yet they then want to affirm the existence of the self as an independent agent (Hoffman, 1998). While some relational analysts advocate for a singular, cohesive self that is subject to change yet endures over time (Fosshage, 2003; Lichenberg, Lachmann, & Fosshage, 2002), others prefer to characterize selfhood as existing in multiplicity: rather than one self there are "multiple selves" (Bromberg, 1994; Mitchell, 1993). But how is that possible? To envision multiple "selves" is philosophically problematic on ontological grounds, introduces a plurality of contradictory essences, obfuscates the nature of agency, and undermines the notion of freedom. Here, we have the exact opposite position of indistinguishability: multiple selves are posited to exist as separate, distinct entities that presumably have the capacity to interact and communicate with one another and the analyst. But committing to a self-multiplicity thesis rather than a psychic monism that allows for differentiated and modified self-states introduces the enigma of how competing existent entities would be able to interact given that they would have distinct essences, which would prevent them from being able to intermingle to begin with.

This brings us back to question the separateness of the self if the self is envisioned to belong to a supraordinate emergent agency that subordinates the primacy of individuality and difference. For relationalists who uphold the centrality of an intersubjective ontology, the self by definition becomes amalgamated within a relational matrix or intersubjective system. Beebe, Lachmann, and

Jaffe's (Beebe, Jafee, Lachmann, 1992; Beebe & Lachmann, 2003) relational systems or dyadic systems approach specifies that each partner's self-regulation is mutually regulated by the other and the interactions themselves that govern the system, therefore locating the source of agency within the system itself. But this is problematic. What becomes of the self in the system? Is it free from the causal efficacy of the relational encounter or is it determined by the encounter? Does the self evaporate, or is it merely dislocated, hence demoted in ontological importance? And what about the locus of agency? How can an interactional process acquire any agency at all? Of course, Beebe and her colleagues would say that the self does not vanish, but by attributing agency to a bidirectional, coordinated "system" rather than the intersection, negotiation, and competing autonomous assertions of two individuated "agencies," they open themselves up to charges that they reify the system by turning it into an agentic entity that has the power to execute competing (reciprocal) modes of determination.

We see the same problem in Ogden: "The intersubjective third is understood as a *third subject* created by the unconscious interplay of analyst and analysand; at the same time, the analyst and analysand qua analyst and analysand *are generated* in the act of creating the analytic third. (*There is no analyst, no analysand, no analysis, aside from the process* through which the analytic third is generated)" (Ogden, 1995, p. 697, italics added). Not only does Ogden specifically hypostatize the intersubjective system by making it an existent "subjective" entity, he also asserts that each subject in the dyad is "generated," presumably as a co-construction, yet this is left unexplained. But he also nebulously introduces the notion that the analytic dyad is "generated" through the process of "creating" the analytic third, hence overshadowing his previous claim that the "third" is "created" by the intersubjective dyad, a convoluted thesis that begs for misinterpretation. What I believe Ogden wants to convey is that the analytic dyad is *transformed* in the act of intersubjective engagement, but this assumption is rapidly overturned when he implies that the duality creates the third yet is generated by the third, hence begging the question of what exactly constitutes agency, causal efficacy, and the analytic third. This is evinced by his irrefutable erasure of personal identity all together by claiming that there is "no" analyst or analysand—hence a negation—independent of the "process" that bought the third subject into being to begin with, thereby collapsing his argument into a tautology or self-contradiction.

I believe the relational turn would be better served to indubitably acknowledge that the intersubjective system, field, or matrix is not an agentic subject, being (*Sein*), or entity (*ens*), but rather a "space" forged through transactional psychic temporal processes. By conceiving the relational matrix as intersubjective space instantiated through temporal dynamic mediacy generated by separate subjective agencies in dialogue, the ontological problematic of an emergent, systemically constituted (hence created) entity or analytic third is ameliorated. From my account, there is no third subjectivity or agency, only experiential space punctuated by embodied, transactional temporal processes that belong to the unique contingencies of the human beings participating in such interaction, whether this be from the developmental perspective of the mother–infant dyad to the therapeutic encounter. To speak of a third subject or subjectivity that materializes out of the vapor of dialogical exchange is to introduce an almost impossible problematic of explaining how a noncorporeal entity could attain the status of being *qua* being (ὄν), let alone how such entity could claim to have agentic determination over the dyad. But this is not to say that the intersubjective dyad does not introduce a new movement or generative element within the analytic milieu, what we may refer to as a "new presence," the presence of affective and semiotic resonance echoed within an unconscious aftermath born from the spontaneity of the lived phenomenal encounter. This is what I believe the best intentioned writers are thinking of when they speak of a relational field theory, not as an entity, but as a complex succession of temporal processes that mutually transpire yet are asymmetrically (not equally) generated from within the intrapsychic configurations of each person's psyche interjected and instantiated within interpersonal transactions—both transitive and mimetic yet under degrees of freedom—that are mutually projected, filtered, incorporated, assimilated, transfigured, and reorganized within each participant's internality; hence, temporal psychic processes that dialectically unfold and are realized through actively constituted intersubjective space. This is not a third subject or agency, only the product of enriched, complex interactional transmutations, partially co-constructed, but ultimately conditioned on the unique contingencies (unconscious, historical, developmental, etc.) and teleological (purposeful) trajectories that inform each participant's inner experience, choice, and actions within any interpersonal encounter.[10]

Illegitimate attacks on classical psychoanalysis

What is perhaps the most salient transgression repeatedly made by relational psychoanalysis is its unrelenting misinterpretation of Freudian theory. What is so vexing to many analysts is the polemical denunciation of classical thought, which is used by many relational analysts to advocate for their position, arguably a politically driven ideology, at the expense of providing accurate scholarship. Masling (2003) has recently criticized Mitchell for setting this trend among the relational tradition, thereby leading to continued unsubstantiated claims that are overstated, provocative, confrontational, brazen, and taken out of context. Richards (1999) argues that the relational school has constructed a false dichotomy between drive theory and relational theory, when in fact Freud's mature theoretical system clearly accounts for relational concepts (Reisner, 1992), a position Frank (1998a) cogently reveals began in Freud's early career. Furthermore, Lothane (2003) recently and persuasively argued that Freud was an interpersonalist, while Roazen (1995) and Lohser and Newton (1996) show that Freud was at times quite relational in his therapeutic actions as evinced by testimonials acquired from the firsthand accounts of his patients.

Let us first examine the exaggerated polarization the relational turn has created between the concepts of relation and drive, an antithesis it has capitalized on to serve as a launching pad for its "new" theory. Mitchell (1988) specifically tells us that his approach is "a purely *relational* mode perspective, unmixed with drive-model premises" (p. 54). Here, Mitchell clearly wants to create a fissure between his relational matrix theory and drive theory in order to advocate for why his framework is superior to Freud's, a position he reinforced throughout his entire body of works to the point that it has become an entrenched trademark of relational lore. Unlike Greenberg (1991) who was concerned with reconciling classical drive theory with contemporary relational perspectives, Mitchell was not only not interested in attempting to account for drive theory, let alone reappropriate it within his alleged "paradigm," rather he wanted to debunk it entirely. Here, he introduces a major flaw to his theory, for he jettisons the primacy of embodiment. What becomes of our corporeality in a relational field theory if drives are no longer acknowledged as basic constituents of psychic activity? Mitchell's intent is to overturn their importance within psychic life, but he does so through an extreme position of negation—not merely displacement. Mitchell's denunciation of the drives is tantamount to a fundamental denial of our embodied facticity.[11]

Freudian drive theory is an ontological treatise on unconscious organization, human motivation, and psychic development. Unlike Mitchell, Freud was deeply engaged in the problem of nature, hence the empirical *and* speculative investigation of our embodiment. Freud had to account for our embodied, sentient life within human motivation and behavior in order for psychoanalysis to be legitimately viewed as a human science, so his solution was to develop a philosophy of organic process that could potentially account for all forms of psychic and cultural phenomena: namely, the doctrine of drives. What sets Freud's drive theory apart from any other theory in the history of psychoanalysis is that he systematically attempts to philosophically address the ontological foundation or *a priori* ground of all psychic activity anchored in unconscious process. It is not enough (let alone sufficient) to claim that everything is relational or intersubjective without attempting to explain how relationality is constituted to begin with, that is, how it comes into being; and for this reason alone the relational school can hardly claim to have a sophisticated metaphysical position on the matter. In fact, it was Freud who first explained how relationality was made possible through the transmogrification of the drives (Mills, 2002b).

It is beyond the scope of this critique to offer a justification for Freud's theory of mind, a topic I have addressed elsewhere in considerable length (see Mills, 2002a, 2005); however, a few points of clarification are in order. Freud (1915) used the term *Trieb*—not *Instinkt*—to characterize the ontological basis of inner experience, not as a fixed, static, immutable tropism belonging to animal instinct, but rather as a malleable, purposeful, transforming and transformative telic process of directed mental impetus, impulse, or endogenous urge.[12] For Freud (1915), *Trieb* was pure psychic *activity*: while drives have their source (*Quelle*), hence not simply their motivation,[13] rooted in biologically based somatic processes, the "essence" (*Wesen*) of a drive is its pressure or force (*Drang*), namely its press, demand, or motion toward action (p. 122). Freud has to account for the question of origin, what I refer to as the "genesis problem" (Mills, 2002b), and this is why he could not omit the importance of our organic (hence constitutional) nature when describing the organization of mental life, what Merleau-Ponty refers to as the question of flesh. The mistake many relational theorists make is to equate drive with material reduction, a position Freud abandoned after he could not adequately reconcile his psychophysical mind $\neq$ body thesis envisioned in the *Project*.[14]

Because *Trieb* becomes an expansive bedrock of psychic activity, Freud (1926) stipulated that the dual instantiation of drives properly introduced in 1923 are derived from a developmental monistic ontology (see p. 97; also see Freud, 1933, pp. 76–77): that is, drives are the initial impetus underlying the evolution and sublimation of the human soul (*Seele*) and civilization (*Kultur*). What is most interesting about Freud's notion of drive is that he ostensibly introduces the presence of otherness within the very fabric of libidinal and aggressive motivation. A drive has a *telos*, hence an aim (*Zeil*)—It (*Es*) seeks, yearns, pines for satisfaction, for fulfillment—which may only be sated through an object (*Objekt*), what Freud mainly considered to be other people, but it could be any object or part-object coveted for satisfaction. In fact, Freud says that an object is the "most variable" aspect to drive activity, but he ultimately privileges human connection. In other words, the force or impetus of a drive is to seek human contact and relatedness in order to fulfill its aims. To speak of the destiny of a drive without other people becoming the object of its aims is a vacuous and ludicrous proposition, for a drive without an object is blind and empty. And of course, what Freud meant by a human object was in fact a subject, namely, another individual who was separate from the self. Yet Mitchell (1988) avers that "Freud … eschew[ed] any role for primary relatedness in his theory and reli[ed] instead solely on drive economies" (p. 54). This tenet is naively fallacious: let us examine why.

Not only is Freud's object relations theory predicated on his seminal 1915 paper, "Drives and their Fate" (*Triebe und Triebschicksale*), thus making a conceptual clearing for "primary relatedness," he specifically elevates the process of identification, hence an interpersonal dynamic, to the status of a relational phenomenon. Freud (1921) specifically tells us that identification is "the earliest expression of an emotional tie with *another person*" (p. 105, italics added). Later, he reiterates this point more clearly: "Identification (*Identifizierung*) … [is] the assimilation of one ego [*Ich*] to another one, as a result of which the first ego behaves like the second in certain respects, imitates it and in a sense takes it up into itself" (Freud, 1933, p. 63). Freud goes on to say that it is "a very important form of *attachment* to someone else, probably the very first, and not the same thing as the choice of an object" (p. 63, italics added). Here, he is deliberately wanting to differentiate the psychic importance and affective value of internalizing a parent or dependency figure rather than merely coveting any arbitrary object for libidinal gratification. And Freud (1931) specifically concedes that for each gender the mother becomes the original and most important object of identification (see p. 225) "established unalterably for a whole lifetime as the first and strongest love-object and as the prototype of all later love-relations—for both sexes" (Freud, 1940, p. 188). Here Freud ostensibly says that "love has its origin in attachment" beginning with the appropriation of the mother's body (p. 188). If the emotional processes of identification, attachment, and love are not forms of "primary relatedness," then I don't know what would be. From these passages, Freud is clearly describing an intrapsychic process of incorporating the attributes and qualities of another subject (in German, *Person*) encountered through ongoing intersubjective, relational exchange.

It is understandable why Freud would invite misinterpretation and controversy. He transcended his early neurophysiological footholds yet retained his commitment to natural science, wrote in ambiguous fashions augmented by metaphoric prose, and often changed his views over the course of his burgeoning discoveries. Feminists generally abhor Freud for his biologicalization of gender, and humanist reactionaries are sensitive to any form of material explanation. I can see why relational theorists would become confused when reading his early work on drives amongst the backdrop of his evolving theoretical variances. Yet by the time Freud introduced the notion of identification and attachment, such ambiguities are sufficiently remedied. This only points toward a lack of familiarity with Freud's mature texts.

Freud (1921) fully appreciated the social phenomenon involved in psychic development and he clearly tells us so: "rarely and under certain exceptional conditions is individual psychology in a position to disregard *relations* of this individual to others. In the individual's mental life someone else is invariably involved … so from the very first individual psychology … is at the same time social psychology" (p. 69, italics added). Freud was not particularly impressed with having to think the same thing all the time: his ideas went through massive evolutionary changes with regard to both theory and technique, and by the time Eros was elevated to a supraordinate drive to account for narcissism, libidinal object love, self-preservation, and that of the species (1940, p. 148), the role of relationality was an indissoluble aspect of his mature theory of human nature. But it may be argued that relational concepts were implicit in Freud's early work all along: Oedipalization is based on coveting one's parents, to possess him or her, to extract their desired attributes, to *be* them. Despite the fact that Freud did not use terms such as "interpersonal" or "intersubjective," Lothane (2003) rightfully points out that therapy was always characterized in terms of dyadic, interpersonal terms manifesting in all aspects of the treatment including resistance, transference, working-through, and the free associative method. Freud (1912) defines one facet of technique as the analyst's ability to "turn his own unconscious like a receptive organ towards the transmitting unconscious of the patient" (p. 115), hence arguably a dynamic that is accomplished by the analyst's attunement of his own subjectivity to the subjectivity of the patient. Yet Mitchell (1988, p. 297) and others (Hoffman, 1998, pp. 97–102) still misrepresent Freud's depiction of the analytic encounter by referring to the analyst as a "blank screen," when Freud (1912) actually said that the analyst should be "opaque" (*undurchsichtig*) to his patients, hence invoking the metaphor of a "mirror" (*Spiegelplatte*) (p. 118). There is nothing blank about opacity, and a reflective surface is hardly a screen. Take another example: Transference is the reiteration of the internalized presence of another person, hence a relational enterprise, which Freud (1916–1917) flatly tells us depends upon "the personal relation between the two people involved"

(p. 441), namely, the analyst and analysand. We *relate* to our internal objects, that is, the internalized subjectivity of another. It should be irrefutably clear that from Freud's own writings he establishes relatedness as a primary role in personality development and the clinical encounter.[15]

When Freud's theoretical corpus is taken as a whole, the relational tradition's criticism that Freud's theory and method was a "one person" rather than a "two-person psychology" (see Aron, 1996; Mitchell & Aron, 1999; Greenberg & Mitchell, 1983) becomes an insipid, vacuous claim. Furthermore, accusations that Freud's view of the mind is "monadic" (Mitchell, 1988, p. 3) and "isolated" (Stolorow & Atwood, 1992, p. 12), thereby collapsing into "solipsism" (Mitchell, 2000, p. xii), is simply shabby sophistry. What is absolutely inconceivable is that by Freud's own words, which I just presented, he cannot possibly be a solipsist who favors a view of the psyche as existing in isolation from other people. Yet, this is the relational propaganda that has been uncritically circulating in psychoanalytic publications for more than two decades. When one closely examines even the secularity of the relational platform, many take a nihilistic critique of classical psychoanalysis based on misinterpretations (and sometimes blatant distortions) of Freud, omitting what he actually said in his mature texts—let alone reading them in German, and thus erecting a foundation of theoretical novelty based on straw man arguments. Not only is this not accurate scholarship, but it conditions the next generation of students, mental health professionals, and analysts to erroneously conclude that Freud's views were fundamentally flawed, antiquated, and reductionistic, without having to bother to read Freud's texts directly to decide for themselves, simply because credible authorities dissuade them from doing so. I believe this also sends the wrong information to the public who is generally naive about the historical terrain defining theory and practice, let alone psychoanalytic politics. What is unnecessarily unfortunate is that these invented schisms between classical and relational viewpoints, which only serve to differentiate contemporary approaches from previous schools under the guise of betterment and novelty, create more polarization and tension rather than unity and collective identification despite having many shared affinities based upon a common calling. What is of further irony, perhaps in part unconsciously informed, is that although relational analysts advocate the value of relatedness—not opposition or difference—many relational writers use the language of objection and difference to advance their cause.

In addition to these adumbrated criticisms, I have often speculated that the current preoccupation with Freud bashing among mainstream American psychoanalytic psychologists is due in part to an unconscious renunciation and dis-identification with what classical theory represents to a collective group narcissism identified with particular ideals within contemporary sensibility. What I particularly have in mind is the virulent need to reject Freud who is seen as a cold, depriving, critical father figure for the fantasy of the unconditional acceptance, warmth, nurturance, empathy, and reciprocal recognition from an idealized loving mother whom forms the role model for a way of being in the consulting room, which from my perspective personifies the relational turn. In some ways, we may not inappropriately wonder if this is due to an unresolved Oedipus complex from within this collective group informed by preoedipal dissatisfactions that continually strive to recover the lost presence of an idealized, albeit fallible, mother, what Ferenczi intimates in his correspondence to Groddeck as possessing "too little love and too much severity" (Ferenczi & Groddeck, 1982, p. 36). While there are many historically documented reasons to conclude that Freud had at times an intractable personality, this is not good enough nor a sufficient reason to discredit let alone jettison his ideas without giving them their proper due. It is with equal understanding and personal longing why the maternal function is such a prized commodity within ideological preferences informing our unconscious identifications with particular revisionist theoretical and technical priorities. And if attachment theory is correct, we may appreciate even more deeply why we are compelled to do so.

Therapeutic excess

Frank (1998a) argues that the relational tradition has overstated its claim to providing an original contribution to the field, instead giving the "appearance" of a unique position when it is merely the reappropriation of old paradigms with a makeover, what Giovacchini (1999) calls "old wine in murky bottles." I would say that this is not entirely the case. From the standpoint of redefining therapeutic intervention, analytic posturing, and technical priority, relational analysis is a breath of fresh air. Having questioned, disassembled, and revamped the classical take on neutrality, anonymity, and abstinence, analysts now behave in ways that are more personable, authentic, humane, and reciprocal rather than reserved, clinically detached, and withholding. While it is indeed difficult to make generalizations about all relational clinicians, which is neither desirable nor possible, one gets the impression that within the consulting room there is generally more dialogue rather than monologue, less interpretation and more active attunement to the process within the dyad, more emphasis on affective experience over conceptual insight, and more interpersonal warmth conveyed by the analyst, thus creating a more emotionally satisfying climate for both involved. No longer do we get an image of the sober, cerebral, emotionally sealed-off analyst who greets the analysand with a curt social acknowledgment, then walks back to his chair saying nothing, standing in thick uncomfortable silence with an expressionless face waiting for the patient to lie on the couch or sit down. Rather, we imagine the analytic encounter aspiring toward an interpersonal ideal of relational fulfillment and mutual recognition that serves a nurturing and validating function for both the patient and therapist alike, similar to the consummate holding environment envisioned by Winnicott or a milieu of optimal empathic attunement identified by Kohut, with the supplementary exception that the analyst is also recognized.

Relational and intersubjective viewpoints have convincingly overturned the dogmatic inculcation of Americanized classical training and encourage free thinking, experimentation, novelty, spontaneity, creativity, authentic self-expression, humor, and play. And here is what I believe is the relational position's greatest contribution—the way they practice. There is malleability in the treatment frame, selectivity in interventions that are tailored to the unique needs and qualities of each patient, and a proper burial of the prototypic solemn analyst who is fundamentally removed from relating as one human being to another in the service of a withholding, frustrating, and ungratified methodology designed to provoke transference enactments, deprivation, and unnecessary feelings of rejection, shame, guilt, and rage. Today's relational analyst is more adept at customizing technique to fit each unique dyad (Beebe & Lachmann, 2003; Greenberg, 2001), what Bacal (1998) refers to as a specificity of intervention choice, and rallies against a blanket standardization or manualization of practice. Because of these important modifications to methodology, one may not inappropriately say that a relational approach can be a superior form of treatment for many patients because it enriches the scope of human experience in relation to another's and validates their wish for understanding, meaning, recognition, and love; what may very well be the most coveted and exalted ideals that make psychoanalysis effectively transformative and healing.

Despite these noted strengths, relational analysis has generated a great deal of controversy with regard to the question and procedural role of analyst self-disclosure. On one hand, relational approaches break down barriers of difference by emphasizing dyadic reciprocal involvement, which naturally includes the analyst having more liberty to talk about his or her own internal experiences within the session. However, the question arises: Where do we draw the line? Of course, this is a question that may only be answered from within a defined frame of analytic sensibility, is contextually determined, and open to clinical judgment. But this question has led many critics of the relational turn to wonder about the level of what Jay Greenberg (2001) refers to as "psychoanalytic excess," or what Freud (1912) called "therapeutic ambition." Equally, we may be legitimately concerned about the undisciplined use of self-disclosure, countertransference enactments, uninhibited risk taking, and flagrant boundary violations that have the potential to materialize within this evolving framework of analytic practice. While I believe that most relational analysts are very sound clinicians, it is incumbent upon us to flag potentially questionable or experimental practices in order to bring them into a frank and open discussion on exactly what constitutes a legitimate execution of analytic method. Recall that the earliest relational analysts within Freud's inner circle were borne out of extreme and excessive forms of experimentation: Jung, Rank, Ferenczi, and Groddeck displayed palpable sexual transgressions under the illusion of analytic treatment, and they were also advocates of mutual analysis (Rudnytsky, 2002), which is not unlike the current trend to return to an emphasis on mutuality, reciprocity, and equality.

On the one hand, relational analysts are commendably brave to report case studies where their own internal processes and intimate experiences are discussed openly in professional space, which I find of great service to the community because it breaks down oppressive taboos surrounding restrictive attitudes on analytic disclosure, self-censorship, dishonesty among colleagues, and creates a clearing for acknowledging the value of the analyst's phenomenology in analytic work. On the other hand, we are introduced to material that evokes questions of potential misuse. There is always a danger with the overexpression of personal communications, countertransference disclosures, and the insistence on providing reciprocal revelations that may reveal more about the needs of the analyst rather than the patient's. While relational analysts operate with degrees of variance and specificity with regard to the employment of disclosure, this description from Lewis Aron (1991) may serve as an example: "I encourage patients to tell me anything that they have observed and insist that there must have been some basis in my behavior for their conclusions. I often ask patients to speculate or fantasize about what is going on inside of me, and *in particular I focus on what patients have noticed about my internal conflicts* … I assume that the patient may very well have noticed my anger, jealousy, excitement, or whatever before I recognize it in myself" (pp. 252–253, italics added). This statement leaves the reader wondering whom is the one being analyzed, thus raising the question of whether a relational approach is more in the service of the analyst's narcissism.

Presumably Aron is conducting his practice under the guidance of mutuality, what he specifically says is "asymmetrical" (Aron, 1996), or what I prefer to call proportional. The acceptance of mutuality within relational discourse is often unquestioned due to the systemic emphasis on dyadic reciprocal relations, dialogic exchange, and the value of the analyst's presence and participation in the therapeutic process. But we may ask: What do we mean by mutual? Is everything mutual or are there independent forces, pressures, and operations at play that are defined in opposition to difference? When relational analysts employ the notion of mutuality, do they really mean equality, such as having the *same* relationship, or are they merely inferring that something is shared between them? Modell (1991) refers to mutuality as a form of "egalitarianism," specifically canceling the notion of difference in favor of equality. In fact, relational analysts often equate mutuality with equality, when I believe this is misguided.

Equality implies that there is no difference between each subject in the dyad, that they are identical, and that they have the same value. This position seems to ignore the substantial individual differences that exist between the analyst and the analysand, not to mention the power differentials, role asymmetry, and purported purpose of forming a working relationship to begin with. Here, mutuality merely means existing in relation to another subject who despite harboring individual differences still share collective values that define us all as human beings, but they are far from being equal (*aequalis*). We all have competing needs, agendas, defenses, caprices, ideals, and wishes, and these clash with others. So, mutuality is merely a formal category of coexistence, not the qualitative implications it signifies. This is why I prefer to refer to analytic mutuality as defined through proportional exchange, whereby a patient, namely, one who suffers (*patiens*), seeks out my professional assistance as an identified authority and pays me a large fee to help. There is nothing equal about it: I'm not the one being analyzed. One cannot help but wonder how the overtly self-disclosing analyst reconciles the tensions that inevitably occur when the patient's personality or therapeutic process radically resists wanting to know anything personal about the analyst at all, let alone the analyst's "internal conflicts." Here, I have in mind patients with histories of developmental trauma, attachment disruptions, abuse, and/or personality disorders whom are generally mistrustful of any kind of relationship. And narcissistic analysands will be the first to let you know that they are not paying you to talk about yourself, let alone demand mutual recognition. Of course, we as analysts want to be recognized and appreciated by our patients, not only because the desire for recognition is a basic human need, but because our work is laborious and we wish some gratitude. Despite how intrinsically rewarding our work can be, we often serve as a filter and container for a plethora of pain, hate, and rage with some emotional cost to ourselves, therefore external validation is affirmative and rewarding. But we must be mindful that we need to be sensitive to the patient's unique needs and not foist or superimpose our own for the sake of our desires for gratification despite identifying with a certain therapeutic ideal. When this happens naturally and unfolds organically from within the intimate parameters of the treatment process, it becomes an aesthetic supplement to our work, and moreover, to our way of being, which speaks of the depth of attachment therapeutic relatedness affords.

Abend (2003) has recently questioned the purported advantages of analyst self-disclosure, particularly alerting us to concerns over radical self-revelation. Ehrenberg (1993), for example, radicalizes the emphasis on countertansference disclosures and argues that direct articulation of the analyst's own experience is the fulcrum for analytic work. We do not require much effort to imagine how this dictum could potentially lead to disastrous consequences, including unethical behavior and gross boundary violations. At a recent conference, a senior analyst delivered a shocking confession to a bewildered audience that she had broken the confidentiality of a former analysand to her current patient (who was in previous treatment with her analysand) by revealing that her former analysand was sexually abused. Regardless of the circumstances surrounding the intervention, it becomes too easy to see how therapeutic excess can have possible detrimental effects. Other relationalists have forayed into what certainly looks like excess, at least out of context, including the disclosure of erotic feelings (Davies, 1994), lying to patients (Gerson, 1996), and even screaming while invading personal body space (Frederickson, 1990). Wilber (2003) confessed to a patient that he had had a sexual dream about her, and she reportedly became furious. If we were only to focus on the content of these interventions without taking into account the context and the overall process of treatment, then these enactments could be simply deemed as unethical, if not outrageous. My main point here is to draw increasing attention to how relational analysts are bringing their own personalities into the consulting room, presumably under appropriate discretion guided by clinical intuition and experienced judgment, as well as having the courage to discuss their countertransference enactments in professional space.

It has been argued time and again that it is far too easy for someone outside the lived analytic encounter to become an armchair quarterback and call all the plays after the game. While certainly no intervention is beyond scrutiny nor reproach, what strikes me about some of these therapeutic transactions is their humanness and authentic spontaneity despite seeming excessive. The hallmark of a relational approach to treatment is that it approximates the way real relationships are naturally formed in patients' external lives including the rawness, tension, and negotiability of the lived encounter, with the exception that the process falls under analytic sensibility. This is why the relationalists demand malleability in the treatment frame rather than applying a rigid, orthodox, or authoritarian procedure because malleability is necessary in order to cater to the unique contingencies of each dyad; and this necessitates abolishing any illusory fixed notions of practice that can be formulaically applied to all situations. I believe most analysts can buy into this premise, but regardless of its pragmatic value, it still begs the question of method. If every intervention is contextually based, then it is relative and subjectively determined, hence not open to universal applications. The question of uniform technique becomes an illegitimate question because context determines everything. The best we can aim for is to have an eclectic skill set (under the direction of clinical judgment, experience, self-reflectivity, and wisdom) to apply to whatever possible clinical realities we may encounter. But perhaps I am being too naive or idealistic in assuming that every analyst is capable of achieving this level of professional comportment. Here I am wondering how this revisionist relational methodology affects training, supervision, pedagogy, and practice. Hoffman (1994) tells us to "throw away the book" once we have mastered it. Fair enough. But what if a neophyte were reading the relational literature and took such statement literally? What about reliability and treatment efficacy if there is no proper method to which we can claim allegiance? Could this not lead to an "anything goes" approach conducted by a bunch of loose cannons justifying interventions under the rubric of relationality? Yet, the same potential for abuse exists when applying any approach rigidly, whether it is a formal procedure, orienting principle, or general technical considerations; thus, the question of method will always remain an indeterminate question with some approaches being more justifiable than others.

In contrast to the relational analyst, let us examine an intervention from Bion. Bion (cited in Klein, M., Heimann, P., & Money-Kyrle, R.E. [Eds], 1957) offers an example of his work with a schizophrenic whom he had been seeing for five years in a five-day-a-week analysis:

PATIENT: I picked a tiny piece of my skin from my face and feel quite empty.

BION: The tiny piece of skin is your penis, which you have torn out, and all your insides have come with it.

PATIENT: I do not understand … penis … only syllables and now it has no meaning.

BION: You have split my word "penis" into syllables and now it has no meaning.

PATIENT: I don't know what it means, but I want to say, "if I can't spell I can't think."

BION: The syllables have been split into letters; you cannot spell—that is to say you cannot put the letters together again to make words, so now you cannot think. (p. 229)

It goes without saying that, like the examples listed from the relational literature, we don't know the nature or quality of Bion's relationship with his patient, nor the historical or developmental contingencies, what the past content of sessions revealed, nor even the affective, unspoken, or behavioral cues of the current context that may be influencing Bion's choice of intervention. We may even concede that in principle we have no way of knowing what is beneficial or detrimental in this therapeutic exchange, nor would the patient necessarily be in a position to know himself. But what is clear is the authoritative tone, hubris, and brazen certainty in which Bion delivers his interpretations, what Thompson (2004) calls "messages from the gods" (p. 118). Perhaps this is merely an artifact of his classical training, his personality, or both. After all, he was a tank commander in World War I. But he was also analyzed by Melanie Klein, herself analyzed by Ferenczi and Abraham, thus modeling the way analysis "should" be done. Let us examine a vignette from her work.

In Klein's (1961) *Narrative of a Child Analysis*, she analyzes a 10 year old boy named Richard whose treatment took place during the second World War. This is what transpired during the *very beginning* of the fifth session:

> Richard began by saying that he felt very happy. The sun was shining. He had made friends with a little boy about seven years old and they played in the sand together, building canals. He said how much he liked the playroom and how nice it was. There were so many pictures of dogs on the walls. He was looking forward to going home for the weekend. The garden there was very nice but, when they first moved in, "one could have died" when one saw the weeds. He commented on Lord Beaverbrook's change of job and wondered if his successor would be as good.
>
> *Mrs. K.* interpreted that the playroom was "nice" because of his feelings about her, the room also standing for her. The new friend represented a younger brother. This was bound up with his wish for a strong father who would give Mummy many babies (the many dogs). She also interpreted his concern that, if he pushed Daddy out … he would take Daddy's place but would be unable to make babies and hold the family together. He was also happy because he was going home and, in order to keep the family life friendly, he wished to inhibit his desire to take Daddy's place. The weeds stood for himself when he upset the family peace by his jealousy and competition with his father. He has used the expression "one could have died" when referring to the weeds, because they represented something dangerous.
>
> Richard sneezed and became very worried … (p. 34)

Klein goes onto interpret Richard's purported fantasies of primal scenes, penises, dangerous internal objects, and *his wish to have intercourse* with her and his mother. It comes as no surprise that the boy became horrified and immediately wanted to flee from the anxiety she engendered with her interpretations. If the relational camp is to be overly criticized for therapeutic excess, then what should we make of this intervention—therapeutic ambition, over zealousness, excess, or wild analysis? Whether Klein was correct, semi correct, or incorrect in her interpretations is not the point; we must seriously question whether deep interpretations *in this context* are the most effective form of treatment, especially with a child. Most relational analysts who place currency on the forms of relatedness that are cultivated in sessions would surely conclude that this analytic method is abusive and potentially traumatizing to patients.

Since its inception, psychoanalysis has always received criticism for not measuring up to the propounded status of a legitimate "science." But clinical case material is what we mainly rely on as legitimate sources of qualitative, empirical data.[16] As Safran (2003) points out in his survey of psychotherapy research, there are many empirically derived conclusions that address the question of treatment efficacy. Once taking into account the patient's developmental and life history, we may be alerted to the following conditions that remain the major criteria in which to evaluate the merit and/or limitations of a treatment and the specific interventions employed: the (a) qualitative degree of the working alliance, including (but not limited to) the level of trust and capacity to form an attachment with the analyst; (b) mutual agreement with regard to the process and goals of treatment; and (c) the patient's assent to professional authority as indicative of his or her level of satisfaction (with or without symptom improvement).

As I have stated elsewhere (Mills, 2005), in my opinion psychoanalysis is ultimately about process over anything else—perhaps even above technical principles, theory, and interventions—for it relies on the indeterminate unfolding of inner experience within intersubjective space. In our training, we learn to cultivate an analytic attitude of clinical composure, optimal listening, data gathering, hypothesis testing, critical reflection, clarification and reevaluation—all of which conceptually and behaviorally guide the analytic process. Process is everything, and attunement to process will determine if you can take the patient where he or she needs to go. The analyst has the challenging task of attending to the patient's associations within particular contexts of content and form, perpetuity versus discontinuity, sequence and coherence, thus noting repetitions of themes and patterns, and the convergence of such themes within a teleological dynamic trajectory of conceptual meaning. The clinician has to be vigilant for competing, overlapping, and/or parallel processes that are potentially operative at once, thus requiring shifts in focal attention and process. There are always realities encroaching on other realities, and affect plays a crucial part. Observation becomes a way of being that requires listening on multiple levels of experiential complexity—from manifest to latent content, detecting unconscious communications, recognizing resistance, defense, drive derivatives, transference manifestations, and differential elements of each compromise, tracking the dialectical tensions between competing wishes, fantasies, and conflicts with close attention to their affective reverberations, listening at different levels of abstraction, ferreting out one's countertransference from ordinary subjective peculiarities—to tracing the multifarious interpersonal components of therapeutic exchange. Given such complexity and the overdetermination of multiple competing processes,

I hardly think psychoanalytic technique is capable of being manualized by following a step-by-step method.

Consilience

I imagine some of my relational colleagues will view me negatively for offering this critique. I must reiterate my purpose for doing so is under the intention of advance. Because there is so much that is of importance and value in the relational school, a proper philosophical grounding becomes a necessary requisite in order to lend credibility and validity to its diverse theoretical positions. Ideas without critique are as blind as perceptions without thought; and just as linguistic mediation is a necessary condition for conceptuality, so is self-criticism a necessary dimension for growth and the actualization of further potential. The politics of psychoanalytic infighting is not a new topic. But it seems to me that the relational school has introduced a new tension within the establishment: with the hermeneutic turn, psychoanalysis is drifting away from its scientific foundations to philosophy. Bornstein (2001), Masling (2003), Silverman (2000), and Josephs (2001) reproach contemporary psychoanalysis for the abnegation of a scientific framework based on empirically derived research methodology under the seduction of postmodern hyperbole. While this criticism is not entirely without merit, it also presupposes that psychoanalysis must continue to view itself solely as a scientific discipline modeled after natural science, a presupposition relational analysts have repeatedly drawn into question.

The conception of psychoanalysis as a science was as much a criticism of Freud's time as it is today;[17] and we can see why the empirical proponents of psychoanalysis—mainly academics—have an invested interest is salvaging psychoanalysis from the bog of illegitimacy. Popper (1972) and Grünbaum (1984) argue that psychoanalysis simply fails as a natural science because it is too private, not open to clinical testing or falsification, and not modeled after physics, while Sulloway (1979) and Webster (1995) decry that it must forgo the status of a serious science because it does not conform to Darwinian biology. In a recent defense of psychoanalysis, Marcus Bowman (2002) argues that outdated and misapplied notions of science and positivism erroneously serve as the main resistance against accepting the value of psychoanalysis as a rational inquiry into the essential conditions of internal human conflict. He claims that critics of psychoanalysis hold onto the illusory hope that human science should be modeled on physical science and/or evolutionary biology when these propositions themselves may be interpreted as category mistakes, distort the real practice of scientific observation which is based on consensus and agreement, and generally reflect an exaggeration of the authority of science as a touchstone to truth. Even Freud (1915) himself recognized the limits to the so-called "scientific method": "We have often heard it maintained that sciences should be built up on clear and sharply defined basic concepts. In actual fact no science, not even the most exact, begins with such definitions" (p. 117). For anyone actually working in empirical research, we all know how easy it is to statistically manipulate data: "scientific" reports are primarily based on the theoretical beliefs of the researcher who is attempting to advocate a specific line of argument under the guise of "objectivity." Freud (1912) saw through this game: "Cases which are devoted from the first to scientific purposes and treated accordingly suffer in their outcome; while the most successful cases are those in which one proceeds, as it were, without any purpose in view, allows oneself to be taken by surprise by any new turn in them, and always meets them with an open mind, free from any presuppositions" (p. 114), hence alerting us to the potential interference of the analyst's subjectivity.

I am afraid that the polarity between psychoanalysis as science versus psychoanalysis as hermeneutics will always be a felt tension. On the one hand, disciplines that largely identify with being scientifically (hence empirically) grounded will need to justify their theories through collaborative identification with methodologies that claim to be epistemologically objective, while the hermeneutic tradition is invested in their renunciation because they simply can't buy the premise of an objective epistemology. As a result, a stalemate is unavoidable: each side wishes to annul the validity and justifications of the other rather than seeking a complementary union or consilience.[18] Because psychoanalysis has historically always fought prejudice against its scientific achievements, a phenomenon that dominates mainstream academic psychology and psychiatry, perhaps the relational tradition is finding new momentum in the field because of the felt dissatisfactions inherent in an epistemological scientific framework. And with so many generations of analysts having to labor continually to justify their trade to an increasingly cynical public that wants only quick symptom relief rather than insight, it comes as no surprise that the rejuvenation of subjectivity needs to vanquish objective science by making it the contemporary whipping boy. The problem comes when radical adherents for each side attempt to ground their positions through the negation of the other rather through seeking the fruitful unification that science and hermeneutics have to offer one another as a complex holism. Can the two identificatory bodies of knowledge coexist in some type of comparative-integrative harmony or dialectical order? This I cannot answer. Yet I believe it remains an important task to pursue this possibility in order for psychoanalysis to prosper and reclaim its cultural value.

Following Bowman's work, I believe it is important to reiterate the point that psychoanalysis is a behavioral science and not a natural (hard) science, which consequently elevates the role of subjectivity, negotiation, consensus, and relational exchange when making any observation, interpretation, or epistemological assertion. The implication of this thesis is that any form of science by definition simultaneously becomes intimately conjoined with the humanities. Yet at the same time, any true scientist would not make dogmatic metaphysical statements of irrefutable objective certainty because science (in theory) is always open to the possibility that any theoretical system or methodological framework is an evolving avenue or medium for procuring knowledge, not as fixed, irrefutable determined fact, but as a process of becoming. Given that relational psychoanalysis is enjoying adventures of change by reappropriating philosophy and incorporating the empirical findings of infant observation research, cognitive neuroscience, and attachment theory, this seems to me to be an auspicious sign for our profession.

Endnotes

1. Note that most identified relational analysts are psychologists, as are the founding professionals associated with initiating the relational movement including Mitchell, Greenberg, Stolorow, Aron, and Hoffman, just to name a few.
2. In fact, Mitchell (1988), in his Introduction to *Relational Concepts in Psychoanalysis*, coins his and Greenberg's newly formed relational model as a "paradigmatic framework" by referring to Kuhn's description of the nature of scientific revolutions, a point he emphatically reinstates in the Preface of *Relationality* (2001), p. xiii.
3. Although Stolorow, Atwood, and Orange have defended their positions quite well in response to their critics, often correcting disgruntled commentators on facets of their writings most readers—let alone sophisticated researchers—would not be reasonably aware of without going to the effort of reading their entire collected body of combined works, one lacunae they cannot defend in their intersubjectivity theory is accounting for *a priori* unconscious processes prior to the emergence of consciousness, a subject matter I throughly address elsewhere (see Mills, 2002a, b). Although having attempted to address the role of organizing principles and the unconscious (Stolorow & Atwood, 1992), because they designate intersubjectivity to be the heart of *all* human experience, they commit themselves to a philosophy of consciousness that by definition fails to adequately account for an unconscious ontology, which I argue is the necessary precondition for consciousness and intersubjective life to emerge.
4. Freud (1925) ultimately defined psychoanalysis as "the science of unconscious mental processes" (p. 70).
5. In philosophy of mind, epiphenomenalism is associated with brain–mind dependence. Much of empirical science would contend that any brain state can be causally explained by appealing to other physical states or structural processes. Philosophers typically qualify this explanation by saying that physical states cause mental events but mental states do not have causal efficacy over anything, a point William James first made when he coined the term "epiphenomena" to account for phenomena that lacked causal determinism.
6. It should be noted that Gadamer's hermeneutics is an analysis of the text, not the human subject. Despite this qualification, he does, in my estimate, develop a dialogical model of interpretation as though the text were treated as a "thou," hence a human being we find ourselves in conversation with, and this undoubtingly had special significance for why Stern gravitated toward Gadamer's hermeneutics. It may be argued, however, that Ricoeur has an equally appealing approach because he insisted philosophical hermeneutics was more fundamentally reflective than the methods used in the behavioral sciences for the simple fact that it does not alienate itself from its subject matter unlike the human sciences that view people as objects rather than subjects of inquiry. Ricoeur further believed hermeneutics must serve an epistemological function by incorporating its own critical practices within its mode of discourse, which is not unlike many relational theorists today who criticize how previously held theories and objectivist assumptions have the potential to distort our methods of knowledge and interpretation, thus championing the role of the analyst's participation in analytic space.

7. It has become fashionable for contemporary analysts to abrogate the notion of "essence" within relational discourse (e.g., see Demin, 1991; Young-Bruehl, 1996; Teicholz, 1999). These views are largely in response to medieval interpretations of Aristotle's notion of substance as a fixed universal category. However, it is important to note there are many divergent perspectives on essence that do not adhere to a substance ontology with fixed, immutable, or static properties that adhere in an object or thing. Hegel's (1807, 1812) dialectic, for example, is necessarily (hence universally) predicated on process, which constitutes its structural ontology. From this account, essence does not suggest a fixed or static immutable property belonging to a substance or a thing, rather it is dynamic, *relational*, and transformative. As a result, Hegel underscores the notion that *essence is process*, which is largely compatible with many relational viewpoints today.
8. While some relationalists refuse to be labeled as relativists, James Fosshage (2003) recently attributed relativism to the relational tradition by highlighting a "paradigmatic change from positivistic to relativistic science, or from objectivism to constructivism" (p. 412). I would like to use the term in reference to its original historical significance dating back to preSocratic ancient philosophy, most notably inspired by the Greek sophist Protagoras, that generally denies the existence of universal truths or intrinsic characteristics about the world in favor of relative means of interpretation.
9. Schelling's (1800) *System of Transcendental Idealism* may be said to be the first systematic philosophy that dissolved the subject–object dichotomy by making pure subjectivity and absolute objectivity identical: mind and nature are one. It can be argued, however, that it was Hegel (1807, 1817) who was the first to succeed in unifying the dualism inherent in Kant's distinction between phenomenal experience and the noumenal realm of the natural world through a more rigorous form of systematic logic that meticulously shows how subjectivity and objectivity are dialectically related and mutually implicative. Relational psychoanalysis has left out one side of the equation, or at least has not adequately accounted for it. On the other hand, Hegel's process metaphysics cogently takes into account both subjective and objective life culminating in a holistic philosophy of mind (*Geist*) that both takes itself and the object world within its totality as pure self-consciousness, hence an absolute (logical) epistemological standpoint based on the dynamics of process and contingency within universality. When relational analysts return to the emphasis on subjectivity by negating the objective, they foreclose the dialectical positionality that is inherently juxtaposed and reciprocally intertwined in experience. For example, Hegel arduously shows how objectivity is the developmental, architectonic culmination of subjective life: regardless of our own unique personal preferences and qualities, developmental histories, or individual perspectives, we as the human race live in communal relation to one another constituted by language, social customs, ethical prescriptions and prohibitions, and civil laws we have come to call culture, hence an objective facticity of human invention. Despite Hegel's opacity, here the relationalists can not only find a philosophy embracing the fullest value of subjective and intersubjective life, but also one that describes the unconscious conditions that make objective judgments possible (Mills, 2002a).
10. Here it is important to reiterate the distinction between a climate, ambiance, or emergent process we may generally refer to as a third movement within relational exchange that may include both conscious and unconscious reverberations within each person's subjective interiority within the patient–analyst dyad, thus always in dynamic flux and subject to retransformation, as opposed to a third subject, entity, or agency that materializes out of the analytic encounter.

11. Mitchell was so unfavorably disposed to the notion of embodiment that it led him to make extreme indefensible assertions such as this: "*Desire* is experienced always *in the context of relatedness*" (Mitchell, 1988, p. 3), thus leading Masling (2003) to charge that he was willing to ignore empirically verifiable facts, such as biologically based desires for thirst, hunger, sleep, and sex, in order to magnify the differences between his viewpoint and classical thought.
12. All references to Freud's texts refer to the original German monographs compiled in his *Gesammelte Werke, Chronologisch Geordnet*, 18 Vols., Anna Freud, Edward Bibring, Willi Hoffer, Ernst Kris, and Otto Isakower, in collaboration with Marie Bonaparte (Eds.) (London: Imago Publishing Co., Ltd.). *Triebe und Triebschicksale* appears in Book X., *Werke aus den Jahren*, 1913–1917, pp. 210–232. All translations are mine. Because many English speaking analytic audiences may not have access to such texts, I have cited the page numbers to *The Standard Edition of the Complete Psychological Works of Sigmund Freud*, 24 Vols. (1886–1940), James Strachey (Trans. & Gen. Ed.) in collaboration with Anna Freud, assisted by Alix Strachey and Alan Tyson (London: Hogarth Press).
13. An endemic misinterpretation to many relational critiques on Freudian drive theory is that they often equate the somatic source of a drive with its motivation, the former being biologically conditioned, the later being pluralistically overdetermined in Freud's system. Cf. Frank (2003).
14. It is important to realize that Freud never intended to publish the *Project for a Scientific Psychology*, written in 1895 and posthumously published, a manuscript he almost burned if it was not for the intervention of his daughter Anna who wanted to preserve it for his biographers. Freud's early psychophysical project of mental life, a manuscript written before he established psychoanalysis as a behavioral science, was abandoned because he could not reduce the complexifications of mental phenomena, what in the philosophy of mind is referred to as *qualia*, to "quantitatively determinate states of specifiable material particles" (p. 295). By the time Freud (1900) published the dream book, he "carefully avoid[ed] the temptation to determine psychical locality in any anatomical fashion" (p. 536), a sentiment he reinforced in his public lectures of 1916–1917 and in 1932–1933.
15. George Frank (1998a) nicely enumerates many of Freud's technical papers where Freud invokes the "personal" dimension to treatment. For sake of brevity, I have only listed a few examples here.
16. I am not in agreement with Masling's (2003) claim that clinical data is "not empirical" (p. 597) since it relies on the qualitative enactments and analysis of experience, not merely culled from the analyst's clinical phenomenology, but also empirically investigated by psychoanalytic psychotherapy researchers including Gill, Hoffman, Luborsky, Strupp, and Safran, just to name a few.
17. Freud states: "I have always felt it a gross injustice that people have refused to treat psycho-analysis like any other science" *Standard Edition*, Vol. 20, 1925, p. 58.
18. This word is adapted from Edward O. Wilson's (1998) book, *Consilience*, where he attempts to unify the hybrid nature of scientific and hermeneutic knowledge.

References

Abend, S.M. (2003). Relational influences on modern conflict theory. *Contemporary Psychoanalysis*, 39(3), 367–377.

Aron, L. (1991). The Patient's Experience of the Analyst's Subjectivity. In S. Mitchell & L. Aron (Eds.), *Relational Psychoanalysis: The Emergence of a Tradition*. Hillsdale, NJ: Analytic Press, 1999, pp. 243–268.

Aron, L. (1996). *A Meeting of Minds*. Hillsdale, NJ: The Analytic Press.

Bacal, H. (Ed.). (1998). *How Therapists Heal Their Patients: Optimal Responsiveness*. Northvale, NJ: Aronson.

Beebe, B., & Lachmann, F. (1998). Co-constructing inner and relational processes: Self and mutual regulation in infant research and adult treatment. *Psychoanalytic Psychology*, 15, 1–37.

Beebe, B., & Lachmann, F. (2003). The relational turn in psychoanalysis: A dyadic systems view from infant research. *Contemporary Psychoanalysis*, 39 (3), 379–409.

Beebe, B., Jafee, J., & Lachmann, F. (1992). A dyadic systems view of communication. In N. Skolnick & S. Warchaw (Eds.), *Relational Perspectives in Psychoanalysis*, Hillsdale, NJ: The Analytic Press, pp. 61–82.

Benjamin, J. (1988). *The Bonds of Love*. New York: Pantheon Books.

Bornstein, R.F. (2001). The Impending Death of Psychoanalysis. *Psychoanalytic Psychology*, 18(1), 3–20.

Bowman, M. (2002). *The Last Resistance: The Concept of Science as a Defense Against Psychoanalysis*. Albany: SUNY Press.

Bromberg, P. (1994). "Speak!, that I may see you": Some reflections on dissociation, reality, and psychoanalytic listening. *Psychoanalytic Dialogues*, 4: 517–547.

Cassidy, J., & Shaver, P.R. (Eds.). (1999). *Handbook of Attachment: Theory, Research, and Clinical Applications*. New York: Guilford.

Davies, J. (1994). Love in the afternoon: A relational reconsideration of desire and dread. *Psychoanalytic Dialogues*, 4, 153–170.

Demin, M. (1991). Deconstructing difference: Gender, splitting, and transitional space. *Psychoanalytic Dialogues*, 1(3), 335–352.

Eagle, M. (2003). The postmodern turn in psychoanalysis: A critique. *Psychoanalytic Psychology*, 20(3), 411–424.

Eagle, M., Wolitzky, D.L., & Wakefield, J.C. (2001). The analyst's knowledge and authority: A critique of the "new view" in psychoanalysis. *Journal of the American Psychoanalytic Association*, 49, 457–488.

Ehrenberg, D. (1993). *The Intimate Edge*. New York: Norton.

Ferenczi, S. & Groddeck, G. (1982). *Briefwechsel 1921–1933. Ed. Pierre Sabourin et al.* Frankfurt: Fischer, 1986.

Fichte, J.G. (1794). *The Science of Knowledge*. P. Heath & J. Lachs (Trans & Eds). Cambridge: Cambridge University Press, 1993.

Fonagy, P. (2000). Attachment and borderline personality disorder. *Journal of the American Psychoanalytic Association*, 48(4), 1129–1146.

Fonagy, P. (2001). *Attachment Theory and Psychoanalysis*. New York: The Other Press.

Fonagy, P., Gergely, G., Jurist, E.L., and Target, M. (2002). *Affect Regulation, Mentalization, and the Development of the Self*. New York: Other Press.

Fosshage, J.L. (2003). Contextualizing self psychology and relational psychoanalysis: B-Directional influence and proposed syntheses. *Contemporary Psychoanalysis*, 39(3), 411–448.

Frank, G. (1998a). On the relational school of psychoanalysis: Some additional thoughts. *Psychoanalytic Psychology*, 15(1), 141–153.

Frank, G. (1998b). The intersubjective school of psychoanalysis: Concerns and questions. *Psychoanalytic Psychology*, 15(3), 420–423.

Frank, G. (2003). Triebe and their vicissitudes: Freud's theory of motivation reconsidered. *Psychoanalytic Psychology*, 20(4), 691–697.

Frederickson, J. (1990). Hate in the countertransference as an empathic position. *Contemporary Psychoanalysis*, 26, 479–495.

Frederickson, J. (2005). The problem of relationality. In J. Mills (Ed.), *Relational and Intersubjective Perspectives in Psychoanalysis: A Critique*. Northvale, NJ: Jason Aronson, pp. 71–96.

Freud, S. (1895). *Project for a Scientific Psychology*. Standard Edition, Vol. 1. London: Hogarth Press.

Freud, S. (1900). *The Interpretation of Dreams*. Standard Edition, Vols. 4–5. London: Hogarth Press.

Freud, S. (1912). *Recommendations to Physicians Practicing Psycho-Analysis*. Standard Edition, Vol. 12. London: Hogarth Press.

Freud, S. (1915). *Instincts and Their Vicissitudes*. Standard Edition, Vol. 14. London: Hogarth Press; Triebe und Triebschicksale, Book X., Werke aus den Jahren, 1913–1917, pp. 210–232. In Gesammelte Werke, Chronologisch Geordnet, 18 Vols. Anna Freud, Edward Bibring, Willi Hoffer, Ernst Kris, and Otto Isakower, in colloboration with Marie Bonaparte (Eds.). London: 1940–1952; Frankfurt am Main, 1968.

Freud, S. (1916–1917). *Introductory Lectures on Psycho-Analysis*. Standard Edition, Vols. 15–16, [1915–1917]. London: Hogarth Press.

Freud, S. (1921). *Group Psychology and the Analysis of the Ego*. Standard Edition, Vol. 18. London: Hogarth Press.

Freud, S. (1923). *The Ego and the Id*. Standard Edition, Vol. 19. London: Hogarth Press.

Freud, S. (1925). *An Autobiographical Study*. Standard Edition, Vol. 20. London: Hogarth Press.

Freud, S. (1926). *Inhibitions, Symptoms and Anxiety*. Standard Edition, Vol. 20. London: Hogarth Press.

Freud, S. (1931). *Female Sexuality*. Standard Edition, Vol. 21. pp. 225–243. London: Hogarth Press.

Freud, S. (1933). *New Introductory Lectures on Psycho-Analysis*. Standard Edition, Vol. 22. London: Hogarth Press.

Freud, S. (1940). *An Outline of Psycho-Analysis*. Standard Edition, Vol. 23, [1938], pp. 144–207. London: Hogarth Press.

Frie, R. (Ed.) (2003). *Understanding Experience: Psychotherapy and Postmodernism*. London: Brunner-Routledge.

Gerson, S. (1996). Neutrality, resistance, and self-disclosure in an intersubjective psychoanalysis. *Psychoanalytic Dialogues*, 6, 623–645.

Giovacchini, P. (1999). *Impact of Narcissism: The Errant Therapist on a Chaotic Quest*. Northvale, NJ: Jason Aronson.

Giovacchini, P. (2005). Subjectivity and the ephemeral mind. In J. Mills (Ed.), *Relational and Intersubjective Perspectives in Psychoanalysis: A Critique*. Northvale, NJ: Jason Aronson, pp. 97–116.

Greenberg, J. (1991). *Oedipus and Beyond: A Clinical Theory*. Cambridge: Harvard University Press.

Greenberg, J. (2001). The analyst's participation: A new look. *Journal of the American Psychoanalytic Association*, 49(2), 359–381.

Greenberg, J. & Mitchell, S. (1983). *Object Relations in Psychoanalytic Theory*. Cambridge, MA: Harvard University Press.

Grünbaum, A. (1984). *The Foundations of Psychoanalysis*. Berkeley: University of California Press.

Hegel, G.F.W. (1807). *Phenomenology of Spirit*, trans. A.V. Miller. Oxford: Oxford University Press, 1977.

Hegel, G.F.W. (1812). *Science of Logic*, trans. A.V. Miller. London: George Allen & Unwin LTD., 1831/1969.

Hegel, G.F.W. (1817). *Philosophy of Mind.* Vol.3 of the Encyclopaedia of the Philosophical Sciences, trans. William Wallace & A.V. Miller. Oxford: Clarendon Press, 1827/1830/1971.

Heidegger, M. (1927). *Being and Time.* Trans. J. Macquarrie & E. Robinson. San Francisco: Harper Collins, 1962.

Hesse, E., & Main, M. (2000). Disorganized infant, child, and adult attachment: Collapse in behavioral and attentional strategies. *Journal of the American Psychoanalytic Association*, 48(4), 1097–1127.

Hoffman, I.Z. (1994). Dialectical thinking and therapeutic action in the psychoanalytic process. *Psychoanalytic Quarterly*, 63, 187–218.

Hoffman, I.Z. (1998). *Ritual and Spontaneity in the Psychoanalytic Process.* Hillsdale, NJ: The Analytic Press.

Josephs, L. (2001). The relational values of scientific practice: A response to commentaries by Silverman (2000) and Mitchell (2000). *Psychoanalytic Psychology*, 18(1), 157–160.

Kant, I. (1781). *Critique of Pure Reason.* N.K. Smith (Trans). New York: St. Martin's Press, 1965.

Klein, M. (1961). *Narrative of a Child Analysis.* London: Hogarth Press/Delacorte Press.

Klein, M., Heimann, P., Money-Kyrle, R.E. (Eds). (1957). *New Directions in Psychoanalysis.* New York: Basic Books.

Lacan, J. (1977). *Écrits: A Selection.* Alan Sheridan (Trans). New York: Norton.

Lichtenberg, J.D., Lachmann, F.M., & Fosshage, J. (2002). *A Spirit of Inquiry: Communication in Psychoanalysis.* Hillsdale, NJ: The Analytic Press.

Lohser, B., & Newton, P. (1996). *Unorthodox Freud: A View From the Couch.* New York: Guilford.

Lothane, Z. (2003). What did Freud say about persons and relations? *Psychoanalytic Psychology*, 20(4), 609–617.

Main, M. (2000). The organized categories of infant, child, and adult attachment: Flexible vs. Inflexible attention under attachment-related stress. *Journal of the American Psychoanalytic Association*, 48(4), 1055–1096.

Masling, J. (2003). Stephen A. Mitchell, relational Psychoanalysis, and Empirical Data. *Psychoanalytic Psychology*, 20(4), 587–608.

Mills, J. (2002a). *The Unconscious Abyss: Hegel's Anticipation of Psychoanalysis.* Albany: SUNY Press.

Mills, J. (2002b). Deciphering the "Genesis Problem": On the dialectical origins of psychic Reality. *The Psychoanalytic Review*, 89(6), 763–809.

Mills, J. (2005). *Treating Attachment Pathology.* Northvale, NJ: Jason Aronson.

Mitchell, S.A. (1988). *Relational Concepts in Psychoanalysis: An Integration.* Cambridge, MA: Harvard University Press.

Mitchell, S.A. (1992). True Selves, False Serves, and the ambiguity of authenticity. In N.J. Skolnick & S.C. Warshaw (Eds.), *Relational Perspectives in Psychoanalysis*, Hillsdale, NJ: Analytic Press, pp. 1–20.

Mitchell, S.A. (1993). *Hope and Dread in Psychoanalysis.* Nw York: Basic Books.

Mitchell, S.A. (2000). *Relationality: From Attachment to Intersubjectivity.* Hillsdale, NJ: Analytic Press.

Mitchell, S. & Aron, L. (Eds.) (1999). *Relational Psychoanalysis: The Emergence of a Tradition.* Hillsdale, NJ: The Analytic Press.

Modell, A.H. (1991). The therapeutic relationship as a paradoxical experience. *Psychoanalytic Dialogues*, 1, 13–28.
Ogden, T.H. (1986). *The Matrix of the Mind*. Northvale, NJ: Aronson.
Ogden, T.H. (1994). The analytic third: Working with intersubjective clinical facts. *International Journal of Psycho-Analysis*, 75, 3–19.
Ogden, T.H. (1995). Analyzing forms of aliveness and deadness of the transference-countertransference. *International Journal of Psycho-Analysis*, 76, 695–709.
Orange, D. (1995). *Emotional Understanding*. New York: Guilford Press.
Orange, D.M., Atwood, G. & Stolorow, R.D. (1997). *Working Intersubjectively: Contextualism in Psychoanalytic Practice*. Hillsdale, NJ: The Analytic Press.
Popper, K. (1972). *Conjectures and Refutation*. London: Routledge.
Reisner, S. (1992). Eros Reclaimed: Recovering Freud's Relational Theory. *Relational Perspectives in Psychoanalysis*, N.J. Skolnick & S.C. Warshaw (Eds), pp. 281–312. Hillsdale, NJ: The Analytic Press.
Renik, O. (1993). Analytic Interaction: Conceptualizing Technique in Light of the Analyst's Irreducible Subjectivity. *Psychoanalytic Quarterly*, LXII, 553–571.
Richards, A.D. (1999). Book Review of *Ritual and Spontaneity in the Psychoanalytic Process: A Dialectical Constructivist Point of View*. *Psychoanalytic Psychology*, 16(2), 288–302.
Ricoeur, P. (1970). *Freud and Philosophy*. New Haven: Yale University Press.
Roazen, P. (1995). *How Freud Worked*. Hillsdale, NJ: Aronson.
Rudnytsky, P.L. (2002). *Reading Psychoanalysis*. Ithaca, NY: Cornell University Press.
Safran, J.D. (2003). The Relational Turn, the Therapeutic Alliance, and Psychotherapy Research. *Contemporary Psychoanalysis*, 39(3), 449–475.
Schelling, F.W.J. (1800). *System des transzendentalen Idealismus*. Peter Heath (Trans). System of Transcendental Idealism. Charlottesville: University Press of Virginia, 1978.
Seligman, S. (2003). The Developmental Perspective in Relational Psychoanalysis. *Contemporary Psychoanalysis*, 39(3), 477–508.
Silverman, D.K. (2000). An Interrogation of the Relational Turn: A Discussion with Stephen Mitchell. *Psychoanalytic Psychology*, 17(1), 146–152.
Solomon, J., & George, C. (Eds.) (1999). *Attachment Disorganization*. New York: Guilford.
Spezzano, C. (1997). The emergence of an American middle school of psychoanalysis. *Psychoanalytic Dialogues*, 7, 603–618.
Stern, D.B. (1997). *Unformulated Experience: From Dissociation to Imagination in Psychoanalysis*. Hillsdale, NJ: Analytic Press.
Stern, D.N. (1985). *The Interpersonal World of the Infant*. New York: Basic Books.
Stolorow, R.D. (1998). Clarifying the intersubjective perspective: A reply to George Frank. *Psychoanalytic Psychology*, 15(3), 424–427.
Stolorow, R.D. (2001). *Foreword to P. Buirski & P. Haglund, Making Sense Together: The Intersubjective Approach to Psychotherapy*. Northvale, NJ: Jason Aronson.
Stolorow, R.D., & Atwood, G. (1992). *Contexts of Being: The Intersubjective Foundations of Psychological Life*. Hillsdale, NJ: The Analytic Press.
Stolorow, R.D., Brandchaft, B., & Atwood, G. (1987). *Psychoanalytic Treatment: An Intersubjective Approach*. Hillsdale, NJ: The Analytic Press.
Sulloway, F. (1979). *Freud: Biologist of the Mind*. London: Harper Collins.
Teicholz, J. (1999). *Kohut, Loewald, and the Postmoderns*. Hillsdale, NJ: The Analytic Press.
Thompson, M.G. (2004). *The Ethic of Honesty: The Fundamental Rule of Psychoanalysis*. Amsterdam/New York: Rodopi.

Webster, R. (1995). *Why Freud was Wrong.* New York: Basic Books.
Wilber, W. (2003). Hope, Play and Emergent Unconscious experience. *Paper presentation at 23rd Annual Spring Meeting of Division of Psychoanalysis (39), American Psychological Association*, April., Minneapolis, MN.
Wilson, E.O. (1998). *Consilience: The Unity of Knowledge.* New York: Knopf.
Young-Bruehl, E. (1996). *The Anatomy of Prejudices.* Cambridge: Harvard University Press.

2 Contextualizing is not nullifying

Reply to Mills

Robert D. Stolorow, George E. Atwood, and Donna M. Orange

Abstract: In omitting crucial words and sentences, neglecting relevant citations, and overlooking important distinctions, Jon Mills' (2005) critique of relational psychoanalysis significantly misrepresents the authors' viewpoint. This viewpoint seeks to contextualize, but not to nullify, individual worlds of experience and their limiting horizons.

Mills' (2005) "A Critique of Relational Psychoanalysis" is sweeping, erudite, and overall, quite damning. We are in agreement with several of his points. For example, we too believe that relational psychoanalysis (indeed, contemporary psychoanalysis in general) could benefit greatly from philosophical questioning and is in need of more solid philosophical foundations. Indeed, these were central themes in our most recent book (Stolorow, Atwood, & Orange, 2002), which Mills does not cite. Additionally, we share Mills' misgivings about the perils of postmodernism. In another work that he fails to cite, we (Stolorow, Atwood, & Orange, 1999) wrote:

> Our intersubjective contextualism … should not be confused with postmodern nihilism or relativism … Relativity to context is not the same thing as a *relativism* … which considers every framework or interpretation to be as good as the next. Pragmatically, some ideas are better than others in facilitating psychoanalytic inquiry and the psychoanalytic process. The claim that all psychoanalytic understanding is interpretive means that there are no decontextualized absolutes or universals, no neutral or objective analysts, no immaculate perceptions, and no God's-eye views of anything or anyone. But it does not mean that we abandon the search for truth, for lived experience, for subjective reality. We hold that closer and closer approximations of such truth are gradually achieved through an analytic dialogue in which the domain of reflective self-awareness is enlarged for both participants. (p. 387)

Mills' critique raises a host of intriguing questions that could be the focus of lively discussion and fruitful debate for years to come. But prior to any such constructive dialogue, certain lapses in scholarly rigor, concealed beneath his philosophical erudition, must be exposed. Such lapses stem, in part, from his grouping under the one heading, *relational psychoanalysis*, a wide range of psychoanalytic viewpoints that are in important respects opposed to one another. We, for example, have offered our own critique of certain relational concepts (Stolorow, Orange, & Atwood, 2001a), which Mills does not cite, which has not particularly endeared us to some of our relational colleagues. But the take-no-prisoners tone of much of Mills' critique suggests that his lapses in rigor also stem from unstated axes he is grinding. Another clue to the existence of such axes can be found in his citation of Giovacchini (1999), whose idea of scholarly criticism is to diagnose those (Kohut, us) with whom he disagrees as having narcissistic personality disorders. Although Mills targets many other contributors to relational psychoanalysis, here we focus primarily on the deficiencies in his depiction of our ideas.

Let us turn to some specific examples of the sloppiness with which Mills mischaracterizes our views. He notes, and we are grateful for this, that we "are often misunderstood as saying that intersubjective constellations annul intrapsychic life and a patient's developmental history" (Mills, 2005, p. 160), but then in succeeding sentences and paragraphs he seems to treat such misunderstandings as if they were accurate portrayals of our viewpoint. Most egregiously, after granting that we have "attempted to address the role of organizing principles and the unconscious" (p. 160, fn. 3), he groups us with relational analysts for whom he claims "the unconscious has become an antiquated category" (p. 160), citing as his justifying evidence a quotation from a 3-page foreword that one of us (Stolorow, 2001) wrote for a clinical primer on the intersubjective approach:

> In place of the Freudian unconscious … we envision a multiply contextualized experiential world, an organized totality of lived personal experience, more or less conscious. … In this view, psychoanalytic therapy is no longer an archeological excavation of deeper layers of an isolated unconscious mind. (quoted in Mills, 2005, pp. 160–161)

From this damning evidence, Mills concludes that "For Stolorow … psychoanalysis has tacitly become a theory of consciousness" (p. 161), nullifying the importance of the unconscious.

However, Mills is able to make this claim only by omitting from the quotation several important sentences that contradict it. Here is a fuller version of the passage in question, with the crucial words omitted by Mills italicized:

> In place of the Freudian unconscious … we envision a multiply contextualized experiential world, an organized totality of lived personal experience, more or less conscious and more or less contoured according to those organizing principles formed in a lifetime of emotional and relational experience. Instead of a Cartesian container, we picture an experiential system of expectations, interpretive patterns, and meanings, especially those formed in the contexts of psychological trauma. Within such a system or world, one can feel and know certain things, often repetitively and with unshakable certainty. *Whatever one is not able to feel or know falls outside the horizons of a*

> *person's experiential world*, requiring no container. One is always organizing one's emotional and relational experiences *so as to exclude whatever feels unacceptable, intolerable, or too dangerous in a particular intersubjective context.* In this view, psychoanalytic therapy is no longer an archeological excavation of deeper layers of an isolated unconscious mind. Instead, it is a dialogic exploration of a patient's experiential world. … *Such inquiry seeks comprehension of the principles that prereflectively* [that is, *unconsciously*] organize the patient's world and that keep *the patient's experiencing confined to its limiting horizons.* (Stolorow, 2001, pp. xii–xiii, emphasis added)

Now, does the foregoing passage read like "a theory of consciousness" that neglects the unconscious? Mills' mischaracterization of us as neglecting the unconscious is quite disheartening, given that we have been attempting to rethink the various forms of unconsciousness from a contextualist perspective for more than 25 years. Our most recent article on the unconscious (Stolorow, Orange, & Atwood, 2001b), which Mills does not cite (Is there a pattern here?), lists the relevant references going all the way back to 1980. In the article, we summarize some of this work on forms of unconsciousness in addition to unconscious organizing principles as follows:

> Two closely interrelated but conceptually distinguishable forms of unconsciousness were pictured as developing from situations of massive malattunement. When a child's experiences are consistently not responded to or are actively rejected, the child perceives that aspects of his or her own experience are unwelcome or damaging to the caregiver. These regions of the child's experiential world must then be sacrificed in order to safeguard the needed tie. Repression was grasped here as a kind of negative organizing principle … determining which configurations of conscious experience were not to be allowed to come into full being. In addition, we argued, other features of the child's experience may remain unconscious, not because they have been repressed, but because, in the absence of a validating intersubjective context, they simply were never able to become articulated. (pp. 48–49)

According to this formulation, as we stated in an earlier book (Orange, Atwood, & Stolorow, 1997) that Mills does cite, the repression barrier, that is, "the boundary between conscious and unconscious," is seen not as a fixed intrapsychic structure housed within a Cartesian isolated mind, but as a "fluidly shifting propert[y] of ongoing dynamic, dyadic, intersubjective systems" (p. 76).

Clearly, we have not in the slightest degree nullified the importance of the unconscious. We have, instead, sought to contextualize its multiple dimensions. In so doing—and Mills is right about this point—we have challenged its a prioricity, which is a central assumption of Freudian and Kleinian theory and apparently of Mills' viewpoint as well.

Let us consider another instance of Mills' sloppiness. In the next paragraph after declaring that ours is a theory of consciousness, he tacitly links our conception of an intersubjective field or system with Ogden's (1994) notion of an "analytic third" and then later contends that we "reif [y] intersubjectivity" (p. 167), a damning charge indeed against authors who have spent more than three decades challenging the reifications that run rampant in all manner of psychoanalytic theory. But we have never embraced Ogden's notion and have, in fact, been sharply critical of his viewpoint (Stolorow, Orange, & Atwood, 2001a). Indeed, we completely agree with Mills' criticisms of Ogden's idea of a "third subjectivity." So why does Mills imply that Ogden's idea is in harmony with our views? Just because Ogden and we use the term "intersubjectivity" does not mean that we mean the same thing by it. An intersubjective system, in our view, is not a concretely existent entity in the same way that a person or human agent is. As Heidegger (1962/1927) might put it, the 2 do not have the same kind of being.

There is more. After citing a claim by one of us (Stolorow, 1998) that "objective reality is unknowable by the psychoanalytic method" (quoted in Mills, 2005, p. 166), Mills notes that it is important for analysts to make objective judgments about such things as suicidality, and then faults "Stolorow [for] making an absolute claim … that 'reality is unknowable'" (p. 167). Note Mills' clever rhetorical device here of leaving out the crucial last four words of Stolorow's claim: "*by the psychoanalytic method.*" Of course, every psychiatric resident and psychology intern is taught the importance of assessing for suicidality, long before he or she is practicing psychoanalytic method. Years ago, one of us had the harrowing experience of talking a patient down as she held a loaded gun to her head. Did this have anything whatsoever to do with psychoanalytic investigative method? Mills surely is aware that analysts, in dealing with clinical exigencies, often must do things that fall well outside the domain of psychoanalytic investigation and its epistemic horizons.

Mills sweepingly declares that "Relationalists and intersubjectivists fail to adequately account for the problem of agency, freedom, contextualism, the notion of an enduring subject or self, and personal identity," and that "relational thinking dissolves the centrality of the self … decomposes personal identity … ignores the unique phenomenology … of lived experience," and "annuls individuality, distinctiveness, and otherness" (p. 169). Damning indictments, indeed, of contributors who have devoted their professional lives to the investigation and illumination of individual worlds of experience. It seems to us that what Mills does here is collapse the distinction between phenomenological description and theoretical explanation. As subject matter investigated by the psychoanalytic method, phenomena such as agency, freedom, enduring selfhood, personal identity, individuality, distinctiveness, and otherness are always and only grasped as dimensions of personal experiencing. Explanations of these dimensions, or of disturbances in them, in terms of their taking form within intersubjective systems do not in any way imply a neglect or annulment of them. Mills is, of course, certainly free to challenge such explanatory accounts, but they in no way nullify personal phenomenology in the way he claims that they do. Contextualizing is not nullifying.

Lastly, contrary to Mills' mischaracterization, our critique of "the myth of the isolated mind" (Stolorow & Atwood, 1992; Stolorow, Atwood, & Orange, 2002) in traditional psychoanalysis is not tantamount to a naive claim that Freud had no appreciation of "the social phenomenon involved in psychic development" (Mills, 2005, p. 175). The myth of the isolated mind, as we see it, is a philosophical doctrine, handed down from Descartes (1989/1641), which has been transformed by history into Western common-sense psychology, and which, as philosopher-psychoanalyst Marcia Cavell (1993) demonstrates, can be shown to pervade Freudian theory. We (Stolorow, Atwood, & Orange, 2002) describe it thus:

> This doctrine bifurcates the subjective world of the person into outer and inner regions, reifies and absolutizes the resulting separation between the two, and pictures the mind as an objective entity that takes its place among other objects, a "thinking thing" that has an inside with contents and that looks out on an external world from which it is essentially estranged. (pp. 1–2)

In our article on the unconscious (Stolorow, Orange, & Atwood, 2001b), we characterized the Freudian unconscious, which Mills seems to be championing, as a "sealed-off, underground chamber within the Cartesian isolated mind" (p. 43). It seems to us that Mills is emerging as a defender of Cartesianism against the challenge of contextualism in psychoanalysis.

Mills' critique raises many important questions concerning the philosophical underpinnings of relational psychoanalysis, questions that are of great interest to us. But we cannot engage in genuine conversation with him about such questions, so long as he continues the practice of omitting crucial words and sentences, neglecting relevant citations, and overlooking important distinctions en route to a relentless, glaring misrepresentation of our viewpoint.

References

Cavell, M. (1993). *The Psychoanalytic Mind: from Freud to Philosophy.* Cambridge, MA: Harvard University Press.

Descartes, R. (1989). *Meditations.* Buffalo, NY: Prometheus Books. (Original work published 1641.).

Giovacchini, P. (1999). *Impact of Narcissism: The Errant Therapist on a Chaotic Quest.* Northvale, NJ: Jason Aronson.

Heidegger, M. (1962). *Being and time* (J. Macquarrie & E. Robinson, Trans.). New York: Harper & Row. (Original work published 1927.)

Mills, J. (2005). A critique of relational psychoanalysis. *Psychoanalytic Psychology*, 22, 155–188.

Ogden, T.H. (1994). The analytic third: Working with intersubjective clinical facts. *International Journal of Psycho-Analysis*, 75, 3–19.

Orange, D.M., Atwood, G.E., & Stolorow, R.D. (1997). *Working Intersubjectively: Contextualism in Psychoanalytic Practice.* Hillsdale, NJ: Analytic Press.

Stolorow, R.D. (1998). Clarifying the intersubjective perspective: A reply to George Frank. *Psychoanalytic Psychology*, 15, 424–427.

Stolorow, R.D. (2001). Foreword. In P. Buirski, & P. Haglund (Eds.), *Making Sense Together: The Intersubjective Approach to Psychotherapy*, Hillsdale, NJ: Jason Aronson, pp. xi–xiii.

Stolorow, R.D., & Atwood, G.E. (1992). *Contexts of being: The Intersubjective Foundations of Psychological Life*. Hillsdale, NJ: Analytic Press.
Stolorow, R.D., Atwood, G.E., & Orange, D.M. (1999). Kohut and contextualism: Toward a post-Cartesian psychoanalytic theory. *Psychoanalytic Psychology*, 16, 380–388.
Stolorow, R.D., Atwood, G.E. & Orange, D.M. (2002). *Worlds of Experience: Interweaving Philosophical and Clinical Dimensions in Psychoanalysis*. New York: Basic Books.
Stolorow, R.D., Orange, D.M., & Atwood, G.E. (2001a). Cartesian and post-Cartesian trends in relational psychoanalysis. *Psychoanalytic Psychology*, 18, 468–484.
Stolorow, R.D., Orange, D.M. & Atwood, G.E. (2001b). World horizons: A post-Cartesian alternative to the Freudian unconscious. *Contemporary Psychoanalysis*, 37, 43–61.

3 Assertions of therapeutic excess

A reply to Mills

Marilyn S. Jacobs

Abstract: Mills (2005) suggests that the tradition of relational psychoanalysis may hold an inherent risk of "therapeutic excess" which leads to unprofessional behavior. In his critique, Mills constructs an argument based upon a series of unsubstantiated claims which wrongly conclude that a particular theory in psychoanalysis can lead to a particular type of behavior, in this case, of the unethical type. This discussion attempts to clarify the errors in reasoning which this critique contains.

In his wide-ranging and all-encompassing critique of the tradition of relational psychoanalysis, Jon Mills (2005) also considers psychoanalytic relational practice. Under the rubric of "Therapeutic Excess" (p. 176), Mills initially offers that the greatest contribution of the relational and intersubjective viewpoints to psychoanalysis may be "the way they practice" (p. 177). He then develops an argument framed to the opposite effect, that is, that the underside of these strengths is the "the question and procedural role of analyst self-disclosure" (p. 177) and the issue of "where do we draw the line?" (p. 177). This "question" shifts the focus as Mills then proceeds to throw the book at the relational turn, asserting that adherents to this theoretical perspective may engage in "the undisciplined use of self-disclosure, countertransference enactments, uninhibited risk taking and flagrant boundary violations that have the potential to materialize within this evolving framework of analytic practice" (pp. 177–178). Mills then presents an analysis of "how this 'revisionist relational methodology' affects training, supervision, pedagogy, and practice" (p. 180).

Thus, Mills essentially has claimed that inherent to relational and intersubjective theory is a risk of unethical clinical practice. This claim, both preposterous and unsubstantiated, contains serious epistemological errors and raises equally serious professional concerns.

Mills suggests that the structure of relational and intersubjective theories prescribe specific behaviors by the psychoanalyst that may increase the risk of inappropriate behavior leading to ethical lapses. It is quite a leap to assert that a particular theory in psychoanalysis has the potential to give license to a given behavior in which there is a lack of discipline and misconduct. Yet Mills does just that; somehow forgetting that any theory by itself is only a framework for investigative understanding and the building of structures of meaning through the use of language. According to Mills, a theory in and of itself can determine behavior. And he is highly suspicious that relational psychoanalysis can lead practitioners astray.

The ethics of professional practice stress that a system of values in a particular culture defines behavior which is right or wrong. (Bersoff, 1995). A psychoanalyst will commit an ethical violation based upon many idiosyncratic factors, including his or her personality dynamics and immediate circumstance (Gabbard, 1995b). An ethical violation does not follow from a particular theory. Any theory can be used in the service of such actions. Mills' discussion seems particularly anachronistic and polemical given the theoretical pluralism and varied methodologies of relational psychoanalysis and the increasingly diverse backgrounds of individuals undergoing psychoanalytic treatment.

Relational approaches in psychoanalysis evolved as new ways of thinking, developed with the intent to do more effective psychoanalytic work. In some instances, this intent was because of difficult and otherwise intractable clinical problems. These ideas arose as an alternative to the then prescribed rigidity of traditional psychoanalytic technique and the limitations of the medical model. The newer approaches of relational psychoanalysts may seem to some to be risky or experimental. However, the complexity of the relational psychoanalytic process cannot be so simply explained.

I especially take issue with the examples of "therapeutic excess" which Mills provides to his argument. A close read of each of these examples reveals that they are excerpted, presented, or published clinical material which are stripped of important context needed for a full understanding. Moreover, they are quite sensationalistically framed. He cites the work of several prominent relational psychoanalysts as cases in point of the propensity for actual examples of excess with the use of relational theory. He cites an excerpt of a clinical vignette published by Lewis Aron (1996) as "…raising the question of whether a relational approach is more in the service of the analyst's narcissism" (p. 178); he tells us that "Barbara Pizer (2003) delivered a shocking confession to a bewildered audience that she had broken the confidentiality of a former analysand to her current patient…" (p. 177). He then goes on to list other "forays" into excess, including the "disclosure of erotic feelings (Davies, 1994)"(p. 177); "lying to patients (Gerson, 1996)" (p. 177); and that "Wilber (2003) confessed to a patient that he had had a sexual dream about her…" (p. 177). These are cited as examples of potential misconduct. There is a glaringly false logic here in that Mills implies that the use of relational psychoanalysis may have caused these purported actions. Mills further suggests that relational psychoanalysis lacks appropriate levels of "professional comportment" (p. 180).

Mills then goes on to "contrast the relational analyst" (p. 180) with the work of Bion and Klein. The implication is that the theories of classical and Kleinian psychoanalysis are less likely to result in ethical violations. The history of our discipline refutes this contention (Gabbard, 1995a; Aguayo, 2003; Jacobs, 2003).

Many of the psychoanalytic institutes where relational theories predominate have made courses in ethical practice and questions of boundary dilemmas a part of the curriculum of their analytic training programs. In addition, there have been many rich and nuanced discussions over the past decade by relationally oriented psychoanalytic clinicians who have carefully considered the question as to what constitutes appropriate standards of practice. A substantial and eclectic literature reflects this area of inquiry (e.g., Spezzano, 1993; Ehrenberg, 1995; Aron, 1996; Berman, 1997; Stolorow & Atwood, 1997; Cooper, 1998; Mitchell, 1998; Summers, 1999; Brice, 2000; Davies, 2000; Pizer, 2000). In his critique, Mills fails to consider the breadth and scope of such scrutiny.

Furthermore, the *International Federation for Psychoanalytic Education* has concluded that the nature of contemporary psychoanalysis "carries radically different implications for the questions of ethics in psychoanalysis" given its "… rich pluralism of values, systems of beliefs, and ways of thinking about the nature of people, life and psychoanalysis" (IFPE, 2005). The struggle with dialectical issues at the core of relational psychoanalysis does not mean bad practice.

The nature of the practice of psychoanalytic psychotherapy invariably leads to complex clinical and ethical questions. As psychoanalysts, we are trained to continually evaluate and recognize how well we are adhering to our professional codes. As Gabbard (1995b) has discussed, theory isn't enough; we have to always be mindful of process, regardless of our theory. We all make mistakes (Casement, 2002). To ascribe those mistakes to a particular theory is a grave error.

References

Aguayo, J.R. (2003, September). Historical context of psychoanalytic boundary management. Paper presented at the *Fall Meeting of the Institute of Contemporary Psychoanalysis*, Los Angeles.

Aron, L. (1996). On knowing and being known: Theoretical and technical considerations. regarding self disclosure. In: *Meeting of the Minds: Mutuality in Psychoanalysis*. New York: The Analytic Press. pp. 221–253.

Berman, E. (1997). Mutual analysis: Boundary violation or failed experiment. *Journal of the American Psychoanalytic Association*, 45, 569–571.

Bersoff, D.N. (1995). *Ethical Conflicts in Psychology*. Washington, DC: The American Psychological Association.

Brice, C.W. (2000). Spontaneity versus constraint; Dilemmas in the analyst's decision making. *Journal of the American Psychoanalytic Association*, 48, 549–560.

Casement, P. (2002). *Learning from our Mistakes: Beyond Dogma in Psychoanalysis and Psychotherapy*. New York: The Guilford Press.

Cooper, S.H. (1998). Analyst subjectivity, analyst disclosure, and the aims of psychoanalysis. *The Psychoanalytic Quarterly*, 67, 379–406.

Davies, J.M. (2000). Descending the therapeutic slopes—slippery, slipperier, slipperiest. *Psychoanalytic Dialogues*, 10, 219–229.

Ehrenberg, D.B. (1995). Self disclosure: Therapeutic tool or indulgence? Countertransference disclosure. *Contemporary Psychoanalysis*, 31, 213.

Gabbard, G.O. (1995a). The early history of boundary violations in psychoanalysis. *Journal of the American Psychoanalytic Association*, 43, 1115–1136.

Gabbard, G.O. (1995b). *Boundaries and Boundary Violations in Psychoanalysis*. Washington, DC: American Psychiatric Publishing, Inc.

International Federation for Psychoanalytic Education (IFPE). (n.d.). *Psychoanalysis and ethics committee*. Available at http://www.ifpe.org/psy_ethics_com.html. Accessed July 10. 2005.

Jacobs, M.S. (2003, September). Between risk and safety in psychoanalytic work: Ethical Dilemmas and the survival of the unconscious: Discussion of presentations. Paper presented at the *Fall Meeting of the Institute of Contemporary Psychoanalysis*, Los Angeles.

Mills, J. (2005). A critique of relational psychoanalysis. *Psychoanalytic Psychology*, 22, 155–188.

Mitchell, S.A. (1998). The emergence of features of the analyst's life. *Psychoanalytic Dialogues*, 8, 187–194.

Pizer, B. (2000). The therapists' routine consultations: A necessary window in the treatment frame. *Psychoanalytic Dialogues*, 10, 197–207.

Spezzano, C. (1993). A relational model of inquiry and truth: The place of psychoanalysis in human conversation. *Psychoanalytic Dialogues*, 3, 177–208.

Stolorow, R.D., & Atwood, G.E. (1997). Deconstructing the myth of the neutral analyst: An alternative from intersubjective systems theory. *The Psychoanalytic Quarterly*, 66, 431–449.

Summers, F. (1999). Psychoanalytic boundaries and transitional space. *Psychoanalytic Psychology*, 16, 3–20.

4 "Neither fish nor flesh"

Commentary on Jon Mills

Stuart A. Pizer

Abstract: Mills (2005) offers a wide-ranging critique of relational psychoanalysis, seeking to point out its theoretical shortcomings and its clinical hazards. Although he declares an evenhanded and nonpolemic approach, promotes "accurate scholarship," and decries "illegitimate attacks" on psychoanalytic literature, Mills' thesis is rife with rhetorical excesses, unsubstantiated allegations, and misrepresentations of clinical moments unlinked from their contexts. This commentary highlights where Mills supports his opinions through evocative and mystifying rhetoric rather than scholarly and substantiating evidence.

In his "Critique of Relational Psychoanalysis," Jon Mills (2005) writes, "I imagine some of my relational colleagues will view me negatively for offering this critique" (p. 182). I, for one, do not view negatively any honest intellectual effort to critique the relational literature. Our field grows through vigorous and open discourse and the careful and reflective articulation of differences. Thus, Mills' ideas about the risks of applying philosophical concepts outside their embeddedness in a philosophical context, and his speculations about the problematics of attributing agency to a third as entity (even if he does dip into a sarcastic style), strike me as well worth our attention and further consideration. But I do view quite negatively much of what Mills has done in his article. And here is why. Mills claims explicitly, "I do not intend to polemically abrogate or undermine the value of relationality in theory or practice" (p. 157). He further argues for "accurate scholarship" (p. 172) and decries "blatant distortions" and "straw man arguments" (p. 176). However, Mills fails to live up to his own declared standards. Indeed, he is guilty on all counts.

First, regarding his style, I hope to demonstrate where Mills argues by rhetoric and innuendo rather than by scholarship. For example, early in his essay, Mills refers to relational analysts as a "politically powerful and advantageous group" (p. 156). Subtly and deftly in passing, I think Mills' rhetoric here serves to conjure the paranoid position in any reader who might fear a relational takeover. He is, in other words, setting up the relational "group" as something it is not—at least no more than other psychoanalytic "groups"—in order to arouse a sense of danger to the psychoanalytic field.

After this tonal set up, Mills sets up Stolorow, with *reductio ad absurdum* zeal, as a straw man representing relational theory without acknowledging the many divergent, even contending, views on intersubjectivity (see, e.g., Benjamin, 1995; Mitchell, 2000) within the broad spectrum of relational contributors. This is another of Mills' rhetorical devices: The one stands for the many, as if his salvo at one simplifies his case against them all. Thus Mills bypasses the heterogeneity of our literature.

Mills proclaims, "What is clearly privileged in the relational *platform* [is a political campaign implied here, or a consensus agenda?] *over and above* the unique internal experiences and contingencies of the individual's intrapsychic configurations is the intersubjective field or dyadic system.... The primary focus here is not on the object, as in relatedness to others (object relations) or the objective (natural) world, or on the subject, as in the individual's lived phenomenal experience; rather the emphasis is on the system itself" (p. 161, italics added). Mills goes so far as to allege that "the relational platform" gives "supremacy" to the system. Mills is entitled to his opinion, but his readers are justified in rejecting it if he does not support it adequately, or if he fails to cite the readily available views that contradict his own. Jessica Benjamin (1995), for example, asserts that the relational project is to take into account the intrapsychic and the interpersonal at the same time. Stephen Mitchell (1988) builds his thinking on the history of an individual's internalized object relations witnessed through the enactments of transference repetitions and proposes (1997) that the aim of psychoanalytic treatment is the widening of experience in an individual analysand who comes to own the analytic process within herself. Donnel Stern (1997) writes a book about a model of the mind based on unformulated experience. I have written (1998) about the essential and ongoing negotiation of a paradoxical bridging between the internal and the external, the individual and the interrelated.

These writings contradict Mills' summary judgment. Of course Mills rightly observes that relational writers have given emphasis to what goes on between people. It is accurate to say that relational people focus on relational phenomena. But it is erroneous to conclude that this is tantamount to "privileging" the system over the individual or ascribing "supremacy" to the intersubjective field, except as it is constituted by the interplay of autonomous yet interrelated individuals. Mills verges close to the edge of that old dismissive gambit in which an opposing view is labeled "not psychoanalytic."

In a subsection of Mills' article, under the title of "Illegitimate Attacks on Classical Psychoanalysis," he perpetrates his own illegitimate attack on Stephen Mitchell with his proclamation that "Mitchell's denunciation of the drives is tantamount to a fundamental denial of our embodied facticity" (p. 172). With this rhetorical device, Mills invites the reader to picture the silliness of Mitchell's thinking. Mills, of course, ignores such sources as Mitchell's (2000) discussions of Loewald, in which he expresses his resonance with Loewald's ideas about the origins of experience in a primal density close to the body and primary process modes. The specious basis for Mills' characterization of Mitchell is in Mitchell's statement that "Desire is experienced always in the context of relatedness." Mills lands on the word "desire" to allege that Mitchell is negating biologically based tension states. But why does Mills slice that linguistic pie at the word "desire"? If we, instead, focused on the word "experienced," we might then ask what is entailed in the individual's experience of desire. We might then think differently about Mitchell's sentence.

Mills proceeds to quote Freud's wonderful statement on "the social phenomenon" involved in psychic development. Indeed, Mills very nicely indicates the relationality that runs through Freud's writings. I quite agree and have always valued these very same aspects of Freud's thinking. And I disagree that the relational community is invested in Freud bashing. But two questions arise for me: If we juxtapose Mitchell's statement with Freud's (e.g., "in the individual's mental life someone else is invariably involved"), why does Mills not also accuse Freud of negating our corporeality? My guess is that, in the service of his argument, it suits Mills to read Mitchell selectively and tendentiously in order to promote his opinion that by turning from the primacy of biologically based drives as the irreducible human motivational system toward a relationally contextualized model of the emergence, experience, and development of needs, wishes, and passions, Mitchell had categorically denied our embodied facticity. In my reading of Mills, his failure to make his case on the evidence is underscored by his own selectively juxtaposed quotations from Mitchell and Freud. My second question: Is Mills not employing the old rhetorical device of "Mitchell and his relational group are wrong, and besides, they have no claim to originality because Freud said it earlier"? Again, what I am emphasizing here is that rather than a short circuiting of debate with dismissal, we need more dialogue between competing theoretical models that, in this day and age, can make equal claims to validity.

Perhaps Mills wants the body to be regarded as the basis of experience and for relational experience to be contextualized in embodied experience. This point of view is entitled to make its claim of validity, but equally, an alternative point of view (closer to Mitchell's) would argue for relational experience to be regarded as the basis of experience and for embodied experience to be contextualized in relational experience. This second perspective does not deny embodied facticity. It is just a competing, constructivist point of view that has to be contended with through the integrity of scholarly debate. But Mills, in his straw man use of Mitchell, makes it seem as if there is *a* reality and a *denial* of that reality. Again, critique morphs into dismissal.

On page 177, Mills warns against overgeneralizing about a group. On the previous page, he had already indulged in the absurd blanket diagnostic formulation that, as a "collective," relationalists suffer from a particularly extreme form of unresolved Oedipal complex along with maternal idealization and a pandemic narcissistic disorder. The International Association for Relational Psychoanalysis and Psychotherapy has, at last count, more than 1,000 members internationally (26 countries). How does a serious scholar like Mills apply such a blanket diagnosis to so many people?

In his discussion of Aron (p. 178), I believe that Mills misreads, or ignores, Aron's (1992) clear conceptual distinction between mutuality and symmetry/asymmetry.

Further, what Mills writes about "equalization" (p. 178–179) conveniently omits: Mitchell (1997) on the analyst's authority, and responsibility as "designated driver"; Aron (1992) on asymmetry; Hoffman (1998) on the analyst's clinically necessary ritual authority; S. Pizer (1998) on the analyst's non-negotiable clinical responsibilities; B. Pizer (2003, 2005) on the analyst's personal responsibility and discipline; Slavin and Kriegman (1998) on inherent conflicts of interest. This constitutes, for me, what Mills terms "blatant distortions."

Finally, I must comment on what I consider to be the single most blatant distortion in Mills' article. Mills, writing about "direct articulation of the analyst's experience" (p. 179), sets up his depiction of the clinical work of B. Pizer by conjuring the specter of "unethical behavior and gross boundary violations." Let me first remind Mills that spurious and baseless allegations of ethical impropriety are, themselves, a violation of the Ethics Code of the American Psychological Association.

Mills writes that at a recent conference Barbara Pizer "delivered a shocking confession" to a "bewildered" audience. He claims, in writing, that Pizer "had broken the confidentiality of a former analysand to her current patient (who was in previous treatment with Pizer's analysand) by revealing that her former analysand was sexually abused" (p. 179). I participated on that panel in the Minneapolis spring meeting of Division 39. I witnessed no "bewilderment" in the audience. Was Mills there? The fact is that there is no reference in B. Pizer's paper to her former analysand being sexually abused. Mills has made a seriously untrue—indeed libelous—statement in print in the journal of our Division. I deplore such a breach on the part of author and editorial staff. Further, the paper so grossly misrepresented by Mills is unpublished. The readership of this journal cannot check the facts unless and until this paper is published. (Fortunately, it is in press in *Contemporary Psychoanalysis*, where readers will find the true substance of B. Pizer's exploration of ethical dilemmas and the hierarchy of ethical responsibilities in clinical practice.) Mills' libelous use of this unpublished material without the author's permission strikes me as a significant boundary violation.

Finally, I am left to my own "bewilderment" by Mills' writing—in the space of the same paragraph—both that "regardless of the circumstances surrounding the intervention" this is "therapeutic excess" with "possibly detrimental effects" and that we should focus not merely on the "content of these interventions" (with their implicitly unethical and outrageous malfeasance), but also recognize the "appropriate discretion" and the "clinical intuition and experienced judgment" exercised in the consulting room along with the courage manifested "in professional space." Mystifyingly, Mills in short order both indicts and praises the same acts of relational sensibility. Thus Mills proposes that his praise of relational technique in practice is "my main point here" (p. 179). In the wake of his unsubstantiated allegations, this assertion leaves me spinning. I am reminded of Falstaff's reference to Mistress Quickly as an "otter": "Neither fish nor flesh; a man knows not where to have her" (Shakespeare, *Henry IV, Part 1*, Act III, iii, 126–127).

Mills has imagined being viewed "negatively." Mills' support of his legitimate opinion with rhetorical spin rather than scholarship is what I view negatively in what purports to be a scholarly contribution in a professional journal.

References

Aron, L. (1992). Interpretation as expression of the analyst's subjectivity. *Psychoanalytic Dialogues*, 2, 475–507.

Benjamin, J. (1995). *Like Subjects, Love Objects*. New Haven: Yale University Press.

Hoffman, I.Z. (1998). *Ritual and Spontaneity in the Psychoanalytic Process*. Hillsdale, NJ: The Analytic Press.

Mills, J. (2005). A critique of relational psychoanalysis. *Psychoanalytic Psychology*, 22, 155–188.

Mitchell, S. (1988). *Relational Concepts in Psychoanalysis*. Cambridge, MA: Harvard University Press.

Mitchell, S. (1997). *Influence and Autonomy in Psychoanalysis*. Hillsdale, NJ: The Analytic Press.

Mitchell, S. (2000). *Relationality: From Attachment to Intersubjectivity*. Hillsdale, NJ: The Analytic Press.

Pizer, B. (2003). When the crunch is a (knot): A crimp in relational dialogue. *Psychoanalytic Dialogues*, 13, 171–192.

Pizer, B. (2005). Passion, responsibility, and "Wild Geese": Creating a context for the absence of conscious intentions. *Psychoanalytic Dialogues*, 15, 57–84.

Pizer, S.A. (1998). *Building Bridges: The Negotiation of Paradox in Psychoanalysis*. Hillsdale, NJ: The Analytic Press.

Slavin, M., & Kriegman, D. (1998). Why the analyst needs to change: Toward a theory of conflict, negotiation, and mutual influence in the therapeutic process. *Psychoanalytic Dialogues*, 8, 247–284.

Stern, D. (1997). *Unformulated Experience: From Dissociation to Imagination in Psychoanalysis*. Hillsdale, NJ: The Analytic Press.

5 A response to my critics

Jon Mills

Abstract: The author responds to criticisms in defense of his recent controversial article on a critique of relational psychoanalysis. Critics charge that Mills fails to live up to scholarly standards, uses rhetorical devices to unjustly discredit certain relational authors, takes clinical material out of context, and has committed unethical and libelous acts. Mills attempts to show that these criticisms largely lack solid rationale, distort or ignore crucial textual evidence, rely on *ad hominem* arguments and emotional polemics, and fail to convince the author of their genuine merit.

The expressed purpose of "Commentary" is to serve as a forum for dialogue in response to articles published in this journal. Commentary on my work preceded its publication in this journal. For this reason, it is important for the readership to be aware of the historical background that informs my response to my critics. At last year's conference of the Division of Psychoanalysis of the American Psychological Association held in New York City, I was chair and moderator of a panel titled, "Relational Psychoanalysis: A Critical Dialogue." There I delivered a paper called, "Why Freud was Right: A Response to the Relational School." This presentation was a subsection of a much larger article that subsequently appeared in *Psychoanalytic Psychology* under the title of "A Critique of Relational Psychoanalysis," (Mills, 2005), the subject matter of this reply. At the conference as well as in print, I charged the relational school with illegitimate attacks on classical psychoanalysis by radically misrepresenting and distorting what Freud actually said in his original texts. Such inaccuracies show poor scholarship and are overstatements that serve to promote an unwarranted theoretical divide between drive theory and relationality, which I allege is due, in part, to informal fallacies construed to politically advance a "new" relational paradigm at the expense of understanding what Freud truly has to offer us.[1]

At the end of the panel presentations and commentary provided by a respondent, a highly charged and emotional incident transpired between myself and two distinguished analysts, the details of which I have described elsewhere (Mills, 2006, p. 198; 2012, pp. 141–143; 145–158) and has been corroborated by others (Sound Images, Inc., 2005; Frie, 2007). This event symbolizes a much larger problem within psychoanalysis. The history of our discipline is replete with competition and contention, divided group loyalties, tendencies toward splitting and character slander, narcissistic displays of superiority and grandiosity, rigid collective identifications that oppose competing points of view, and political ostracism under the emotional direction of retribution, abuse of power, and intolerance of difference for perceived transgressions against what any school believes is unadulterated dogma. No wonder why critics have bemoaned psychoanalysis for its mismanagement by its adherents. This politic has fueled splintering and factions in psychoanalysis since its inception, and I doubt it will ever change. But when key leaders of the relational movement succumb to such emotional polemics based on a simple economy of intolerance for difference, it hurts us all in a discipline whose goal is the pursuit of meaning, knowledge, truth, and potentially wisdom.

What I believe is fundamentally dangerous is the inability to engage leading relational proponents in genuine dialogue about contemporary ideas, despite the fact that they profess to uphold such ideals. Only our discipline can properly appreciate such a contradiction, for it speaks to a broader voice, namely, the echo of human nature. We all get emotionally attached to our ideas because we identify with their value and invest them with personal meaning. When they are challenged we understandably feel threatened and frequently wish to lash out, alienate, or aggress upon our perceived or projected enemy. And we need to have enemies. What would psychic life be like if we all agreed on the same thing? I for one would find it boring. But ideological intolerance of difference is simply unacceptable in any academic or scientific discipline: It does nothing but lead to stasis and exploitive, corrupt power differentials that erode the advancement of any intellectual pursuit. The minute we are prohibited or dissuaded to engage in critique, let alone reviled for doing so, we betray our intellectual integrity as a behavioral-social-human science and lose all credibility as a discipline. And what became of the so-called "dialogue" after the imbroglio? It vanished, chalked-up as "pseudo dialogue" by the respondent.

If these exchanges are accurate representatives of the relational tradition, and I hope they are not, then this would lead any reasonable person to question its viability and leadership. Such undisciplined display of emotion directed at me in public professional space based on theoretical differences reflects to me their insecurity, narcissistic fragility, and intellectual vulnerability. What is ironic is that while this movement launched its claim to fame by abnegating Freud, this behavior unequivocally mirrors Freud's own narcissistic pursuit of power, tenacious demand for loyalty, and unsavory tendency to alienate anyone who challenged his authority. A cult bases its practice on indoctrination, prohibition of autonomy, and the oppression of free thought and speech. If you dare question cult doctrine, you are immediately seen as a heretic and promptly excommunicated. I have both personally and professionally felt the backlash.

At least Bob Stolorow, George Atwood, and Donna Orange have some professional integrity to address my arguments directly, and for this they have my respect. Let me first of all say that I have admired much of their work, for we are all interested in seeing psychoanalysis broaden its horizons, to use their metaphor, by embracing philosophical principles. I am on the same page in many respects with their overall project, yet we simply happen to have differences in emphasis, not to mention scholarly disagreements when it comes to key aspects of their collective writings. They have introduced many important philosophical concepts to a psychoanalytic audience that has either remained oblivious to or simply uninterested in properly engaging. In doing so, they have done a great service to our field.

In response to their particular criticisms of my characterization of their work, let me address a few points in turn. To me, the overarching complaint they have is that I "fail" to cite all of their work. As I stated specifically in my article, my critique could not possibly address every relational analyst's point of view, theoretical allegiance, or philosophical preferences that are associated or identified with this movement let alone Stolorow et al.'s "entire collected body of combined works" (Mills, 2005, p. 160, fn 3). Instead I carefully inform the reader that "I hope to approximate many key tenets of relational thinking that could be reasonably said to represent many analysts' views on what relationality represents to the field" (p. 157). What they charge as a "failure to cite" as "lapses in scholarly rigor" or as "sloppiness" is in fact merely my choice not to read all their publications. No author is reasonably expected to know every aspect of other authors' works, especially with colleagues who are as prolific as Stolorow, Atwood, and Orange. This criticism in itself does not negate my critique of their ideas they once held, which unbeknownst to me, they may have amended at a later time. I am actually pleased to see that they wish to distinguish themselves from other relational analysts who displace the notion of the unconscious. Yet their particular views still remain a point of theoretical difference between us. Let me explain why.

Stolorow et al. claim that because I do not adequately situate the context of their writings when quoting or interpreting their work, I annul the notion of the unconscious in their combined theories, which they uphold. But this in not accurate. I specifically stated in my article that they account for the notion of the unconscious (p. 160; fn 3) but it is "decentered," not annulled. Instead, I say the very thing they criticize me for allegedly omitting in their response, namely, that they "privilege" conscious experience, to which they give "priority" (p. 160), over unconsciousness. Although I readily concede that the authors object to being equated with other relationalists who do not adequately address the nature and being of the unconscious in contemporary discourse, Stolorow et al. still bear the onus of explaining their own textual contradictions.

They quote a long passage from Stolorow (2001) where they italicize "crucial words" that I allegedly leave out in my article, hence claiming that I mischaracterize their project. As I originally stated, "it becomes easy to see why Stolorow invites misinterpretation" (p. 160). Here Stolorow (2001) italicizes various phrases to emphasize his affirmation of an unconscious, such as subjective defenses that "*exclude whatever feels unacceptable, intolerable, or too dangerous in a particular intersubjective context*" (p. xii–xiii). But this statement could imply a defense model of dissociation that does not necessarily require a dynamic unconscious based on repression theory, a point that Freud attempted to distinguish from contemporaries such as Morton Prince, Charcot, and Janet. Moreover, Stolorow uses the term *prereflective* in his original text. Here in his reproduction of that passage, he inserts the qualification "*[i.e., unconsciously]*," which he places after the word "prereflectively," a descriptor not included in his original text. He obviously wants to equate or associate prereflexivity with unconsciousness. But this equivalence does not necessarily follow, at least it is not transparent to this reader. It is incumbent on Stolorow to define his terms in language that is customary to a certain readership, and not simply invoke language that means different things to different philosophers that come from different philosophical traditions.[2]

Other points of scholarly misunderstanding stem from Stolorow's use of the term "experience," a word almost exclusively used by phenomenologists. With the exception of Alfred North Whitehead (1929) who speaks of the cosmos as "throbs" or "drops of experience," which I have articulated in the context of a wider unconscious ontology (Mills, 2003), the only other author I am aware of in the relational literature that systematically invokes the notion of "unconscious experience" is Donnel Stern (1997) who, from my reading, prefaces his thesis on postmodern principles that privilege language and linguistic social structures, hence a conscious enterprise, over a dynamic unconscious that prepares such processes to emerge in the first place. In their quoted passage (Stolorow, Atwood, & Orange, 2001, pp. 48–49), they attempt to distinguish two forms of unconsciousness, each of which emerge from conscious experience. They attempt to describe that which is repressed, although this could be interpreted as merely being dissociated, as well as that which was "never allowed to come into full being" or that which was "never able to become articulated." To me Stolorow et al. appear to be saying the same thing Don Stern describes as unformulated experience. The question still remains whether the unconscious precedes or is forged through conscious experience. If intersubjectivity is privileged as a totalistic category of experience, then we are reasonably led to speculate that the unconscious is created by conscious (linguistic) experience, hence becoming a repository for shapes of consciousness—thus subordinated in its causal efficacy, agentic functions, and dynamic teleology—or it is dispensed with altogether. Here, relational authors have to attend to these conundrums more carefully rather than merely throwing the word "unconscious" around and assuming we all understand its meaning when these theoretical revisions challenge its very existence, purpose, and function.

Stolorow et al. make a slip in their reply to my article. In their manuscript provided to me by the editor of this journal, upon which I was asked to respond, and before it had gone through any copyediting by the APA office and potentially changed by the authors' during proof reviews, they specifically state the following:

> After citing a claim by one of us (Stolorow, 1998) that "objective reality is unknowable by the psychoanalytic method" (quoted in Mills, 2005, p. 166), Mills notes that it is important for analysts to make objective judgments about such things as suicidality, and then faults "Stolorow [for] making an absolute claim … that 'reality is unknowable'" (p. 167). Note Mills's clever rhetorical

device here of leaving out the crucial last four words of Stolorow's claim: "by the psychoanalytic method."

Notice that I *do* acknowledge his last four words in my article; yet they appear to have effaced this from their memory. I suppose this is a good example of how the unconscious is alive and well in their work; so, my claim that they decenter the role of the unconscious is obviously overstated, to which they have my apology. It is only by accident, hence a faulty achievement, that they could have possibly overlooked such a crucial detail in their reply. What does this suggest? Perhaps Stolorow is the main author of their reply who is personally invested in defending his position to the degree that he is not willing to entertain an objective fact—namely, that "objective reality" *is* knowable.

My main point in the article was to say that the psychoanalytic method, which is based on phenomenal interpretations of shared (albeit separately registered or organized) experience in the analytic encounter, can indeed allow us to render reasonably correct (objective) judgments independent of others' subjective states of mind. Is Stolorow intimating in his criticism that some other method can indeed have epistemic access to objective reality that is foreclosed by psychoanalytic investigation? If so, then what is it? And even if this is his claim, why would we privilege such methodological practices over our own if they also rely on the senses, reason, and subjective interpretations of observable phenomena? When making objectivist claims about reality independent of the subject's mind, all science interprets the natural world through the filter of human subjectivity. This does not negate the epistemic fact that we *can know* certain aspects of the natural world independent of the subject's unique subjectivity that interprets it.

I agree with Stolorow, Atwood, and Orange that contextualizing is not nullifying, it only situates or demarcates a particular object of study, subject matter, or datum for observation, theoretical reflection, or critical inquiry. Yet, there is always a dilemma to context, a discussion that lies beyond the scope of this response. I fully agree with my colleagues that "phenomena … are always and only grasped as dimensions of personal experiencing." What else could phenomena be grasped by? We cannot step outside of our own minds, except only in theory or fantasy, yet this of course is mediated by mind. Regardless of our irreducible subjectivity, this does not necessarily mean that "objective reality is unknowable," a debate we may leave for another time.

The biggest disagreement I have with my learned friends is their constant inaccurate references to Freud's model of the mind as an "isolated Cartesian container." Not only do I think they need to brush-up on their Freud, I do not think that they truly understand Descartes' overall project. Stolorow et al., as well as Mitchell, constantly refer to terms that accuse Freud of adhering to a solipsistic and monadic theory of mind, when Freud neither believed nor stated any such thing in his writings. These are unwarranted conclusions. My colleagues appeal to Marcia Cavell as a premiere authority, a colleague whom I respect and have indeed published in one of my edited books, but this does not give them license to conclude that there are no other ways of situating or interpreting Freud vis-a-vis

Descartes. Here, Stolorow et al.'s rendering of Descartes is something one might find in an introductory philosophy textbook replete with inaccuracies and watered-down summations. In their recent collaboration, *Worlds of Experience* (2002), they barely engage what Descartes actually said in his texts, relying instead on secondary sources and commentaries, and as a result they misinterpret his project. Any Descartes scholar, and I am being kind in saying this, would find their interpretation of Descartes to be elementary at best.[3]

It is important to reiterate to the reader that I never stated that Stolorow, Atwood, and Orange "nullify" the unconscious, only that it is "subordinated" to intersubjective life. This is what I interpret to be their main thesis, even if I am not acquainted with everything they have written. Their suggestion that I am an emerging "defender of Cartesianism against the challenge of contextualism in psychoanalysis" shows that they are not familiar with my work, to which I hold them no fault. As an applied revisionist Hegelian, I have championed in many ways their project of explaining contextual complexity within a developmental monistic ontology that accounts for context to begin with. At the end of their reply, they rebuff me; but I think we can "engage in genuine conversation" if they are open to a meeting of minds.

My next series of replies is in response to Marilyn Jacobs' discontent with my concerns of therapeutic excess reported in the relational literature. Jacobs is essentially charging me with a theory-method confound: namely, that I accuse relational theory—indeed the whole relational tradition—for "determining" the analyst's behavior in the consulting room, concluding that I am saying that relational "theory" "prescribes" "unethical" behavior. First of all, nowhere in my text do I say such as thing because I believe, as she does, that theory and method are differentiated classifications, and that while they may certainly be interdependent, theory in itself does not necessarily "determine" a method or clinical course of action. In fact, she uses the word "suggests" in several places in her reply but she does not cite my actual words. Therefore, her entire refutation is based on a *non sequitur* that misattributes premises and propositional attitudes to my actual position that I do not hold, nor do I state in my article. As a result, her whole argument against me is based on something I do not say, hence it is groundless. That is not to say that her thoughtful points are not legitimate, for they most certainly are, only that they are wrongfully attributed to me. Jacobs can be reassured we are on the same page. Having said this, the issue she raises nevertheless sparks important questions for future inquiry amongst many different psychoanalytic schools.

As I argued, the relational tradition does not present nor possess a systematized view of psychoanalytic theory or practice. My critique was an attempt to give some form, coherency, and voice to a plurality of ideas and approaches that have been identified in some fashion with the relational turn. Of course, any broad critique is bound to have partial success at best, because everyone's contributions to that literature base cannot be sufficiently addressed in the scope of an article. But Jacobs' assertions not only do not adequately convey my project, they also do not acknowledge my caveats and qualifications that I clearly define for the reader. When a subdiscipline such as the relational movement does not hold a unified theory or methodology, it is particularly open to different interpretations in both theory and practice. There are, consequently, larger degrees of discrepancy in freely translating theory into therapeutic action, let alone uniform technique, because un-systematization introduces more ambiguity than systematic thought and procedure. Analysts who are identified with any theory must decipher, interpret, and absorb certain conceptual schemas and convert them into directive principles that inform clinical action, regardless of whether the theory justifies the method or vise-versa. Theory informs method, but it does not "determine" method, a point Jacobs inaccurately attributes to me. In fact, it is important to retain a categorical distinction between the two because a method, in principle, should be able to be potentially applied to diverse and variegated theoretical frameworks that in turn may lend increasing conceptual complexity to explaining therapeutic action. Despite this qualification, adherents of any theoretical model advocate for certain interventions over others that may duplicate, simulate, overlap, oppose, or complement one another; resulting thereby in emphasizing some aspects while de-emphasizing others, or depart entirely from other technical practices based upon theoretical proclivities. If Jacobs is suggesting there exists a complete polarization of theory and method, then I think this is logically untenable.

There is a potential for misuse and abuse that exists with any teachings and in any training milieu, and this is certainly no different in contemporary analytic training environments where the way one comes to subjectively interpret theory, which in turn effects their clinical practice, is influenced by faculty, training analysts, and supervisors who advocate for their own perspectives. Such positions may not be devoid of thoughtfulness, clinical judgment, expertise, and experience, but they are biased, necessarily so, by their preferences, caprices, and prejudices that oppose other credible points of view. To push this discussion further, I *do* believe, as Jacobs is likewise concerned about, that there is an "inherent risk" of therapeutic ambition in *any* psychoanalytic tradition, not just the relational movement. I am accentuating the issue here, in my discussion of therapeutic excess, involving some of the behaviors reported or observed by analysts identified with contemporary relational thought. Just because I draw attention to and question certain technical practices or theoretical tenets does not mean relational theory is decisively wrong; let alone do I claim it ethically condones or "prescribes" "unprofessional behavior," as Jacobs accuses me of saying. The issue at hand, in this context, is how one interprets theory, not the theory itself.

Jacobs charges me with indicting the relational "tradition" itself when I in fact am alerting others to various behaviors I question as potentially excessive or overly ambitious, and which, I believe, we need to talk about more openly in professional space. Jacobs rightly points out that this is already happening in the relational field, a subject matter I was remiss not to be aware of. I am happy to be informed of this because these ongoing discussions are likely to be very fruitful for us all. But Jacobs is wrong to say that I am advocating that classical approaches cited in the works of Bion and Klein are "less likely to result in ethical violations," when in fact a close reading of my actual text conveys the opposite. I unambiguously say that "what is clear is the authoritative tone, hubris, and brazen certainty with which Bion delivers his interpretations" and that Klein's treatment of her child analysand is "abusive and potentially traumatizing" (Mills, 2005, p. 181).

Jacobs is obviously upset, as is Pizer, that I report clinical events out of context, however, I specifically acknowledge this on several occasions. For instance, I state that: "If we were to focus only on the content of these interventions without taking into account the context and the overall process of treatment, then these enactments could be simply deemed unethical" (Mills, 2005, p. 179). One point I wanted to convey in my adumbrated and excerpted examples of "excess" is the overdetermined motivations and multiple implications embedded within an intervention. A careful reading of that section of my article will show both praise for the technical liberation the relational tradition has introduced as well as the potential for ethical concern and admonishment. The main issue here becomes a serious inquiry into the ground, breadth, and impediments to psychoanalytic method. This is an important area in the relational field that needs further discussion and debate, a subject that Jacobs and I are seemingly in agreement.

This brings us to the last commentary by Stuart Pizer, which is quite inflammatory to say the least. Pizer accuses me of using rhetorical ploys to discredit the relational school, and that I further make "unsubstantiated allegations" that have no "scholarly" merit or "evidence." Pizer's criticisms of my article begin with an abbreviated analysis of the alleged motives informing the formal structure and writing of my article, namely, that I wish to make the reader "paranoid" by arousing a "sense of danger" of a "relational takeover." He then goes on to imply—but not deny—that the relational movement has no political agenda.

Pizer admonishes me for not acknowledging the diversity of the relational literature, a common complaint Stolerow, Atwood, and Orange, Jacobs, and Pizer all share. As I stated earlier, these criticisms all conveniently omit my careful caveats, qualifications, and disclaimers outlining the scope and limits of my critique. Here Pizer is essentially saying: "Because you don't quote me and my buddies, then your criticism is invalid." So far Pizer is grasping at straws.

His next substantial criticism is to say that I don't properly understand Mitchell's views on embodiment because Mitchell appreciates and acknowledges the work of Loewald. Whether Mitchell's later thought resonates with Loewald does not erase the fact that he built his relational theory on the denunciation of drives. I specifically quote Mitchell in several places in my critique where he unabashedly negates the primacy of the drives, hence the foundation of classical psychoanalytic theory, which is unquestionably grounded in the question and nature of embodiment. Pizer wants to challenge my interpretation of Mitchell's meaning of desire when he states that: "*Desire* is experienced always *in the context of relatedness*" (Mitchell, 1988, p. 3, italics in original), which Pizer wants to chalk-up to a linguistic construct. But what he omits from Mitchell's text is quite crucial, namely, that Mitchell aligns with the supposition that: "We are portrayed *not* as a conglomeration of physically based urges, but as being shaped by and inevitably embedded within a matrix of relationships with other people"

(p. 3, italics added). While I agree with Mitchell's last statement, as does Freud, why does Mitchell need to negate biology? Pizer then extends his challenge to absurdly ask why I don't criticize Freud as well, who, like Mitchell, acknowledges the value of social relatedness. This is because Freud offers a holistic, coherent, and internally consistent theoretical corpus that does not lend itself to the type of false dichotomies that Mitchell commits by making such overstatements under the guise of theoretical originality. What is further ironic is that Pizer accuses me of using Mitchell out of context to suit my own needs in order to build a straw man against Mitchell, when Mitchell himself has been fervently criticized for distorting previous psychoanalytic traditions, magnifying theoretical differences among schools when little or none exist, and using a variety of concepts out of context and selectively to suit his own theoretical needs (see Meissner, 1998; Richards, 1999; Silverman, 2000; Masling, 2003). The fact is that Mitchell was hell-bent on forging his "new" paradigm through negation rather than seeing how the old could positively inform the new. Perhaps this insight came later when Mitchell became enamored with Loewald, but it does not efface his earlier theoretical commitments that he put to pen.

Pizer pushes the issue of prioritizing relational experience while subordinating embodiment. He states that "an alternative point of view (closer to Mitchell's) would argue for relational experience to be regarded as the basis of experience and for embodied experience to be contextualized in relational experience." Notice Pizer says that relational experience is the "*basis* of experience" (italics added). Here he is saying essentially the same thing as Mitchell without considering the philosophical predicaments he generates. Pizer accuses me of dismissal as a denial of scholarly debate, when I see that he offers no philosophical defense of the mind-body problem that adequately accounts for mind-body dependence. According to most reasonable people I know, it is generally uncontested that: "If you ain't got a body, you ain't experiencing nothin'." Pizer, Mitchell, Hoffman, and others may rightfully think they are "constructing" how they *conceive* of embodiment, which I do not object to nor see as problematic, but they are certainly not constructing their material facticity *ex nihilo*. Embodiment logically and developmentally precedes "constructive," linguistic thought. I think certain relationalists have more thinking to do on this subject.

Pizer's criticisms become more caustic and personal. Moreover, he distorts what I actually say in my text. He charges me with diagnosing relationalists with a "pandemic narcissistic disorder." Although I do believe a collective narcissism exists in any group of people, especially those who are overidentified with certain ideals that by definition oppose others, nowhere in my text do I charge the relational movement with a "narcissistic disorder." But because of the way I have been treated by key people identified with this tradition, perhaps I should reconsider my position.

The most damning charges Pizer launches against me is that I violate the ethical code of professional conduct established by the American Psychological Association and that I have committed an illegal act. Very grave allegations indeed. Pizer accuses me of making "spurious and baseless allegations of ethical impropriety," which he further claims are "untrue" and "libelous." He also "deplore[s] such a breach on the part of author and editorial staff." First let me inform Pizer and the readership that Dr. Joseph Reppen is a man of principled integrity and would not condone unethical or libelous acts if he were aware of them as such. Secondly, my article was subjected to and passed a blind review process. Given that I serve on the editorial board of *Psychoanalytic Psychology*, I know that Reppen does not show favoritism when it comes to publishing articles. He uniformly sends submitted manuscripts to three blind reviewers and determines acceptances, revisions, and rejections based on the reviewers' expertise. And if there are any errors or breaches that were made, they solely rest on the author's shoulders.

But I have made no such breaches and I take full responsibility for what I claim in my article.[4] For the record, I am not making any ethical charge against anyone regarding their therapeutic disclosures, nor am I showing any malice or ill-will toward anyone in the relational field for simply taking their words seriously. I have critiqued people who I find have something of value to say, even if my disagreements have generated bad feelings. If I did not think these issues were important, then I would not have been bothered wasting my time commenting on their work. My intent is to stimulate noteworthy attention and serious debate about these ideas and practices so our profession can continue to prosper and advance.

Pizer says he is left "spinning" by both my praise and indictment of the relational school, invoking Shakespeare to lend profundity to his refutation by *ad hominem*. I am reminded here of Frederick Crews, who, in response to his acrimonious critics, pointed out that no one seemed to respond to his arguments because they were too busy slashing his character. Is this what contemporary psychoanalysis has amounted to—personality worship and self-aggrandizement in a self-congratulatory fraternity among friends—at the expense of legitimate self-critique and intellectual honesty?

Endnotes

1. The reader should be informed that despite the fact that I practice as a relational analyst in the consulting room, and hence feel qualified to critique the relational school from within its own realm of discourse, I am also a Freud scholar by philosophical training. I can appreciate differences of interpretation, explanation, scholarly distinctions, and redirecting shifts in emphasis that have informed the history of the psychoanalytic domain, and I actually think it is a good thing to promote a healthy debate of ideas, but I do not feel most representatives of the relational tradition have accurately understood Freud's mature theoretical corpus nor have they fully grasped the relational aspects or implications of Freud's thought. In fact, relational psychoanalysis has made its claim to originality and popularity "based on the radical rejection of drive" (Greenberg, 1991, p. vii). This was one of my main points at the conference.
2. The notion of prereflectiveness is associated to several continental philosophers dating back to Hegel and Fichte, but it is most notably associated to Sartre who, inspired by Brentano's notion of intentional versus nonpositional states of

consciousness, disavows Freud's dynamic unconscious for a model of self-deception (*mauvaise foi*) based on prereflective consciousness. Given that Stolorow has often identified himself with the phenomenological tradition (most recently, see Stolorow, 2004b), this could easily confuse any reader familiar with the history of the concept of prereflexivity. For example, Sartre's (1943) magnum opus, *Being and Nothingness*, was a phenomenological project on ontology. Given that Stolorow is now by his own account a graduate student formally studying philosophy (Stolorow, 2004a), he is enamored, rightfully so, with the many diversified, albeit competing and contradictory philosophical theories that challenge traditional psychoanalytic concepts. In fact, due to his response to my critique, I have pleasantly read some of his recent works where we are likely to be in frank agreement. I particularly see a commonality between our attempt to account for the phenomenology of lived experience, developmental trauma, intrapsychic organization, personal meaning and metaphor, and unconscious structure. But our main point of difference, as I can tell, is that I am fundamentally a psychoanalytic ontologist and that Stolorow is a psychoanalytic phenomenologist. He privileges consciousness over unconsciousness, while I have argued extensively (Mills, 1996, 2002) that conscious experience, hence the realm of phenomenology, must be necessarily prepared *a priori* by an unconscious ground (*Ungrund*). Therefore, my main point in my article is to situate Stolorow et al. in the same camp as other relationalists who privilege consciousness over unconscious process, especially given that they concede in their reply that they have "challenged its priority."

3. Stolorow et al. maintain that the Cartesian mind is "estranged" from the external world, essentially alienated, sealed-off, and solipsistic, a philosophical proposition they extend to Freud. I doubt they have ever studied the *Meditations* with any precision. If they had I do not believe they could possibly make such sweeping generalizations. In my opinion, they fundamentally misunderstand what Descartes said and what he intended to convey. In the Synopsis to the *Meditations*, and in his letters of reply to his critics, Descartes clearly defends himself against the accusation that he is a solipsist. Rather, he is making a *categorical distinction* between the human soul or mind and the body—he is not saying that they are estranged or alienated from one another. Here the reader should know that, for Descartes, the body is extended in space and is part of the natural world, hence by Stolorow et al.'s interpretation they are completely separated. Descartes begins his meditations by using a skeptical, epistemological methodology of doubting everything as a tool to overturn unquestioned presuppositions of his time, only to conclude that he is certain of his own inner subjective processes and eventually the external world, but this does not mean that the inner and outer, subject-object, self and world are estranged from one another. On the contrary, he goes on to argue that mind and nature, psyche and substance, consciousness and reality are interconnected. Descartes (1984) specifically says in his Synopsis, summarizing the Sixth Meditation, that "the mind is proved to be really [categorically] distinct from the body, but is shown, notwithstanding, to be so closely joined to it that the mind and the body make up a kind of unit" (p. 11). In the Sixth Meditation, he further states that mental activity, such as "sensory perception and imagination, cannot be understood apart from some substance for them to inhere in, and hence cannot exist without it" (pp. 54–55). Here it is absolutely illegitimate to say, as Stolorow et al. do, that the mind is "estranged" from body, hence a part of the "natural world." There are in fact many connections to the mind, body, and nature in Descartes' overall philosophy—not just

the subject matter of the *Meditations*—that challenge Stolorow et al.'s claims, the details of which are not important to make my point in this context.

4. For complete details of these events, accusations, and my defense, please refer to Mills (2006), pp. 207–208 and Mills (2012), pp. 107–109.

References

Descartes, R. (1984). *The Philosophical Writings of Descartes, Vol. II.* J. Cottingham, R. Stoothoff, D. Murdoch (Trans.). Cambridge: Cambridge University Press.

Frie, R. (2007). Letter to the Editor. *Psychologist-Psychoanalyst*, 27(No. 3: Summer), 5.

Greenberg, J. (1991). *Oedipus and Beyond: A Clinical Theory.* Cambridge: Harvard University Press.

Masling, J. (2003). Stephen A. Mitchell, relational Psychoanalysis, and Empirical Data. *Psychoanalytic Psychology*, 20(4), 587–608.

Meissner, W.W. (1998). Review of *Influence and Autonomy in Psychoanalysis. Psychoanalytic Books*, 9, 419–423

Mills, J. (1996). Hegel on the Unconscious Abyss: Implications for Psychoanalysis. *The Owl of Minerva*, 28(1), 59–75.

Mills, J. (2002). *The Unconscious Abyss: Hegel's Anticipation of Psychoanalysis.* Albany: SUNY Press.

Mills, J. (2003). Whitehead's Unconscious Ontology. *Theory & Psychology*, 13(2), 209–238.

Mills, J. (2005). A critique of relational psychoanalysis. *Psychoanalytic Psychology*, 22(2), 155–188.

Mills, J. (2006). A Response to my Critics. *Psychoanalytic Psychology*, 23 (1), 197–209.

Mills, J. (2012). *Conundrums: A Critique of Contemporary Psychoanalysis.* New York: Routledge.

Mitchell, S.A. (1988). *Relational Concepts in Psychoanalysis: An Integration.* Cambridge, MA: Harvard University Press.

Richards, A.D. (1999). Squeaky chairs and straw persons: An intervention in the contemporary psychoanalytic debate. *The Round Robin*, 14(1), 6–9.

Sartre, J.P. (1943). *Being and Nothingness.* H.E. Barnes (Trans). New York: Washington Square Press, 1956.

Silverman, D. (2000). An interrogation of the relational turn: A discussion with Stephen Mitchell. *Psychoanalytic Psychology*, 17, 146–152.

Sound Images, Inc. (2005). *Being and Becoming: 25th Annual Spring Meeting of the Division of Psychoanalysis (39) of the American Psychological Association*, April 13–17, New York. Tape No. D3905-CDROM; Recorded by Sound Images, Inc., www.soundimages.net.

Stern, D.B. (1997). *Unformulated Experience: From Dissociation to Imagination in Psychoanalysis.* Hillsdale, NJ: Analytic Press.

Stolorow, R.D. (1998). Clarifying the intersubjective perspective: A reply to George Frank. *Psychoanalytic Psychology*, 15(3), 424–427.

Stolorow, R.D. (2001). *Foreword to P. Buirski & P. Haglund, Making Sense Together: The Intersubjective Approach to Psychotherapy.* Northvale, NJ: Jason Aronson.

Stolorow, R.D. (2004a). Phenomenology, Hermeneutics, and Contextualism: Summer reading notes. *Psychologist-Psychoanalyst*, 23(4), 28–29.

Stolorow, R.D. (2004b). The relevance of early Lacan for psychoanalytic phenomenology and contextualism: Preliminary communication. *Psychoanalytic Psychology*, 21(4), 668–672.

Stolorow, R.D. Atwood, G.E., & Orange, D.M. (2001). World horizons: A post-Cartesian alternative to the Freudian unconscious. *Contemporary Psychoanalysis*, 37, 43–61.

Stolorow, R.D. Atwood, G.E., & Orange, D.M. (2002). *Worlds of Experience*. New York: Basic Books.

Whitehead, A.N. (1929). *Process and Reality*. Corrected Edition, D.R. Griffin, & D.W. Sherburne (Eds.). New York: Free Press, 1978.

6 Conundrums: A critique of contemporary psychoanalysis

Interview on *New Books in Psychoanalysis*

Jon Mills and Tracy D. Morgan

Abstract: In this interview, Canadian philosopher, psychologist, and psychoanalyst Jon Mills speaks with us about his book *Conundrums: A Critique of Contemporary Psychoanalysis* (Routledge, 2012). In the book he discusses current tenets in North American psychoanalytic thinking and practice that he finds to be concerning and problematic. Focusing on the relational and intersubjective turn currently popular in the field, he articulates what he believes are the faulty ways in which some contemporary analytic thinkers make use of philosophy and, therein, particularly postmodernism. Though relationally influenced himself, in that he is drawn towards a more flexible, less removed approach in the consulting room, he questions the denigration of the drives and what appears to be a seeming disinterest in life before the acquisition of language. Mills wonders about the ways in which ideas associated with postmodernism and the practice of a psychoanalytic hermeneutics have been used to drum thinking about the body out of psychoanalysis and what impact that has on our clinical encounters. In this interview, the discussion ranges from the problem of therapeutic excess via analytic self-disclosure to the fate of the drives in relational and intersubjective thinking to the emphasis on meaning-making, and the role of philosophy in psychoanalysis. Also discussed are psychoanalytic politics, analytic training, and the relational critique of the analyst's authority. While in this interview Dr. Mills asks some hard questions, particularly of the relational approach, and particularly its philosophical underpinnings, he does so gently and with great seriousness.

Host introduction

Hi, welcome to New Books in Psychoanalysis. My name is Tracy Morgan, your host; and today we'll be interviewing Dr. Jon Mills about his most recent publication, *Conundrums: A Critique of Contemporary Psychoanalysis* published by Routledge. Dr. Mills is a philosopher, a psychologist, and a psychoanalyst. He's on the editorial board of *Psychoanalytic Psychology*, is the editor of two book series, as well as the author of 11 books including, *Origins: On the Genesis of Psychic Reality*, which was published by McGill-Queens University Press, 2010. Dr. Mills, like New Books in Psychoanalysis, is a winner of the Gradiva Award from the National Association for the Advancement of Psychoanalysis. He won for his book *Origins* in 2011, and New Books in Psychoanalysis, we're proud to say, just won in the category of New Media in 2012. Dr. Mills maintains a private practice as well as runs a mental health corporation in Ontario, Canada, and today we'll be speaking with him about his critique of the relational turn and its philosophical underpinnings. He raises questions about the use of postmodernism, whither goest the body, the unconscious and drives, in the turn toward the here-and-now and toward relating, and ways of relating as being made primary in the consulting room. I think that people who are interested in these issues of self-disclosure, critiques of the analyst's authority—Who knows? Does the analyst know anything anyway? And should the analyst be in a position of the one who is supposed to know?—and other critiques the relational movement has leveled on many classical analytic approaches: all of those kinds of topics are going to be taken up here, and hope that you'll enjoy. We encourage you to go and like us on Facebook, Why not? And we also encourage you to write in if you have commentary on, and do let people know about this interview and about this program. So, let's move forward to the interview without further ado.

TM: Hi, and welcome to the New Books in Psychoanalysis. My name is Tracy Morgan, your host, as always, and today we'll be speaking with Dr. Jon Mills about his book *Conundrums*, which has a subtitle of, *A Critique of Contemporary Psychoanalysis*, published by Routledge. Welcome Dr. Mills to New Books in Psychoanalysis.

JM: Thank you for having me.

TM: You're very welcome. We're excited to have you here today. In fact, when I read your book, I thought, I'm not trained in philosophy, but I was extremely interested in many of the ideas. The book has a critique of the relational psychoanalytic movement, and that I found very compelling. These were some ideas, I guess unthought knowns, that were floating around in my mind for quite some time, and in reading your book, it was almost like putting thoughts that I had and had not articulated, putting into words, so it's a treat to have you here. Would you tell us a bit and set it up for the listeners? Tell us about your book.

JM: Well broadly, I believe it is a contribution to the history of ideas in terms of where psychoanalysis has come from and where it is today. I am primarily interested in this project in explicating various types of paradigms within contemporary thought, and that is mainly within the relational camp, as well as intersubjective and postmodern theories. I am trying to provide a systematic critique of the contemporary field, but I am certainly not inclusive. I do not entertain contemporary empirical research, or neuroscience, or other dimensions that certainly are worthy of looking at. I just had to limit the scope of this project to mainly those three areas. I am broadly looking at theory, as well as modes of practice, as well as politics, ethical parameters of our practice, and also approaching some type of consilience in the field. So in a nutshell, that is what I am trying to broadly get at.

TM: What drew you to focus, as I think you do, a bit more on relational work as opposed to intersubjective work? What was it about relational thinking that seems to capture your attention and got you wanting to speak to that tradition?

JM: Well, for one, I would want to say that I practice as a relational analyst; so I'm very much drawn to the freedom and humanness, and in the flexibility that the relational movement has brought to the field in terms of opening up a certain permissible space for us to act in the consulting room in ways that, perhaps, the classically trained analyst, or caricature of the analyst, might appear like. So that is one reason why I was drawn to reading the literature, because I found in many ways a refreshing point of view. But also, within my way of doing research, in reading a variety of different people, I was also struck by a certain lack of philosophical sophistication, and particularly looking at how relationality is being pitted against, in a binary fashion, Freudian metapsychology; and in my view, that is misguided and not necessary. So I think there was certainly a critique along the lines of theory as I'm reading, but at the same time feeling an identification with the liberties of practice.

TM: You think, I wonder, as I've read a lot of and interviewed a number of relational thinkers, Why is this an American phenomena? I know you're Canadian, so you can look at this culturally, as you have a different vantage point. Let's put it this way, it strikes me as a very American movement. I'm wondering, is it possible that the emphasis on relatedness has made psychoanalysis, somehow, I've heard people say this, more palatable, less frightening? It's more civilized than, let's say, the emphasis on the drives and the unconscious. Do you have any thoughts about that?

JM: Well, it's a broad topic. I would think on one hand, you're absolutely correct, when we talk about—What do you do? How do you relate to people? What exactly do you say in your sessions?—the last thing that people would probably expect is for someone to be silent, say nothing, withhold certain humanness, then spew out interpretations down the road. I don't think that any of us would probably keep very many people in our practice if that's how we acted.

TM: Right.

JM: But in terms of jettisoning the notion of drives and the unconscious, I just cannot fathom how that would be a very useful, let alone productive, or a fruitful project, because that would be jettisoning the very foundations of our profession. And it's important that we historically understand where we come from, as well as the key tenants that undergird what we buy into. One thing is that classical theory is certainly not dead by any means, and we have to appreciate the nature of embodiment. When we speak about drives, that's what we are really getting at—how the complexities of our embodiment are enacted. And clearly, if we are to jettison the notion of that, we are precariously having to displace an unconscious ontology. So I cannot envision psychoanalysis flourishing without reconnecting to, at least in some fashion, its original unconscious and embodied theses.

TM: I was reading Rosemary Balsam—I'm not sure if you're familiar with her work, and she has a new book called *Women's Bodies in Psychoanalysis*, and she has a quote that I think is pretty interesting when it comes to the contemporary response to drive theory. She says: "If drive theory and conflict-defensive operations are dismissed as irrelevant, then penis envy, castration anxiety, and the denigration of the clitoris do thankfully disappear as focal to a developmental theory about women. Yet the proponents of the alternative theories [and I think here she's referencing the relational and the intersubjective] do not offer us any developmental theory that pays us close attention to the body as Freud did." I think what she's suggesting is that, what we have are some feminist critiques of the more classical approach, such as privileging penis envy or the Oedipal in a certain way, and so it's an attempt to move away from a biological essentialism. But can we have drives without biological essentialism?

JM: First of all, what you read was quite in simpatico in many ways with my line of thinking.

TM: Totally.

JM: But with the issue of jettisoning drives, we have to ask ourselves, What do we mean by a drive? Traditionally, I don't believe the field really even knows what Freud was saying. They have probably never read his works, particularly in German, and there is an entirely different feel. What we have are these English translations, such as "instinct," but there is also a conditioning that I think we undergo when we do our training, that somehow these are antiquated categories. So the notion of embodiment or the gendered body is something that, of course, cannot be simply dismissed. It would be like dismissing an empirical fact, such as we have hunger or that we have to sleep or eat, or have sex. These are things that are just given. It's the way we go about interpreting how they provide a basis for experience. And experience is, of course, organized on much higher realms and in different spheres of psychic reality. I really think there can be all these discourses that are valid and operative, but some are going to be more relevant, particularly to practice, than others. I think we've replaced the term drive with desire.

TM: Yeah.

JM: And our desires, of course, lead to conflicts; they lead to affective dysregulations, which are still part of our embodiment. Not that we have to separate them out, such as drives are separate from feelings or emotions, or that they are separate from motivation, or separate from cognition—these are all very much operative together. And yet the way we go about talking about it, sometimes we don't always understand people's discourses.

TM: Yeah, I was also thinking that in the book you have a number of chapters that you move sequentially through, and after your introduction you begin with a critique of the use of postmodernism in psychoanalysis. I guess I wanted to ask first of all, Why do you think psychoanalysis, aside from this being a contemporary moment, and postmodernism is a theory, a school of thought, a theory, a philosophy that's very popular in the last twenty-five to thirty years, but, Why do you think psychoanalysis has gotten itself so involved with postmodern thinking? What's the relationship there as you see it?

JM: Well, it can be appealing on many levels. I think, particularly for those who have a certain element of personal experience where they cannot relate to other people, or they have identified with certain groups, such as those who have been historically disenfranchised, whether this be feminists or postfeminists, racial or ethnic groups, or those who just simply don't fit into the establishment, the GBTLQ populations, people where their difference is magnified and they are comparing themselves to the so-called "norm"—this would draw attention to them. But the one thing that the postmodern project brings is a number of conundrums. So we have to be careful about the political and ethical motivations behind adopting the postmodern turn, versus what theoretical contributions they uniquely bring.

TM: As I was reading your chapter on postmodernism, you can always sit with the patient and you can really feel stupid, like you have no idea what's happening for a long time, and you have to tolerate feeling stupid, and in the dark, and insignificant, and unsure, and I began to think about the turn toward postmodernism as giving people a way that maybe the classical theory didn't, to reckon with or in order to make it okay having some of those feelings. Does that make any sense to you?

JM: Maybe it would help for me to understand, What do you mean by postmodernism?

TM: Well that's a good question. I might be thinking of the sort of critique that, the idea that, "There's no Self," "That you can't fully know one's self," "That there's a limit that is perspectival," "That I only see you within the limits of my own contexts," etc., etc. Some of those ideas I see floating around and being used by analysts in writing about postmodern thinking in the psychoanalytic frame.

JM: Yes, well I guess I would have to challenge a number of these things. One would be, and this could be perceived to be quite pejorative, but it's ridiculous to think that we don't have a self. Who doesn't have a self? (laughs) Understanding what one is, or what oneself is, is another issue.

TM: Right.

JM: The thought that, How could we even have any communication, let alone some type of organized internal experience without some type of self-organization? –seems unbelievable to me. But I imagine that people are not thinking about the philosophical parameters of when they say that. It's another thing to say, "I don't really know who I am fully, or completely," and I would fully agree with that. Of course we don't.

TM: Right.

JM: We are in a process of becoming. So I guess it really depends on those specific kinds of things people are writing about, and yet at the same time, I can identify with that. I can identify with saying that I don't fully know. I don't pretend to know. I'm in the pursuit or some type of process of looking for truth, or universals, or meaning in life, and there are many forms and many different perspectives that I can fully agree with. So maybe we are not so far off in our vocabularies or tensions than we think.

TM: Interesting. I guess I'm also thinking that my sense is that the use of postmodern thinking in the psychoanalytic context can also focus on a critique of authority. The analyst's authority has importantly, and I don't work this way, so I think that authority is not a bad thing in the consulting room, but in the spirit of 1968 the analyst's authority has been thrown into question. I wonder about how you would think about the impact of that on the clinical encounter?

JM: Yeah, it's a very important topic and I certainly am in sympathies with that line of thinking. If we are to assume that there is an authority figure out there as the one who knows, let's say the objective scientist, those who claim to possess absolute knowledge, then we think that's preposterous. It's also a defense of grandiose narcissism or pretense, but honestly, I don't think I've ever encountered anybody like that in the real world. If we are setting up a straw man to attack, then that's one thing, but I have encountered, of course, many people who feel they are right and they're intolerant to critique or different points of view. One might be reminded of one's professors or ones you know, like supervisors or training analysts, or whoever you've encountered that pretend to be the one who knows, and if you don't cater to that then there's going to be some real consequences. So I very much think that those stances need to be challenged.

TM: But I also think, as I made the comment before, about tolerating feeling stupid in the consulting room and I'm thinking that the one who's supposed to know never has to sit with that feeling of not knowing (laughs), and really being profoundly in the dark. My question is, in the relational reformulation of the postmodern, it seems that everything becomes about the here and now; there's this idea of co-creation, which you write about in the book, and that somehow objectivity and epistemology find themselves disavowed, so, Where's the unconscious? When these ideas are at play, it just seems like the focus is more on something much more conscious, this co-creation. Do you have thoughts about this?

JM: Well, I agree with that. It seems like that is where the emphasis is, at least from the readings people present in their work. It seems that the focus is upon the attunement to the here-and-now situation where the parameters of two subjects are feeling one another out, and that have a certain presence to bear on each other. And while I would certainly contend that's true and that does happen, it does appear that we've lost our third ear, or we are not listening with that anymore. But to be fair to people, we don't know how everybody practices.

TM: Right.

JM: We don't know how they have amalgamated different theories over the years, what they have identified with or what they have renounced, or how they have uniquely developed their own way of facilitating a professional relationship; and these kinds of nuances are very difficult to write about. I can only go on my own experiences, and that is, we are looking for patterns, whether they be defensive patterns, whether they be repetitions, whether they be transference enactments. That is part of my work, and simply not to dismiss the fact that the person who is coming to see you is bringing their historical past to bear on coming to see you as a professional. And from that point of view, there is an element of authority that we as analysts or clinicians bring. If that wasn't the case, why would someone pay me an obscenely high amount of money to see me?

TM: Umm hum. In your book, you also write a lot about the hermeneutical turn. I'm not sure that I think making meaning is curative. What do you think? Is making meaning curative, and if so, how?

JM: That's an interesting thesis you put forward, that you don't see it is as curative. I guess we have to ask, What does that mean? If we are using the metaphor of cure, such as it is like inoculating against some kind of disease, then clearly meaning might not serve that purpose. I'm reminded of what Freud said: that the best we can do is to turn neurotic misery into ordinary unhappiness. But there is something essentially healing to meaning-making. Even if we don't like it, even if we find that truth unsavory, at least one's level of awareness has been expanded. It may open up a whole other "can" that we don't like, but nevertheless it is what it is, and it's up to us to then take that information and integrate it in some meaningful fashion. I think ultimately there has to be some curative element to the pursuit of meaning even if we never get there.

TM: Let me add something to my question or flush it out a little bit further because one of the things I wonder about in this focus on co-creation and mutuality and self-disclosure: these are key tenets of relational work. I always think, What about the pre-Oedipal or preverbal, or the more narcissistically fragile patient who, when confronted with me, do? One of the things you say in the book is that the conscious mind seems to be perhaps privileged within the relational. I always put myself in the position of the patient: What if I were in a fragile state? How do I work with this analyst's need for recognition? How do I survive that actually?

JM: Very good observations. Yes, it's a good question, because the last thing a narcissistic patient wants to hear is something coming out of your mouth.

TM: Right.

JM: Let alone that we would demand a certain kind of mutual recognition from them.

TM: Right.

JM: So I'm not sure if people are actually practicing in a manner where they would actually foist their own need or desire for their patient to acknowledge them. It may just be something that transpires naturally once the relationship has been developed. But I'm in agreement with you that those who are more regressed, or people who are on more primitive levels or organizations of self-development, whether it be people who are more narcissistically fragile, or people who have more schizoid phenomena, or those on more of a borderline level of organization—that type of technique would probably backfire on you quite quickly.

TM: Yeah, I haven't seen it, and this could be an oversight on my part as I'm well-read in the relational literature, not fully well-read, but I never imagined that patient to be one who has pre-Oedipal or preverbal conflicts, like, Who doesn't? Then how do we work with that aspect of a person using these ideas? For instance, there is an idea about democracy in the consulting room. It's puzzled me. Maybe it's a way of working; it's a theory that is about a more object-related patient. Maybe that's who this way of working works best with, which is fine.

JM: I guess the type of people I see are the same type of people you see.

TM: Yeah (laughs).

JM: They have horrible developmental traumas, and I don't believe I have ever met an Oedipal patient.

TM: Right (laughs).

JM: That would be a delight if I can have someone come in who is the normal, garden variety neurotic who just wants to be like Woody Allen and talk about his day.

TM: Ha, Ha (laughs). Very funny. Yeah, it's an ongoing question in my mind about this particular school of thought. With different schools of thought, you can wrap your mind around the different kind of patient that is drawn to and can be worked with in this way. You spend some time in the book talking about what you term "therapeutic excess" and I was wondering if you could in the context of discussing the relational explain, What do you mean by therapeutic access? And what does it look like? How do we know it when we see it? And what about it that concerns you?

JM: In reading the literature there are certain analysts who have been very open about the way they practice in the consulting room; and to be honest, I really find that valuable because we need to know what people actually say and what they do in order for us to have an honest discourse. So I do admire them in many ways for talking about what they communicate to patients. But some of the material I've read seems to me to be quite dangerous, particularly when we talk about excess. What I mean by that is that there are certain excessive forms of self-disclosure that I've seen certain contemporary practitioners talk about, whether it be a breach in confidentiality, whether it be disclosing sexual feelings to patients in the session, whether it be lying directly to patients, screaming at them while invading their face. Of course we don't know the context of all these things, but there is a certain—at least on the face of things, phenomenon that is happening in contemporary circle's where they just do whatever they want and they act out on certain countertransference processes. So that's where I think we need to be careful about, particularly the realm and range of disclosures that take place in session.

TM: If you compare this sort of straw man of the American 1950s ego psychology movement, where there is this withdrawn or hard to access figure of the analyst, and then we have this other figure contemporarily of the analyst, as you said, screaming in someone's face—it couldn't be any more different. How do you understand this generation—our generation's—such strong reaction? It's almost like a throwing out of the baby with the bathwater to that more reserved figure. The year 1968 is always in my mind when I read the relational work. I don't know if that makes any sense to you, but just in terms of the feelings about authority and about transparency. I may have mentioned this you in our lead up to the interview, I think I said something about being and presenting at an analytic institute, and an analyst said to me that she did not like the use of the term "psychoanalysis," that I "use it too frequently," also in the use of the term "unconscious," and she had very bad associations—even though she's an analyst—to these ideas. I was like, What? I wonder what has taken place to so turn people against the drives, the unconscious?

JM: They were probably mistreated by their own analysts.

TM: Yeah.

JM: And then they probably generalize that, and project that as a transference phenomenon onto theory. Rather than thinking about the logical implications of what one says, such as "There's no such thing as an unconscious." It's amazing that people would write about that or allude to that, like, "Everything is simply language," or is encapsulated by the speech act. It's as if there is no dynamic unconscious activity that is a priori or is operating prior to experience. And you will see that with the relationalists, from Mitchell to Greenberg in particular, who more or less adopt a view that there is no unconscious prior to experience. And I just don't buy that.

TM: Yeah, I think you write some place that: "Mitchell's denunciation of the drives in beyond displacement, it's actually a negation," which of course made me think about what negation is (laughs) and how it always contains within it it's opposite.

JM: Yes, a doubling of the negative.

TM: Yeah, exactly. It's a little painful to read some of the quotes that you have in here from Mitchell because they're so extreme, that you have to wonder, that if the man were alive today, where would he be at with all of this?

JM: We would probably be having a dialogue.

TM: Right. I wonder about the impact of his death on the movement, because if he could have critiqued himself, which I imagine he had that capacity. I sense in your book that you received some very strong reactions to your critique of certain relational concepts and their philosophical underpinning. Your book is unique, certainly in that you have a chapter in which you really go into "Who said what?" regarding difficult exchanges with some key relational thinkers, that there seems to be no room for incorporating new ideas. And I wonder about Mitchell's death and the need to defend the tradition since he's not here.

JM: Yes. I think a lot of Mitchell's close friends have gone on to defend him, and of course there are many loving feelings that they have about this man and they wouldn't want his work to be sullied. But it is really nothing personal.

TM: Right.

JM: I hope people don't take what I do as a direct assault or an attack on them personally. I'm really interested in a critique of ideas, and that's what I think ultimately will push our field along to be more intellectually vibrant. If we don't have an openness to critique and differences of opinion, and in tolerating the reasons for those differences, then we are not going to advance.

TM: Right. Right. And as a field we are always at a risk of extinction. Are we going to survive? Is psychoanalysis going to survive? And these types of battles are not really all that helpful. Another thing is they end up being more destructive than constructive. They end up being less about desire then about the death drive, the way that things were handled. It was something to read in your chapter about the responses you've received, and I think you were censored—I can't remember the journal. I think Sandra Buechler, who I recently interviewed, called it "psychoanalytic color wars," and that we can't seem to stop engaging in them.

JM: I think that as a profession we love gossip.

TM: Right.

JM: And we eat it up, and particularly about people who we may not like.

(laughs)

JM: In some ways I feel like I'm the designated mourner, in some sense. But that's something I've chosen to take on as well. On one hand, there is a nasty side to psychoanalytic politics that is operative in any organization, just as it rears in real life. Unfortunately, when people exert their power differentials and manipulate others, and they don't allow for a process of academic freedom and exchange of ideas to continue, then that's upsetting to me. So I felt the need to talk about these things on a real level and not censor that because this is something that needs to be analyzed, and it needs to be acknowledged. Often people write about these things when other people have died, and they have a confessional.

TM: That's true.

JM: When/if people are behaving badly or unprofessionally, then they are not immune to criticism, and especially around the censoring of academic freedom. So I felt the need to put that in there. I hope it doesn't overshadow the other aspects of the book, because it seems like people are commenting about that more than other aspects.

TM: It's funny. I've read some of the reviews of how people will comment on that. As a culture, we are just thinking of reality, right? Like there's nothing like a documentary, a documentary channel, Reality TV. There's this chapter in your book which does get to a sort of reality, like, "This is real politics," "This is what people said," "This is what happened," and, "This is what 'I' said," and I had the question: There seems to be a turn away in the relational movement from the intrapsychic or the inner world to the interpersonal, and again it's an orientation towards reality. Do you think that the creation of relational analysis is part of the Zeitgeist?

JM: On one hand, I can fully identify with someone who is more warm and open and accepting and inviting rather than someone who is cold, staid, emotionally reserved, or removed, and I think this is the dichotomy of how we present the classical and the relational analyst.

TM: Right.

JM: When in reality, though, there is always a hybrid element. Instead of the bifurcation between the intrapsychic and the interpersonal, they both are operative at once and together; it's just a matter of where is the emphasis being placed. I'm more of a comparative analyst, so I like to look at what people think in terms of theoretical foundations that drive their methodologies. The relational inevitability, as you put it, to recapture the notion of 68, is really to rebel. It's to say: "I don't want to practice like that because this is unnatural" or "This is not meeting the real needs of patients," and you just have to look at your own experience of being in analysis or with your supervisors who will tell you to do things that you think are palpably bizarre.

TM: (laughs)

JM: Or just that are going to drive your patient away or hurt them. In many ways this is what is fostered in analytic institutes: that you're supposed to just listen to Daddy and do what you're told, rather than to think through something and have your own your mind about it and have a real discussion. But everybody's worried about failing, about being judged, about being shamed, and unfortunately that kind of environment is not conducive to an intellectual kind of debate.

TM: It's almost as if working analytically in some institutes only happens in the consulting room with the patient but it doesn't happen in the training analysis or the supervision.

JM: So I am told by many people.

TM: Yeah (laughs), so I hear. I don't have that complaint about my institute, but I do hear that a lot—the feeling that you have to do what you're told, and that people are hiding things from their supervisor because the supervisor wouldn't want to know about these things, or judge the candidate for having certain kinds of feelings and reactions to patients. It's pretty bleak to think that people are being exposed to something very unanalytic in their training and with their analyst.

JM: Well put.

TM: Yeah. I was at a meeting the other night and Otto Kernberg was there. We were with a group called the *Unbehagen*, which is a group here in New York of people in training, or people who left training midway, or are considering training, and are asking the question about the formation of the analyst—so there's many Lacanians there, but not just. I'm Modern; there is interpersonalist there, many relational people, and we're asking the question, What makes one an analyst? This group is sort of outside of analytic training. We meet and have clinical study days, and we just do things. We have speakers come and Kernberg came to address the group, and now I forgot what my question was, so funny, Oh, and he came to address the group and was talking to us about training. You know he's written these articles, like "Thirty Ways to Kill the Creativity of a Candidate." And a question I asked him, I said, "You know when people graduate from an institute they also graduate from supervision and analysis. And then the institutes become—'they run amok.' People force-feed their trainees, and all their analytic candidates. Why do we give up so quickly our supervision in our analysis once we enter institute life?" I don't know if that's what goes on in Canada (laughs), but it does go on here.

JM: Well, I can't speak for everybody in Canada.

(laughs)

JM: But I'm going to echo that sentiment in some circles.

TM: Yeah. Yeah. I wanted to also ask you, Does psychoanalysis need philosophy? You are trained as a philosopher as well as a psychologist and a psychoanalyst, What do you think of as an ideal relationship, or as close of an ideal relationship, between psychoanalysis and philosophy, contemporarily?

JM: I'm not sure it needs it, but I would argue that ultimately it is enriched by it; particularly when we are working with complex ideas that evoke, whether they be phenomenological, epistemological, or ontological concerns. And, of course, psychoanalysis does all of that. Not only that, it's even approaching what it means to be an ethical or moral human being. So if you don't have some type of training, even if it's your own self-reading in philosophical circles, you will probably be hindered in understanding the complexity of things.

TM: Yeah.

JM: It used to be that philosophy did not segregate itself from its subject matters, as it was interested in everything.

TM: Right.

JM: I would argue that psychoanalysis has everything to gain by philosophical fortification.

TM: And in terms of the relational movement, which I said is an American homegrown product, do you have any sense of its relationship to various schools of American philosophy? Would you say that James, for instance, resonates within, or in any other traditional American philosophers?

JM: The people who have been writing in the field seem to be more all over the map, but who comes to mind is Donna Orange, who I think is a pragmatist, ultimately. She has adopted James and Pierce's notion of a pragmatic theory of truth, what she refers to as more perspectival. In many ways, American pragmatism could be viewed as operative within contemporary circles because it is asking basic questions, such as, What is useful? What is helpful? What helps people get their goals or needs met? Those pragmatic concerns are also what is driving the public coming into treatment. Does it bake bread? So, "I'm coming into see you, are you going to help me?" And that means one has to be attuned to the interpersonal nuances of tact and pleasantries that perhaps the old school or old guard hasn't always fulfilled.

TM: Right. I hear what you are saying. You have an idea that I think people would be interested in understanding. I believe you have published elsewhere more fully about this, which is the idea of dialectical psychoanalysis. Could you just describe what you mean when you use this term "dialectical psychoanalysis"?

JM: Yes, in a nutshell, it is a neo-Hegelian notion of how the dialectic is operative within a psychoanalytic context, so ultimately I'm interested in offering a psychoanalytic metaphysics that is trying to explain how psychic reality is constituted. I really want to return to a radicalization of unconscious processes, and believe that there is, in fact, an unconscious agency that is operative in everything that we do. And that it conditions all of subjectivity, and particularly consciousness. In fact, it is the a priori ground that makes consciousness possible. It makes relatedness possible, or language. So when contemporary people are writing about "everything is based in language" or "everything boils down to a social construction," they don't realize that they have completely displaced the foundation of our field.

TM: Yeah, I was really interested in how you really laid that out in this book. You have written about it elsewhere, I believe. Is that correct?

JM: Yes, I published a book called *Origins: On the Genesis of Psychic Reality.*

TM: Yeah.

JM: I lay out my system there.

TM: Yes, you have a paragraph in this book that really grabs it, and I felt, as I read it, that really nothing was missing. It struck me that really nothing was missing from that—that there is room for everything. You begin on a substrate that was really humane to me. It is interesting that last weekend, or the weekend before, at the institute where I am training at, we had a conference with Nancy Chodorow, and she was the featured speaker, and I asked her a question, or I made a comment to her, and I said, "You know, around my institute you can hear people ask the question, 'Who were you before you met your mother?'," and she didn't like that question, I don't think. She said "How could there be a you or an I before you met your mother?," but there is something there. And I think that part of your project, if I understand it, is to fight for that aspect of us *before*—where there is an "I" or a "You," and the ability to recognize a "you" and to make sure that is not lost in contemporary psychoanalysis.

JM: Yes, I don't see why we need to exclude anyone or anything. It's really about a matter of emphasis. So I'm certainly the type that would give golden apples all around.

TM: (laughs) All right, we're going to bring our interview to a close. It's been very delightful to hear your ideas and I thank you for being with us at New Books in Psychoanalysis, and keep us posted about what's coming next. Send us your next book, because we're happy to talk to people again. So thank you very much Jon Mills.

JM: Thank you Tracy, and congratulations on your Gradiva Award.

TM: Ah, thank you. That was a delight.

7 Fine-tuning problems in relational psychoanalysis

New directions in theory and praxis

Jon Mills

Abstract: Relational approaches to contemporary psychoanalysis and psychotherapy have garnered international appeal for the way they apply to clinical practice across many mental health disciplines and population groups. Despite the recent success of the relational movement, theoretical fine-tuning problems still persist. Throughout this article I will revisit what I find to be the greatest theoretical challenges to relational perspectives requiring amendment and rectification: namely, the negation of biological drives, and the displacement of the unconscious. After championing the value of relational principles in the consulting room, I offer my own view of what constitutes effective praxis with regards to clinical theory and technique.

Introduction

Relational psychoanalysis and the relational psychotherapy movement have become an international phenomenon. In just over a decade, the International Association for Relational Psychoanalysis and Psychotherapy (IARPP) went from being a New York-based organization to an established international presence with forums and chapters in the United States, Australia, Canada, the United Kingdom, Israel, Mexico, New Zealand, Greece, Spain, Portugal, and Chile. In looking at its success, it becomes easy to appreciate the force, value, and loci of the relational turn:

1. Relational thinking has opened a permissible space for comparative psychoanalysis and psychotherapy by challenging fortified traditions ossified in dogma, such as orthodox conceptions of the classical frame, neutrality, abstinence, resistance, transference, and the admonition against analyst self-disclosure.
2. Relational perspectives have had a profound impact on the way we have come to conceptualize the therapeutic encounter, and specifically the role of the analyst or therapist in technique and practice. The relational turn has forged a clearing for honest discourse on what we actually do, think, and feel in our therapeutic work, thus breaking the silence and secrecy of what actually

transpires in the consulting room. Relational approaches advocate for a more natural, humane, and genuine manner of how the therapist engages the patient rather than cultivating a distant intellectual attitude or clinical methodology whereby the analyst is sometimes reputed to appear as a cold, staid, antiseptic, or emotionless machine. Relational analysts are more revelatory, interactive, and inclined to disclose accounts of their own experience in professional space (e.g., in session, publications, and conference presentations); enlist and solicit perceptions from the patient about their own subjective comportment; and generally, acknowledge how a patient's responsiveness and demeanor is triggered by the purported attitudes, sensibility, and behavior of the therapist. The direct and candid reflections on countertransference reactions, therapeutic impasse, the role of affect, intimacy, and the patient's experience of the analyst are revolutionary ideas that have redirected the compass of therapeutic progress away from the uniform goals of interpretation and insight to a proper holistic focus on psychoanalysis as process.

3. The relational turn has displaced traditional epistemological views of the therapist's authority and unadulterated access to knowledge, as well as the objectivist principles they rest upon. By closely examining the dialogic interactions and meaning constructions that emerge within the consulting room, relational psychoanalysis has largely embraced the hermeneutic postmodern tradition of questioning the validity of absolute truth claims to knowledge, objective certainty, and positivist science. Meaning, insight, and conventions of interpretation are largely seen as materializing from within the unique contexts and contingencies of interpersonal participation in social events, dialogical discourse, dialectical interaction, mutual negotiation, dyadic creativity, and reciprocally generated co-constructions anchored in an intersubjective process. This redirective shift from uncritically accepting metaphysical realism and independent, objective truth claims to reclaiming the centrality of subjectivity within the parameters of relational exchange has allowed for a reconceptualization of psychoanalytic doctrine and the therapeutic encounter.

No small feat indeed. But with so many relational publications that largely dominate the contemporary psychoanalytic scene, we have yet to see relational paradigms undergo a proper conceptual critique from within its own frame of reference. With the exception of Jay Greenberg (2001), who had turned a critical eye toward some of the technical practices conducted within the relational community today, most of the criticism comes from those outside the relational movement (see Frank, 1998a, 1998b; Richards, 1999a, b; Silverman, 2000; Eagle, Wolitzky, & Wakefield, 2001; Josephs, 2001; Eagle, 2003; Lothane, 2003; Masling, 2003). To my knowledge I have provided the most comprehensive critique of the relational movement to date (see, Mills, 2005a, b; Mills, 2012), and here I wish to further expound upon where I believe the relational school could improve upon its conceptual and technical practices.

Displacement of drive theory

From his early work onward, Stephen Mitchell (1988) stated that the relational model is "an alternative perspective which considers relations with others, *not drives*, as the basic stuff of mental life" (p. 2, emphasis added), thus declaring the cardinal premise of all relational theorists. He clearly wanted to advocate for a "purely" relational model that is opposed to drive theory when he declares that "the concept of drive, as Freud intended it, has been omitted" (p. 60) from the relational perspective. Greenberg (1991) makes this point more forcefully: The relational model is "based on *the radical rejection of drive* in favor of a view that *all motivation* unfolds from our personal experience of exchanges with others" (p. vii, emphasis added). Echoing Mitchell, Greenberg (1991) makes a universal proclamation attributed to all relational theorists when he states: "Analysts operating within the relational model of the mind are united in their claim that it is misguided to begin theorizing with drive" (p. 69). This attitude holds steadfast today to the degree that it has become the relational movement's motto emblazoned on the IARPP website:

> Relational Psychoanalysis is the term that has evolved in recent years to describe an approach to clinical work that attracts many practitioners in different parts of the world. Although not a hard and fast set of concepts and practices, one core feature is the notion that psychic structure–at the very least, those aspects of psychic structure that are accessible to psychotherapeutic intervention–derive from the individual's relations with other people. This, of course, is intended as *an alternative to the classical view that innately organized drives and their developmental vicissitudes are, at root, the basis of psychic structure* (emphasis added).[1]

Notice the theoretical presupposition that "psychic structure … *derive(s)* [sic] from the individual's relations with other people" (emphasis added). So according to the flagship organization, psychic structure does not derive from the drives (*Triebe*), what is commonly translated into English as instincts, but rather derives from other people.

As I have elaborated with precision elsewhere (2010), this tenet is unfathomable and ultimately indefensible because you cannot have relationships without a body. We are embodied beings who cannot deny our evolutionary and material facticity. In fact, our embodied psychic processes such as drives, urges, pulsions, innate desires, organic impulses, yearnings, compulsions, evolutionary pressures, internal regulatory catalysts, motivations, and the like need a corporeal foundation lest we return to a protoscientific model of a caricatured Cartesian *cogito* floating out in space divorced of a physical medium. Moreover, our biological (bodily) and enmattered psychic (mental) activities that constitute "the basis of psychic structure" are a necessary condition for consciousness, object seeking (what Freud [1915] argued was the aim of a drive), and the higher order organizations of mind and relatedness to arise, without which we would not relate to anything.

This single-minded antithesis of relationality versus drive theory is not only an unnecessary and unfortunate false dichotomy, but it is furthermore a philosophical embarrassment that the relational community could easily remedy by modifying its theoretical position.

It is not necessary to negate our biological drives or their psychophysiological-neurocognitive correlates in order to appreciate how relationships with others become internalized within psychic structure. This *either-or* theoretical bifurcation only highlights the political agenda behind the need for reform and revolution. But with the radical rejection of our embodied natures comes further *aporias* when relational theory wants to include the biological-developmental interactions that take place within the mother–infant dyad. And with the revival of attachment theory that has been annexed within relational circles (Mills, 2005b; Beebe & Lachmann, 2014), a biopsychosocial model of relationality is merely a logical corrective. One does not have to defend a flawed conceptual binary or refute the role of drives in order to *emphasize* the primacy of attachment and relatedness to other people. Both are coexistent and coextensive motivations underlying psychic structure: it simply becomes a matter of degree and the level of importance one wishes to highlight in constructing a theory of mind and human nature.

The centrality of interactions with others, forming relationships, interpersonally mediated experience, human attachment, the impact of others on psychic development, reciprocal dyadic communication, contextually based social influence, and the recognition of competing subjectivities seem to be universal theoretical postulates underscoring the relational viewpoint. These are very reasonable and sound assertions, and we would be hard-pressed to find anyone prepared to discredit these elemental facts. The main issue here is that these propositions are nothing new: Relational theory is merely stating the obvious. These are simple reflections on the inherent needs, strivings, developmental trajectories, and behavioral tendencies propelling human motivation; a point that Freud made explicit throughout his theoretical corpus, which became further emphasized by early object relations theorists through to contemporary self psychologists. Every aspect of conscious life is predicated on human relatedness by the simple fact that we are thrown into a social ontology as evinced by our participation in family interaction, communal living, social custom, ethnic affiliation, local and state politics, national governance, and common linguistic practices that by definition cannot be refuted nor annulled by virtue of our embodied and cultural facticity, a thesis thoroughly advanced by Heidegger (1927) yet originally dating back to antiquity. But what is unique to the relational turn is a philosophy based on antithesis and refutation: namely, the abnegation of the drives. As the relational tradition moves forward, I hope it will attend to and rectify these theoretical fallacies.

What about the unconscious?

Another difficulty in determining the philosophical merit of relational theory is its perspective on the force and ubiquity of the unconscious. If relationality rejects the drives, does it not open itself up to accusations that it ignores, or even refutes, unconscious dynamic processes? Perhaps contemporary relationalists would concede that unconscious processes do exist, if they are not cast into the abyss of dissociation, and they would acknowledge the internalized nature of other people over drive derivatives, which I would support, such as the way introjects, part objects, self and object representations, and environmental encounters are incorporated and arranged within internal experience based on the unique configurations of self-organization that transpire in relation to others and one's being in the world. But this does not necessitate the abnegation of drive, nor does relational theory have to overstate its position in order to make the point that the experiential quality of relatedness to others is paramount to mental functioning and personality development. But the emphasis on consciousness, relationality, and intersubjectivity in contemporary theory and praxis naturally challenges the fundamental principle of psychoanalytic doctrine: namely, that mind is the epigenesis and outgrowth of unconscious process. If the relational mind no longer rests on an unconscious edifice, then we have a very different psychoanalytic model from its classical origins.

Stolorow and his collaborators perhaps best represent the tension between the conscious–unconscious binary. Rather than juxtapose unconscious dimensions in relation to conscious experience, and how there are different and competing realms of psychic reality operative at once, relational proponents make ontological commitments about the nature of mind that are severely encumbered by theoretical biases. For Stolorow and his colleagues, intersubjectivity is ontologically constituted through conscious acts: "experience is *always* embedded in a constitutive intersubjective context" (Stolorow & Atwood, 1992, p. 24, emphasis added). Elsewhere he states that the intersubjective system is the "constitutive role of relatedness in the making of *all* experience" (Stolorow, 2001, p. xiii, emphasis added). Even more recently Stolorow (2010) affirms that "all…forms of unconsciousness are constituted in relational contexts" for "'unconscious organizing principles' are intersubjectively constituted" (p. 7). Notice here that he states that *any* form of unconscious process is intersubjectively—hence relationally—established. This implies that even unconscious drives, which are part of our embodied biological constitutions, are enacted and composed by relational elements; therefore, drives are originally derived from conscious experience. This problematic presupposition goes against contemporary wisdom in the biological sciences. How can the intersubjective system create or co-construct our organic bodies? These absolutist overstatements lend themselves to decentering intrapsychic activity over relational interaction, and draw into question the separateness of the self, the preexistent developmental history of the patient prior to treatment, the prehistory of unconscious processes independent of one's relatedness to others, and *a priori* mental organizations that precede engagement with the social world.[2] These statements appear to replace psychoanalysis as a science of the unconscious with an intersubjective ontology that gives priority to conscious experience.[3] To privilege consciousness over unconsciousness, to me, appears to subordinate the value of psychoanalysis as an original contribution to understanding human experience. Even if we as analysts are divided by competing theoretical identifications, it seems difficult at best to relegate the primordial nature of unconscious dynamics to a trivialized backseat position implicit in much of the relational literature. For Freud (1900), the "unconscious is the true psychical reality" (p. 613), which by definition is the necessary condition for intersubjectivity to materialize and thrive.

Although there are many contemporary analysts who are still sensitive to unconscious processes in their writings and clinical work, it nevertheless appears that on the surface, for many relational analysts, the unconscious has become an antiquated category. While Stolorow, Atwood, and Orange have certainly advocated for revisionist interpretations of unconscious processes, Stolorow (2001) in particular specifically relates a theoretical sentiment that is common among many relationalists: "In place of the Freudian unconscious…we envision a multiply contextualized experimental world, an organized totality of lived personal experience, *more or less conscious*" (p. xii, emphasis added). Here, we have a radical departure from Freud's original contributions to psychology.

Developing a relational treatment philosophy

By contemporary standards, I would be said to favor relational and existential orientations to practice informed by my training in self psychology, the interpersonal schools, and phenomenology; but unlike any identification with a particular theoretical movement, this acknowledgment carries forth certain stipulations. Given my dual training background in clinical psychology and philosophy, I never liked being classified or pigeon-holed into a certain theoretical camp because this tends to limit the scope of self-identity and professional perception as well as dilute the rich and multitextured conceptual body the psychoanalytic domain serves to offer as a whole. Although I largely work clinically as a relational therapist,[4] I may be more accurately considered a comparative analyst heavily indebted to many great intellectuals, practitioners, and contemporaneous trains of thought. Among these, first and foremost is Freud, who has been greatly misunderstood and maligned by relational schools today. Many of his theories have been fundamentally misinterpreted and distorted from their original context, nor critically evaluated within the evolution of his mature theoretical corpus.[5] This is due in part because few have bothered to consult his original texts written in German and have been conditioned by incompetent expositors and introductory textbooks that have little appreciation for accurate scholarship. Therefore, I am not in agreement with the uncritically accepted and erroneous characterizations of Freudian theory as adhering to a one-person psychology (Greenberg & Mitchell, 1983; Mitchell & Aron, 1999) or espousing the belief in a solipsistic, isolated mind (Stolorow & Atwood, 1992), just to name two popularized propaganda circulating today. In my opinion, these claims are invalid, fueled in part by ignorance about what Freud actually said, including the corruption of classical thought by Anglo commentators that is carelessly perpetuated in contemporary training institutes, as well as political idolatry advocated by the American middle group of relational psychoanalysis who are radically opposed to classical paradigms.[6] By the subjective accounts of his patients (Roazen, 1995; Lohser & Newton, 1996), Freud was quite relational, personable, and flexible in his approach to treatment; but unlike some relational clinicians today, he turned a critical eye toward continually uncovering and understanding the myriad unconscious processes that suffuse the analytic encounter including the interpersonal dynamics of resistance, transference, repetition, and working through. Although I do not wish to belabor points of contention between relational and classical thought, suffice it to say that I do not see the radical divide that is professed to exist. Where important and valid discrepancies do exist, they tend to lie in the nature of specific theoretical disputes and renunciations, (e.g., feminist psychology), extensions, and revisionist expansions of technique, which are something radically different than the broad philosophical and technical innovations embedded in the classical tradition that relational perspectives seem to discredit. As I have said elsewhere, psychoanalysis is merely a footnote to Mills (2004a).

I cannot emphasize enough the need for beginning therapists to develop a firm theoretical orientation to their work and to be able to justify its merits and limitations. While there is often a schism between theory and practice, your theoretical orientation guides you on how to think conceptually about case material and informs your approach to treatment. Theory and method are not necessarily synonymous, and they are often confounded to mean one and the same thing. In practice, however, the clinician is informed by multiple perspectives at any given moment, and therefore must be open and flexible to seeing points of connection between the patient's reported lived subjective reality and the diverse theoretical models that may be applied in attempting to lend order and meaning to that process. Beginning therapists need to develop a firm grasp of their theoretical orientation(s) and preferred modes of working clinically for the simple reason that it provides structure and direction for informed therapeutic practice. Whatever preferred modes of conceptualization one adopts in the end, the clinician can never escape from the fact that theory only serves as an orienting guide to the treatment process that is constantly being challenged and confronted by emergent data and the intersubjective contingencies arising in the lived encounter. Just as theory takes on its own dynamic, thus introducing contradiction, evolution, and change, so does the therapeutic dyad itself informed by the psychodynamics and phenomenological novelties of forming a new relationship amongst strangers. When it comes down to it, you and the patient are thrown into an unfamiliar encounter, each with one's own competing subjectivities and individual personalities. This is the existential dimension of treatment that cannot be eluded nor disavowed, for it is here that a new intersubjective reality is forged and negotiated.

Existential, phenomenological, and continental perspectives in philosophy complement psychoanalytic discourse, thus providing a fecundity of overlap in conceptual thought and practice that the relational schools have been increasingly acknowledging over the past two decades. It can be said that psychoanalysis is fundamentally a theory and method geared toward insight, truth, and the amelioration of human suffering, while philosophy is the pursuit of wisdom, truth, human excellence, and rational meaning, what Freud (1927) himself identifies as

Logos. I see these two disciplines as embracing similar convictions that human existence is ultimately about developing our potential, fulfilling our possibilities, and living an authentic life through the liberation of ignorance and the malicious forces that threaten our happiness. This takes courage and fortitude, but it first and foremost takes awareness; for we can only be free through knowledge. In this way, therapy is a *liberation struggle*—Know thyself! This Delphic decree is the psychoanalytic motto. Insight or self-knowledge takes a commitment to educating oneself to what truly lies within—the complexity and competing flux of the inner world—and this is never an easy endeavor. It takes another to nurture and draw this out, to validate and reinforce, to encourage and to guide, to hold and reassure. This begins with the most primary of all relations, the relation of the embryonic self to its mother, then to its family and community at large, and finally to the social institutions that foster and beget the cultivation of self-consciousness. This is why a relational approach to treatment mirrors the natural process of self-development, for the self is given over to the other equiprimordially, and the other to the self: the subject–object split is foreclosed. Each are dynamically informed by a dialectical system of mutual implication, interaction, exchange, negotiation, and force.

Therapy as a way of being

When I was a predoctoral intern in Chicago, I was assigned a training and supervising analyst at the Chicago Institute for Psychoanalysis to supervise two of my cases. When I first met the man, he opened his office door onto a vestibule where I was sitting, which was used as a common waiting area for several other offices. When he called me by name, I stood up and entered his office greeting him with a handshake and a hello. He pointed with his hand to where I should sit and then walked over to his chair and promptly sat down. He stared at me and said nothing. I was waiting for some sort of an appropriate social greeting, introduction, or question of some sort, but instead I received the cool impression that I was to be observed and analyzed like I imagined he behaved toward his patients. Close to a minute had passed before I broke the ice and began to speak. It was clear to me that I was not going to be treated as a colleague, nor even as an advanced graduate student about to receive his doctorate, but as an object under a microscope. Whether this was the man's personality or his style of clinical supervision, the immediate impression he created was intractable: he was a jerk. Whether he was a brilliant supervisor or not is inconsequential: his very mode of relatedness was enough to create unease, intimidation, and resistance. This was not the way I wished to be treated, and I immediately thought how this too must feel for patients who are in an even more vulnerable situation. Simply put, his behavior was uncalled for and certainly not the treatment approach I wanted to emulate.

There were many instances like this one during my training days where I learned more about how *not* to act rather than about the so-called "appropriate" technique or demeanor I should adopt as a therapist. Ask yourself this question: How would you feel if you were in the patient's shoes? In the real world of private practice outside of the academy, this type of behavior is a good way to lose business: if people are made to feel interpersonally uncomfortable, then they are more likely than not to discontinue coming to treatment because they feel as though you have already judged or demeaned them. It is common throughout the psychoanalytic literature to read of authors who are quick to blame or condemn the patient as being resistant, defensive, acting out, deficient, limited, disturbed, narcissistic, or pathological in some way when they fail to return or commit to treatment, when in turn they may be simply reacting to the normal feeling of being belittled in some fashion—even dehumanized—by a cool, staid, or threatening first impression the analytic encounter can sometimes generate. And dependent and deprived patients will sometimes masochistically submit themselves to this form of treatment with the unconscious hope of winning over their analyst's approval, when in all likelihood this acquiescent submission is motived from abnormal forces dictated not only by transference repetition, but by the recalcitrant need to win recognition from a cold, depriving object in the here and now.

Although the analyst is always a transference figure, s/he can also generate extratransferential phenomena that may be more of the result of unspoken or expressed power differentials which truly belong to the analyst's pathological inclinations. If you act superior, aloof, removed, and/or clinically detached, then the message is clear: you don't want to get too close. So how could you expect patients to open up or trust you? If you create the slightest impression of being contemptuous, then the patient's "shit detector" immediately turns on and the relational milieu becomes soiled. Putting aside for the moment the notion of projection and transference, you are accountable for how you come across: your subjectivity, demeanor, interpersonal style and accord, and so forth influence the patient's perceptions, defense activations, relatedness patterns, and the negotiation of individuality within the intersubjective frame of treatment. If you don't concede that you bring something into the picture, then you can erroneously collude with the false impression that the patient is solely responsible for the reaction s/he orchestrates in others, when in actuality this is a two-way relational street.

Therapy is a *way of being*, not some contrived state, nor just another job, role, or hat one puts on only to be removed at the end of the day. I once had a patient whom I worked with for a few years. Approximately a year and a half into the treatment, during a particularly poignant disclosure, I commented on how I felt for her in that moment. In a dismissing tone, she told me: "That's your job, you're supposed to." Since we had already reached a degree of intimacy in the therapy, I was surprised at her dismissal and replied: "As if I couldn't possibly, truly care about you." This led to her confession that it hurts when others show her sympathy or genuine concern because she feels that deep down she does not deserve it, so she brushes it away by finding an ulterior motive in the other's behavior. When you develop a genuine relationship with a patient, you cannot help but open up your own soul to the experience of the other and feel *with* them and *for* them, even though you may not disclose this directly. When this happens, and when it develops naturally—not acted or manufactured—I find this to be an aesthetic supplement and intensification of empathy, what Heidegger (1927) calls care or concernful solicitude, or what Binswanger (1962) calls an extension of love.

I am always suspicious of those who say that they leave their occupation at the office. How can you just turn off your mind? I simply cannot shut off my fundamental orientation toward existence, namely, to think dynamically and critically about most aspects of life, and to open up my emotional world in the process—my total being. Deep understanding gives me a greater sense of purpose and meaning, even if certain discoveries are unsavory or distressing. Regardless of what we encounter or come to know through the analytic process, psychoanalysis makes our suffering more tolerable. Establishing a sound theoretical orientation for treatment efficacy takes thoughtfulness, justification, critical review, and revision. The lazy therapist who is only worried about what to say and not how to think dynamically will be eaten alive by certain patient populations, such as character disorders, and personally embarrassed when confronted with more intellectually sophisticated clients. One needs a personal commitment to ongoing professional development, and that means personal development. It means reading the literature (both disciplinary and interdisciplinary) and critically thinking about your own thoughts and experiences rather than consulting the identified expert on what is acceptable and what is not. Along with introspection and ongoing self-analysis, this critical function is a necessary (albeit not sufficient) condition for lasting professional growth that transcends the ossified dogma that can potentially serve to create stasis and ostracization from actualizing genuine potential.

In many distinct ways, one's theoretical orientation often complements the clinician's personality or individuality, and consequently, what is more often the case than not, the personality of the therapist largely determines the course of the therapy. It is the analyst's personality that allows for genuine engagement, thus making a clearing for authentic relatedness. One's own personality cannot help but be interjected in every aspect of the treatment, for every disclosure is value laden and communicates a great deal about the clinician, even during silence.

In order to establish and maintain ongoing professional identity, the therapist needs to think critically about their own worldview and adopt approaches that are congruent with that worldview in order to appear trustworthy and credible to patients. Beginning therapists often ask themselves: What do I do or say when the patient says *x* or *y* ?, as if there is a bag of tricks or general skill set to apply to each and every situation when a similar dynamic unfolds. In my experience teaching and supervising graduate students and postgraduate professionals, it appears to be a common phenomenon that what they initially want is a tool bag to reach into in order to fix something in the patient. They have done some reading, have some pat phrases down, are testing out or playing a role, hence trying it on for fit and size, rather than consulting their own personality tempered by thoughtful self-awareness and the process that guides it. Those who take the "bag of tricks" approach will be mediocre at best, and usually stifle the treatment because patients will inevitably feel that they come across as gimmicky, stilted, pedantic, and unnatural. This does not foster genuine relatedness, which is what many patients need, especially those with attachment vulnerabilities, in order to live more fulfilling and functional lives.

Developing a personal treatment philosophy should authentically reflect the way in which clinicians actually live their lives in order *to be* genuine to the patient. Do you really believe what you tell patients? Do you hold yourself to the same standards? If not, you should reevaluate your premises and the reasons that dictate your approach to treatment. Clinical and theoretical refinement demands work, reading, experimentation, thoughtfulness, contemplation, supervised experience, and ongoing training. You are only going to take a person as far as you have been yourself (Erikson, 1964). If you can't recognize the dynamic forces that influence your own psychic reality, then how will you recognize what is going on in others? Every conscientious clinician should know thyself, get personal therapy or undergo analysis, and live an introspective and contemplative life. This is both a preparatory and ongoing attitude or sensibility that grounds your theoretical beliefs and convictions, guides your clinical work, and offers stability in professional identity and therapeutic efficacy. This takes time and erudition, experience and technical refinement, openness and flexibility, creativity and humor, and as Kohut (1971) would say, a "modicum" of wisdom.

The value of relationality in clinical practice

Relational and intersubjective viewpoints have convincingly overturned the dogmatic inculcation of Americanized classical training and encourage free thinking, experimentation, novelty, spontaneity, creativity, authentic self-expression, humor, and play. And here is what I believe is the relational position's greatest contribution—the way they practice. There is malleability in the treatment frame, selectivity in interventions tailored to the unique needs and qualities of each patient, and a proper burial of the prototypic solemn analyst who is fundamentally removed from relating as one human being to another in the service of a withholding, frustrating, and ungratifying methodology designed to provoke transference enactments, deprivation, and unnecessary feelings of rejection, shame, guilt, and rage.

Today's relational analyst is more adept at customizing technique to fit each unique dyad (Greenberg, 2001; Beebe & Lachmann, 2003), what Bacal (1998) refers to as a specificity of intervention choice, and rallies against a blanket standardization or manualization of practice. Because of these important modifications to methodology, one may not inappropriately say that a relational approach can be a superior form of treatment for many patients because it enriches the scope of human experience in relation to another's and validates their wish for understanding, meaning, recognition, and love; what may very well be the most coveted and exalted ideals that make psychoanalysis effectively transformative and healing. In short, unlike the caricature of the classical analyst, the relational practitioner treats the patient as a real person who has needs, conflicts, and wishes that the analyst is obliged to address, and if possible, meet or fulfill simply because it is the humane thing to do.

Traditionalists and contemporary Freudians may have a legitimate criticism that the "new view" analysts gloss over the goal of uncovering unconscious conflicts; but in their defense, they would likely say that uncovering unconscious material for the sake of pure discovery is not as therapeutically important as other pursuits. To be fair to the classicists, however, in enumerating various criticisms, contemporary practitioners by and large could be accused of: (1) not focusing on the deeper stratification of unconscious structure and their dynamics processes; (2) largely failing to focus on the genetic past and their symbolic manifestations in the transference; (3) are inattentive to unconscious fantasy; (4) are too permissive in maintaining a permeable treatment frame, one which largely lacks contained or well-defined boundaries, including consensual rules for participation; and (5) focuses too much on the here and now, where the emphasis is placed on co-constructing a relationship rather than exploring the patient's dynamic past. But, in practice, this is much more likely to be a matter of emphasis.

In response, the contemporary practitioner would likely question the value of unconscious interpretation as a primary therapeutic goal over the lived reality of the present moment that is far more pressing and important to the client. Here, interpretation for the sake of interpretation out of the analyst's need to pursue truth or to be right, to interject self-importance in the session, or to trump the patient's take on their own inner experience is not deemed to be the main mission of analysis. In fact, the principle of the primacy of interpretation that traditionally characterizes the technical method of psychoanalysis could be the very bane of treatment for many patients simply because it is not helpful. Not only can premature or imposed (let alone intrusive), adduced interpretations drive patients away from treatment due to their misattunements or stinging exposures based on a lack of tact, they can arguably be clinically counter-indicated. The last thing patients want is their analyst to analyze with a hammer.

The *interpretive imposition*—the calling card of shame—is often an authoritarian epistemology foisted upon the analysand as an illusory objective observation toted under the banner of truth, when it is simply superimposed power on a dubious subject. The personal (sometimes narcissistic) need for the clinician to spew forth gems of wisdom, or point out unconscious motives based on the analyst's internal muses (qua constructive fantasies) and passing them off as so-called quasiscientific facts, perpetuates a hubris that betrays the spirit of psychoanalysis as a catalyst for self-knowledge. A methodology that privileges interpretation over self-discovery, disclosedness, and unconcealment, what the ancients refer to as *aletheia* (ἀλήθεια), undermines the value of self-exploration as a confrontation with the dialectic of truth and uncertainty.

Since its inception, psychoanalysis has always received criticism for not measuring up to the propounded status of a legitimate "science." But clinical case material is what we mainly rely on as legitimate sources of qualitative empirical data.[7] As Safran (2003) points out in his survey of psychotherapy research, there are many empirically derived conclusions that address the question of treatment efficacy. Once taking into account the patient's developmental and life history, we may be alerted to the following conditions that remain the major criteria in which to evaluate the merit and/or limitations of a treatment and the specific interventions employed: the (a) qualitative degree of the working alliance, including (but not limited to) the level of trust and capacity to form an attachment with the analyst; (b) mutual agreement with regard to the process and goals of treatment; and (c) the patient's assent to professional authority as indicative of his or her level of satisfaction (with or without symptom improvement). In the end, what is likely most indicative of clinical efficacy is whether or not the client likes the therapist and feels safe in the treatment.

As I have stated elsewhere (Mills, 2005b), in my opinion psychoanalysis is ultimately about process over anything else—perhaps even above technical principles, theory, and interventions—for it relies on the indeterminate unfolding of inner experience within intersubjective space. In our training, we learn to cultivate an analytic attitude of clinical composure, optimal listening, data-gathering, hypothesis testing, critical reflection, clarification and reevaluation—all of which conceptually and behaviorally guide the analytic process. Process is everything, and attunement to process will determine if you can take the patient where he or she needs to go. The analyst has the challenging task of attending to the patient's associations within particular contexts of content and form, perpetuity versus discontinuity, sequence and coherence, thus noting repetitions of themes and patterns, and the convergence of such themes within a teleological dynamic trajectory of conceptual meaning. The clinician has to be vigilant for competing, overlapping, and/or parallel processes that are potentially operative at once, thus requiring shifts in focal attention and microdynamic attunement. There are always realities encroaching on other realities, and affect plays a crucial part. Observation becomes a way of being that requires listening on multiple levels of experiential complexity—from manifest to latent content; detecting unconscious communications; recognizing resistance, defense, drive derivatives (i.e., unconscious desire), transference manifestations, and differential elements of each compromise; tracking the dialectical tensions between competing wishes, fantasies, and conflicts with close attention to their affective reverberations; listening at different levels of abstraction; ferreting out one's countertransference from ordinary subjective peculiarities—to tracing the multifarious interpersonal components of therapeutic exchange. Given such complexity and the overdetermination of multiple competing processes, I hardly think psychoanalytic technique is capable of being manualized by following a step-by-step method.

What patients remember the most about you is not necessarily what you say, but how you relate to them, how you model a way of being; and this is what gets internalized and transmuted within psychic structure. No one wants to be related to as a thing. Traditional approaches, whether intended or not, implicitly foster (if not encourage) a detached scientific, experience-far observer paradigm, while the relational approach sees the inherent value of being real, genuine, and fostering an experience-near, co-participant observer stance, whereby the patient is related to as a nonobjectified person.

It becomes difficult to define the overall purpose or meaning of therapy because the clinical encounter is always mediated by context and contingency. For rhetorical purposes, if I had to pinpoint the essence of treatment, I would say therapy is a *process of becoming*, a process of creative self-discovery, a process that requires the presence and influence of the other. Therefore, therapy is about forming and being in a relationship, one that is healthier and more genuine than what patients know only too well in their private lives. Having the opportunity to say what they truly think, and feel how they truly feel, is one of the most beautiful experiences and more curative dimensions of analysis; and having this recognized, understood, and validated by another person serves to encourage and instill a new set of values and ideals for what it truly means to have a fulfilling relationship. When this occurs naturally and developmentally over time, the patient comes to identify with and pursue a new way of being that is modeled on authentic relationality.

Endnotes

1. IARPP Website, About Us: Who We Are. http://iarpp.net/who-we-are/ Downloaded on January 22, 2016.
2. Although Stolorow, Atwood, and Orange have defended their positions quite well in response to their critics, often correcting critics on facets of theirwritings most readers—let alone sophisticated researchers—would not be reasonably aware of without going to the effort of reading their entire collected body of combined works, one lacuna they cannot defend in their intersubjectivity theory is accounting for *a priori* unconscious processes prior to the emergence of consciousness, subject matter I thoroughly address elsewhere (see Mills, 2002a, 2002b). Although having attempted to address the role of organizing principles and the unconscious (Stolorow & Atwood, 1992), because they designate intersubjectivity to be the heart of *all* human experience, they commit themselves to a philosophy of consciousness that by definition fails to adequately account for an unconscious ontology, which I argue is the necessary precondition for consciousness and intersubjective life to emerge (Mills, 2010).

   In their criticism of my assessment of their philosophy, Stolorow et al. (2006) claim that because I do not adequately situate the context of their writings when quoting or interpreting their work, I "annul" the notion of the unconscious in their combined theories, which they uphold. But this is not accurate. Although they account for the notion of the unconscious, it becomes decentered, not annulled. They do not deny the significance of the unconscious, they simply privilege conscious experience, to which they give priority due to the primacy of intersubjectivity. Although I readily concede that the authors object to being equated with other relationalists who do not adequately address the nature and being of the unconscious in contemporary discourse, Stolorow et al. still bear the onus of explaining their own textual contradictions.
3. Freud (1925) ultimately defined psychoanalysis as "the science of unconscious mental processes" (p. 70).

4. I wish to distinguish myself from some forms of clinical practice that are common among relational analysts today including the overexpression of personal communications, countertransference disclosures, and the insistence on reciprocal revelations that may reveal more about the needs of the analyst rather than the patient's. I am much more conservative when it comes to these matters and am cautious about the risk of too much self-disclosure.
5. These issues are explored in depth in *Rereading Freud: Psychoanalysis through Philosophy* (Mills, 2004a) and *Psychoanalysis at the Limit: Epistemology, Mind, and the Question of Science* (Mills, 2004b).
6. While I do not intend to provoke enemies among my respected colleagues over theoretical turf wars, I do feel it is vitally important to be open to self-critique within any preferred camp throughout the history of the psychoanalytic movement in order to be able to prosper and advance psychoanalysis as a whole. Even though I readily concede that I practice as a relational clinician, I am not so impressed with the need to elevate relationality by vilifying classical approaches.
7. I am not in agreement with Masling's (2003) claim that clinical data is "not empirical" (p. 597) since it relies on the qualitative enactments and analysis of experience, not merely culled from the analyst's clinical phenomenology, but also empirically investigated by psychoanalytic psychotherapy researchers including Gill, Hoffman, Luborsky, Strupp, and Safran, just to name a few.

References

Bacal, H. (Ed.) (1998). *How Therapists Heal Their Patients: Optimal Responsiveness.* Northvale, NJ: Aronson.

Beebe, B., & Lachmann, F. (2003). The relational turn in psychoanalysis: A dyadic systems view from infant research. *Contemporary Psychoanalysis*, 39 (3), 379–409.

Beebe, B., & Lachmann, F. (2014). *The Origins of Attachment.* London: Routledge.

Binswanger, L. (1962). Ausgewählte Werke Band 2: Grundformen und Erkenntnis menschlichen Daseins. M. Herog & Has-Jürgen Braun (Eds.). Heidelberg: Asanger, 1993.

Eagle, M. (2003). The postmodern turn in psychoanalysis: A critique. *Psychoanalytic Psychology*, 20(3), 411–424.

Eagle, M., Wolitzky, D.L., & Wakefield, J.C. (2001). The analyst's knowledge and authority: A critique of the "New View" in psychoanalysis. *Journal of the American Psychoanalytic Association*, 49, 457–488.

Erikson, E.H. (1964). *Insight and Responsibility.* New York: W.W. Norton.

Frank, G. (1998a). On the relational school of psychoanalysis: Some additional thoughts. *Psychoanalytic Psychology*, 15(1), 141–153.

Frank, G. (1998b). The intersubjective school of psychoanalysis: Concerns and questions. *Psychoanalytic Psychology*, 15(3), 420–423.

Freud, S. (1966–95 [1886–1940]). *The Standard Edition of the Complete Psychological Works of Sigmund Freud*, 24 vols. Trans. and gen. ed. James Strachey, in collaboration with Anna Freud, assisted by Alix Strachey and Alan Tyson. London: Hogarth Press.

Freud, S. (1900). *The Interpretation of Dreams.* Standard Edition, Vols.4–5. London: Hogarth Press.

Freud, S. (1915). *Instincts and Their Vicissitudes.* Standard Edition, Vol. 14. London: Hogarth Press.

Freud, S. (1925). *An Autobiographical Study*. Standard Edition, Vol. 20. London: Hogarth Press.

Freud, S. (1927). *Future of an Illusion*. Standard Edition, Vol. 21. London: Hogarth Press.

Greenberg, J. (1991). *Oedipus and Beyond: A Clinical Theory*. Cambridge: Harvard University Press.

Greenberg, J. (2001). The analyst's Participation: A new look. *Journal of the American Psychoanalytic Association*, 49(2), 359–381.

Greenberg, J., & Mitchell, S. (1983). *Object Relations in Psychoanalytic Theory*. Cambridge, MA: Harvard University Press.

Heidegger, M. (1927). *Being and Time*. Trans. J. Macquarrie & E. Robinson. San Francisco: Harper Collins, 1962.

Josephs, L. (2001). The relational values of scientific practice: A response to commentaries by Silverman (2000) and Mitchell (2000). *Psychoanalytic Psychology*, 18(1), 157–160.

Kohut, H. (1971). *The Analysis of the Self*. New York: International Universities Press.

Lohser, B., & Newton, P. (1996). *Unorthodox Freud: A View from the Couch*. New York: Guilford.

Lothane, Z. (2003). What did Freud say about persons and relations? *Psychoanalytic Psychology*, 20(4), 609–617.

Masling, J. (2003). Stephen A. Mitchell, relational psychoanalysis, and empirical data. *Psychoanalytic Psychology*, 20(4), 587–608.

Mills, J. (2002a). *The Unconscious Abyss: Hegel's Anticipation of Psychoanalysis*. Albany: SUNY Press.

Mills, J. (2002b). Deciphering the "Genesis Problem": On the dialectical origins of psychic reality. *The Psychoanalytic Review*, 89 (6), 763–809.

Mills, J. (2004a). *Rereading Freud*. Albany, NY: SUNY Press.

Mills, J. (2004b). *Psychoanalysis at the Limit*. Albany, NY: SUNY Press.

Mills, J. (2005a). A critique of relational psychoanalysis. *Psychoanalytic Psychology*, 22(2), 155–188.

Mills, J. (2005b). *Treating Attachment Pathology*. Northvale, NJ: Aronson.

Mills, J. (2010). *Origins: On the Genesis of Psychic Reality*. Montreal: McGill-Queens University Press.

Mills, J. (2012). *Conundrums: A Critique of Contemporary Psychoanalysis*. New York: Routledge.

Mitchell, S. A. (1988). *Relational Concepts in Psychoanalysis: An Integration*. Cambridge, MA: Harvard University Press.

Mitchell, S., & Aron, L. (Eds.) (1999). *Relational Psychoanalysis: The Emergence of a Tradition*. Hillsdale, NJ: The Analytic Press.

Richards, A.D. (1999a). Book review of *Ritual and Spontaneity in the Psychoanalytic Process: A Dialectical Constructivist Point of View*. *Psychoanalytic Psychology*, 16(2), 288–302.

Richards, A.D. (1999b). Squeaky chairs and straw persons: An intervention in the contemporary psychoanalytic debate. *The Round Robin*, 14(1), 6–9.

Roazen, P. (1995). *How Freud Worked*. Hillsdale, NJ: Aronson.

Safran, J.D. (2003).The relational turn, the therapeutic alliance, and psychotherapy research. *Contemporary Psychoanalysis*, 39(3), 449–475.

Silverman, D.K. (2000). An interrogation of the relational turn: A discussion with Stephen Mitchell. *Psychoanalytic Psychology*, 17(1), 146–152.

Stolorow, R.D. (2001). Foreword to P. Buirski & P. Haglund, *Making Sense Together: The Intersubjective Approach to Psychotherapy*. Northvale, NJ: Jason Aronson.

Stolorow, R.D. (2010). A phenomenological-contextual psychoanalyst: Intersubjective-systems theory and clinical practice. Interviewed by A. Sassenfeld. *Psychologist-Psychoanalyst*, 30(3), 6–10.

Stolorow, R.D., & Atwood, G. (1992). *Contexts of Being: The Intersubjective Foundations of Psychological Life*. Hillsdale, NJ: The Analytic Press.

Stolorow, R.D., Atwood, G., & Orange, D. M. (2006). Contextualizing is not nullifying: Reply to Mills (2005). *Psychoanalytic Psychology*, 23(1), 184–188.

8 Introduction to the relational approach and its critics

A conference with Dr. Jon Mills

Aner Govrin

Abstract: In February of 2015, a symposium was held at Bar-Ilan University, titled *The Relational Approach and its Critics: A Conference with Dr. Jon Mills*, sponsored by the Israeli forum of the International Association for Relational Psychoanalysis and Psychotherapy (IARPP) and the Department of Hermeneutics and Cultural Studies at Bar-Ilan University. The distinguished keynote speaker was Jon Mills, the Canadian philosopher, psychoanalyst, and clinical psychologist who has become the most important and profound spokesman to critique the relational psychoanalytic movement. We asked two relational psychologists, together with an independent school psychologist, a Kleinian psychoanalyst, and a researcher of hermeneutics and culture to respond to Mills' address, each from their own unique vantage point. This symposium created a chance for a scholarly, comprehensive evaluation of current relational thought that ranged from the clinical to the philosophical, emphasizing anew the vitality of interdisciplinary dialogue.

In February 2015, a symposium was held at Bar-Ilan University, titled *The Relational Approach and its Critics: A Conference with Dr. Jon Mills*, sponsored by the Israeli forum of the International Association for Relational Psychoanalysis and Psychotherapy (IARPP) and the Department of Hermeneutics and Cultural Studies at Bar-Ilan University. The distinguished keynote speaker was Jon Mills, the Canadian philosopher, psychoanalyst, and clinical psychologist who has become one of today's most important critics of the relational psychoanalytic movement. The aim of the symposium was to expose the Israeli psychoanalytic community to Jon Mills' critique as presented in several of his published articles (Mills, 2005; 2010), as well as his book *Conundrums: A Critique of Contemporary Psychoanalysis* (2012). Dozens of conferences convene each year with analysts engaging in dialogue with others who embrace the same viewpoints as themselves. This symposium was meant to accomplish something different; something that would trigger critical thought, discussion, and a lively public debate.

During the revolutionary phase of the relational approach to psychoanalysis at the end of the 1990's and beginning of the 2000's Mitchell (1993) emphasized the limits and constraints of human knowledge. The relational approach was preoccupied with epistemology, and thus in direct conflict with the conventionally accepted worldview of positivism and correspondence theory of truth that classical analysts traditionally endorsed. But now, we are beyond this point. In the course of the last decade, preoccupation with epistemological issues has, to a great extent, declined. One of the main reasons for this change is that the relational movement together with contemporary understanding of truth and knowledge have had a huge impact on the psychoanalytic world (including more traditional schools).

It has become rare to find analysts who claim there is one correct and complete way of understanding a patient's experience. As a result, the centrality of the question "What does the analyst know?" has been replaced with the practical consequences and implications of a relational point of view. A return to epistemology and theory is important. Without it we overlook an important dimension of psychoanalysis and remove ourselves from the fascinating discourse of contemporary philosophy. Mills has brought these epistemological premises back, through his consistent engagement with a variety of philosophical approaches to the fundamental problems facing relational psychoanalysis.

Mills identifies himself as a relational psychologist who endorses a number of fundamental principles of this point of view. At the same time, he is scathingly critical of the practical implementation of relational psychoanalytic theory and of various practices and methodologies adopted by relational therapists. Moreover, with his broad and enlightened philosophical view, Mills is particularly doubtful about the ways in which relational theories are formulated and crafted, and concerned about the lack of a metapsychological formulation which would endow relational theory with an underlying rational foundation.

We have brought together some prominent clinicians and thinkers in our field and asked them to discuss and respond to Mills' critique. Chana Ullman counters Mills by strongly urging us to view the relational approach as one that endorses universals rather than one supporting relativism. Shlomit Yadlin-Gadot suggests we may be able to solve the issues Mills raises by admitting multiple epistemologies into analytic discourse. Boaz Shalgi posits that the problem with Mills' arguments is not that he condemns the primacy of intersubjectivity, but that he authorizes the precedence of objectivity. Merav Roth offers a Kleinian perspective into the complex ideas raised by Mills concentrating on a critique of self-disclosure and the analyst's subjectivity. Finally, Liran Razinsky defends postmodernism in its more nuanced and balanced form, applying the philosophical approach of Jacques Derrida.

Despite psychoanalysis' basic humanistic values, the discipline has, from its very beginnings, been witness to endless bitter confrontations. Saucy stories of exclusion, expulsion and personal vilification are familiar to us from Freud's time and continue till this day. It is conceivable that this is embedded in the manner in which every polemicist becomes attached to his chosen theories; but it may also be that this is not much more than an enactment of the destructive drives Freud first discussed.

The relational approach emphasizes the vital importance of the encounter between two disparate subjectivities. The capacity of these two differing subjectivities to recognize one another culminates in mutual realization of their common humanity. But this encounter with otherness also brings with it potential dangers of misrepresentation, and perhaps even destruction. Truth and meaning evolve from the dialogue between or among people with truly diverse points of view, their own histories, cultural backgrounds, experiences and intellectuality. In other words, truth emerges from two or more subjectivities.

In our view, in terms of both content and process, the symposium demonstrated the relational principles of mutual recognition at their best. Out of differences of view, unfamiliarity and alienation, there flowered productive dialogue and a generative space in which to think and relate. The Jewish book of oral law, *The Mishnah*, says that when a dispute arises for the sake of heaven, the intentions of the disputants are to clarify the truth; and at the end of this type of generative discussion, both sides will continue to exist and be remembered for having been involved in the debate. This is because the clarification of the truth can only come about through a dialogue of differences. It is the *dispute itself* that clarifies the truth (Lev Pirkei Avot Commentary, Chapter 5, *Mishnah* 17).

I believe that the relational approach possesses a remarkable capacity for self-reflexive humor (see Dimen, 2014, p. 508) and an acceptance of criticism both from within and beyond. For example, in recent years I published an article in JAPA (Govrin, 2006) arguing that in terms of formulating a new psychoanalytic theory the relational approach was problematic. The first person to congratulate me was Lew Aron, one of the founders of the relational movement. The relational school of thought permits keen internal debate and embraces sharp differences of view, as is appropriate for a healthy and strong body of knowledge. This is an approach that encourages dialogue and critical inquiry. I believe that the conference with Jon Mills is yet another example of the flexibility of relational psychoanalysis, an approach that is confident, aware of its own worth and of the revolution it has generated, and one that is not afraid of facing critics and engaging in lively debate.

I wish to express my sincere gratitude to everyone who contributed to the success of this conference and to all those who collaborated in the present publication. I am also grateful to the editor of *Psychoanalytic Perspectives* for his invitation to publish the symposium and disseminate it to a wider audience.

References

Dimen, M. (2014). Inside the revolution: Power, sex and the technique on Freud's "Wild Analysis", *Psychoanalytic Dialogues*, 24, 499–515.

Govrin, A. (2006). The Dilemma of Contemporary Psychoanalysis: Toward a "Knowing" Post-Postmodernism. *J. Amer. Psychoanal. Assn.*, 54(2), 507–535.

Lev Pirkei Avot Commentary, Chapter 5, *Mishnah* 17.

Mills, J. (Ed.) (2005). *Relational and Intersubjective Perspectives in Psychoanalysis: A Critique*. Lanham, MD: Aronson/Rowman & Littlefield.

Mills, J. (2010). *Origins: On the Genesis of Psychic Reality*. Montreal: McGill-Queens University Press.

Mills, J. (2012). *Conundrums: A Critique of Contemporary Psychoanalysis*. New York: Routledge.

Mitchell, S. (1993). *Hope and Dread in Psychoanalysis*. New York: Basic Books.

9 Challenging relational psychoanalysis

A critique of postmodernism and analyst self-disclosure

Jon Mills

Abstract: This essay is based on two lectures given at Bar-Ilan University, Israel, February 13, 2015. These lectures were largely derived from my book, *Conundrums: A Critique of Contemporary Psychoanalysis*, and serve as the focus of critique and rebuttal from five panelists who responded to my lectures delivered at the conference. Here, I provide an adumbrated critique of the adoption of postmodernism within contemporary relational theory and the excessive use of analyst self-disclosure. Although these lectures have been merged into a formal paper, they remain mostly unrevised and represent what transpired at the conference despite being cut in length for the purposes of publication.

I wish to challenge the postmodern turn in relational psychoanalysis for its antimodern tendencies, theoretical contradictions, and the wholesale acceptance of the primacy of language. Because postmodernism denies traditional metaphysical and epistemological paradigms, it also compromises the status of psychoanalysis as a legitimate human science by opposing the notions of objectivity, interpretation, and truth claims about reality. Relational psychoanalysis in particular has selectively adopted various features of pomocentrism that oppose the notions of selfhood, agency, essentialism, and the nature of universals. I wish to advocate for a return to a discourse on the modern tenets of universality, essence, and objectivity that properly appreciates the role of ontology and how it informs all aspects of subjectivity, contextuality, culture, and collective social experience.

A critique of the postmodern turn in relational psychoanalysis

Since Mitchell's (1988) and Greenberg's (1991) instantiation of the relational platform (Greenberg & Mitchell, 1983), contemporary psychoanalysis has increasingly embraced postmodern paradigms originally initiated by several key developments in twentiethcentury European continental philosophy. These genres include (but are not limited to) preoccupations with phenomenology, the hermeneutic tradition, and the linguistic turn. Among these postmodern assumptions are the abnegation of the Enlightenment modern notions of rationality, objectivity, epistemic certainty, truth, universal absolutes, individuality and free will, and positivistic science, just to name a few. What we see abundant today in the analytic literature are constant references to relatedness in lieu of intrapsychic life, an emphasis on intersubjectivity over internality, constructivism versus discovery, context and perspective rather than universal proclamations, contingencies contra absolutes, skepticism over certainty, consensus—not truth—and conscious experience over the primacy of unconscious mentation. And with this new addition to the history of psychoanalysis comes a swing of the pendulum away from the precepts that characterize the sciences and modern philosophy and everything they stand for: namely, claims about the nature of reality, universal laws, objective methodology, logical coherence, epistemological standardization, and truth.

As a psychoanalyst, philosopher, and relational practitioner, I have a great deal of respect for how relational psychoanalysis has created a permissible space for questioning and revamping the theoretical and technical convictions passed down from previous generations; nowhere do we see such a forceful reformation in psychoanalytic practice since Kohut. Indeed, such rehabilitative approaches in the consulting room are perhaps the greatest accomplishments relational psychoanalysis offers our discipline as a whole, a subject matter I will address shortly. But regardless of these advances, on the theoretical side of things, relational psychoanalysis at times lacks philosophical sophistication. What I believe is fundamentally problematic in much of the relational literature is its implicit and naive adoption of the postmodern turn. In its efforts to justify its viability as a behavioral science through engaging the humanities, and without having to adopt the stringent criteria of mainstream empirical science, contemporary psychoanalysis seems to have jumped on the postmodern bandwagon without considering the consequences. In some instances, contemporary writers use the term liberally when they often have no firm grasp of what they mean by *postmodernism* to begin with.[1] Postmodern sensibilities are arbitrarily applied to literature, art, politics, feminism, spirituality, gender and queer theory—even architecture—each having radically different meanings and contextual variations depending upon which discipline you consult. The same arbitrariness and slipshod propositional assertions are being made today within the contemporary psychoanalytic domain, often under the guise of scholarship passed off as legitimate philosophical justification, when the merits for such justification are suspiciously dubious to begin with. I hope to persuade the audience that relational psychoanalysis is in need of theoretical restoration if it plans to prosper and advance. Postmodernism is not the answer.

Relativism, objectivity, and the linguistic construction of the subject

One indelible problem is the nature and meaning of universals that are flippantly disregarded by postmodern relationalists. Another is the antimetaphysical and antiepistemological frameworks that tacitly govern postmodern politics.

Moreover, the ontology of the unconscious, self-experience, freedom, will and agency, moral absolutes, and the existence of an autonomous self become eclipsed by postmodern commitments. My contention is that relational psychoanalysis has everything to gain by returning to a modern discourse on the explication of universals that allows for particularity and contextual complexity. It may do so while avoiding the pitfalls associated with postmodern proclamations that ultimately stand for categorical refutation, relativism, and nihilism under the political, contradictory guise of affirming a particularly biased agenda—itself, ironically, the very thing it wishes to negate.

The word *postmodernism* is so ambiguous that it has virtually become a meaningless term. What exactly do we mean by it? And what is its burgeoning role in psychoanalytic discourse? The lure of postmodernism is widely attractive because it explains the hitherto unacknowledged importance of the analyst's interjected experience within the analytic encounter; displaces the notion of the analyst's epistemic authority as an objective certainty; highlights contextuality and perspective over universal proclamations that apply to all situations regardless of historical contingency, culture, gender, or time; and largely embraces the linguistic, narrative turn in philosophy. Although postmodern thought has propitiously criticized the pervasive historical, gendered, and ethnocentric character of our understanding of the world, contemporary trends in psychoanalysis seem to be largely unaware of the *aporiai* postmodern propositions introduce into a coherent and justifiable theoretical system. Although postmodernism has no unified body of theory, thus making it unsystematized, one unanimous implication is the demise of the individual subject. Postmodernism may be generally said to be a cross-disciplinary movement largely comprising linguistic, poststructural, constructivist, historical, narrative, deconstructivist, and feminist social critiques that oppose most Western philosophical traditions. As a result, postmodern doctrines are antimetaphysical, antiepistemological, and anticolonial, thus opposing realism, foundationalism, essentialism, neutrality, and the ideal sovereignty of reason. Although postmodern sensibility has rightfully challenged the omnipresence of historically biased androcentric and logocentric interpretations of human nature and culture, it has done so at the expense of dislocating several key modern philosophical tenets that celebrate the nature of subjectivity, consciousness, scientific discovery, and the teleology of the will. Consequently, the transcendental notions of freedom, liberation, individuality, personal independence, authenticity, and reflective deliberate choice that comprise the essential activities of personal agency are altogether disassembled. What all this boils down to is the dissolution of the autonomous, rational subject. In other words, the self is anaesthetized.

Postmodernism has become very fashionable with some relationalists because it may be used selectively to advocate for certain contemporary positions, such as the co-construction of meaning and the disenfranchisement of epistemic analytic authority, but it does so at the expense of introducing antimetaphysical propositions into psychoanalytic theory that are replete with massive contradictions and inconsistencies. For example, if meaning is merely a social construction, and all analytic discourse that transpires within the consulting room is dialogical, then meaning and interpretation are conditioned on linguistic social factors that determine such meaning, hence we are the product of language instantiated within our cultural ontology. This means that language and culture are *causally determinative.* Donnel Stern (1997) nicely summarizes the contemporary psychoanalytic platform:

> This view of language, along with psychoanalytic constructivism itself, are outgrowths of the many streams of contemporary thought (philosophy of science, post-structuralism, pragmatism, and contemporary hermeneutics) that join together in the one great postmodern conclusion: *All experience is linguistic.* (p. 7, emphasis added)

Stern is unmistakably clear: "language is the condition for experiencing" (p. 7). If all experience is linguistic, then what becomes of unconscious mental processes? How would you account for "prelinguistic" organizations that belong to the experiential world of an infant, such as sentient, sensorial, and affective reverberations? If language is the ground or condition for experience, then by definition this excludes biologically based regulatory processes, such as the teleonomic and teleological pressures inherent to the drives (see Mills, 2010).

The implications of such positions immediately annul metaphysical assertions to truth, objectivity, free will, and agency, among other universals. For instance, if everything boils down to language and culture, then by definition we cannot make legitimate assertions about truth claims or objective knowledge because these claims are merely constructions based upon our linguistic practices to begin with rather than universals that exist independent of language and socialization. So, one cannot conclude that truth or objectivity exist. These become mythologies, fictions, narratives, and illusions regardless of whether we find social consensus. Therefore, natural science—such as the laws of physics, mathematics, and formal logic are merely social inventions based on semantic construction that by definition annul any claims to objective observations or mind independent reality. In other words, metaphysics is dead and buried—nothing exists independent of language.[2]

What perhaps appears to be the most widely shared claim in the relational tradition is the assault on the analyst's epistemological authority to objective knowledge. Stolorow (1998) tells us that "objective reality is unknowable by the psychoanalytic method, which investigates only subjective reality… there are no neutral or objective analysts, no immaculate perceptions, no God's-eye views of anything" (p. 425). What exactly does this mean? If my patient is suicidal and he communicates this to me, providing he is not malingering, lying, or manipulating me for some reason, does this not constitute some form of objective judgment independent of his subjective verbalizations? Do we not have some capacities to form objective appraisals (here the term *objective* being used to denote making reasonably correct judgments about objects or events outside of our unique subjective experience)? Is not Stolorow making an absolute claim despite arguing against absolutism when he says that "reality is unknowable?" Why not say that knowledge is proportional or incremental rather than totalistic, thus subject to modification, alteration, and interpretation rather than categorically negate the category of an objective epistemology? Are there no objective facts? Would anyone care to defy the laws of gravity by attempting to fly off the roof of a building by flapping their arms?

Because postmodern perspectives are firmly established in antithesis to the entire history of Greek and European ontology, perspectives widely adopted by many contemporary analysts today, relational psychoanalysis has no tenable metaphysics, or in the words of Aner Govrin (2006), no real "metatheory." This begs the question of an intelligible discourse on method for the simple fact that postmodern sensibilities ultimately collapse into relativism. Since there are no independent standards, methods, or principles subject to uniform procedures for evaluating conceptual schemas, postmodern perspectives naturally lead to relativism. From the epistemic (perspectival) standpoint of a floridly psychotic schizophrenic, flying donkeys really *do* exist, but this does not make it so. Relativism is incoherent and is an internally inconsistent position at best. I once had a student who was an ardent champion of relativism until I asked him to stand up and turn around. When he did I lifted his wallet from his back pocket and said: "If everything is relative, then I think I am entitled to your wallet because the university does not pay me enough." Needless to say, he wanted it back.

Relativism collapses into contradiction, inexactitude, nihilism, and ultimately absurdity because no one person's opinion is any more valid than another's, especially including value judgments and ethical behavior, despite qualifications that some opinions are superior to others. A further danger of embracing a "relativistic science" is that psychoanalysis really has nothing to offer over other disciplines who may negate the value of psychoanalysis to begin with (e.g., empirical academic psychology), let alone patients themselves whose own opinions may or may not carry any more weight than the analysts with whom they seek out for expert professional help. Imagine saying to your patient: "I know nothing, now where's my money?" When one takes relativism to the extreme, constructivism becomes creationism, which is simply a grandiose fantasy of omnipotence—"things are whatever you want them to be."[3]

I had a patient who was run over as a pedestrian by a drunk driver and was left permanently disabled. He was so traumatized and enraged by his insurance company who rejected his claim that he started contemplating killing his claims adjuster. This fantasy gradually began to acquire an autonomy of its own to the point that he started developing a concrete plan. When he told me in session that he had been canvassing the insurance building and determined that he could drive a tractor trailer through the building during the smoke break, where he would likely kill the greatest number of employees at once, I told him that if he continued down this path I was certain he would be arrested. He immediately became frightened—scared straight, so to speak. I told him that he must work through his pain and victimization rather than act on it, and I reassured him that if he did this, he would find it healing. We explored how this impulse toward murder was an attempt to seek revenge for his injustice and undo his sense of helplessness, but that he had other options rather than bring about his total self-destruction. Later in treatment my patient referred back to that discussion as one of the most helpful interventions because he needed to know that I knew I could help him. This shows why "to know" is important, and that patients sometimes need us to know.

One thing is for sure (in my humble "relativist" opinion!), relational and intersubjective theorists seem to have a penchant for creating false dichotomies between inner/outer, self/other, universal/particular, absolute/relative, truth/fallacy, and subject/object. For those familiar with the late modern Kantian turn through to German Idealism, phenomenology, and early continental philosophy, contemporary psychoanalysis seems to be behind the times. The subject–object divide has already been closed.[4] Although postmodern psychoanalytic thought is attractive for its emphasis on contextuality, linguistic, gender, and cultural specificity, political reform, postcolonial antipatriarchy, the displacement of pure reason and phallocentrism, and the epistemic refutation of positivistic science, it does so at the expense of eclipsing metaphysical inquiry, which was the basis of Freud's foray into understanding the ontology of the unconscious and establishing psychoanalysis as a science of subjectivity.[5]

Most relational analysts would not deny the existence of an independent, separate subject or self, and in fact have gone to great lengths to account for individuality and authenticity within intersubjective space. A problematic is introduced, however, when a relational or intersubjective ontology is defined in opposition to separateness, singularity, distinction, and individual identity. For example, Seligman (2003) represents the relational tradition when he specifically tells us that "the analyst and patient are co-constructing a relationship in which neither of them can be seen as *distinct* from the other" (pp. 484–485, emphasis added). At face value, this is a troubling ontological assertion. Following from these premises, there is no such thing as separate human beings, which is tantamount to the claim that we are all identical because we are ontologically indistinguishable. If there is no distinction between two subjects that form the relational encounter, then only the dyadic intersubjective system can claim to have any proper identity. Relational analysts are not fully considering the impact of statements such as these when they propound that "everything is intersubjective" because by doing so it annuls individuality, distinctiveness, and otherness, which is what dialectically constitutes the intersubjective system to begin with.

Further statements such as "There is *no* experience that is not interpersonally mediated" (Mitchell, 1992, p. 2, emphasis added) lend themselves to the social-linguistic platform and thereby deplete the notion of individuation, autonomy, choice, freedom, and teleological (hence purposeful) action because we are constituted, hence *caused*, by extrinsic forces that determine who we are. Not only does this displace the centrality of subjectivity—the very thing relationality wants to account for—it does not take into account other nonlinguistic or extralinguistic factors that transpire within personal lived experience such as the phenomenology of embodiment, somatic resonance states, nonconceptual, perceptive consciousness, affective life, aesthetic experience, *a priori* mental processes organized prior to the formal acquisition of language, and most importantly, the unconscious. The confusional aspects to relational thinking are only magnified when theorists use terminology that align them with postmodernism on the one hand, thus eclipsing the self and extracting the subject from subjectivity, yet they then want to affirm the existence of the self as an independent agent (Hoffman, 1998). While some relational analysts advocate for a singular, cohesive self that is subject to change yet endures over time (Lichtenberg, Lachmann, & Fosshage, 2002; Fosshage, 2003), others prefer to characterize selfhood as existing in multiplicity: Rather than one self there are "multiple selves" (Mitchell, 1993; à la Bromberg, 1998). But how is that possible? To envision multiple "selves" is philosophically problematic on ontological grounds, introduces a plurality of contradictory essences, obfuscates the nature of agency, and undermines the notion of freedom. Here, we have the exact opposite position of indistinguishability: Multiple selves are posited to exist as separate, distinct entities that presumably have the capacity to interact and communicate with one another and the analyst. But committing to a self-multiplicity thesis rather than a psychic monism that allows for differentiated and modified self-states introduces the enigma of how competing existent entities would be able to interact given that they would have distinct essences, which would prevent them from being able to intermingle to begin with.

Universality, essentialism, and the assault on truth

Postmodern doctrines have been selectively embraced by many identified minorities or those who belong to culturally, politically, and racially disenfranchised groups, including women, people of color, ethnic, religious, and nationalist supporters, socialists, GLBTQ (or gay-lesbian-bisexual-transgendered-queer) advocates, and those who simply defy mainstream society or live alternative lifestyles. These groups personify difference, and it is no wonder why they vilify the status quo. Perhaps one of the most avid opponents of postmodernism are feminists of various kinds, from the more virulent radicals to those who simply oppose the androcentric mindset that has dominated ancient thought since the pre-Socratics and Asiatics, which have, in part, historically informed the subjugation and political oppression of women. A similar sentiment may be found among other disenfranchised groups as well—such as the racially or ethnically encumbered—thereby informing disparate subcultures based on a philosophy of antiestablishment.

We want to be sensitive to the emotionality that often accompanies such reactionary motives to forsake antiquated philosophies, especially if they have contributed to personal, collective, or political prejudices that have directly or indirectly harmed an identified group; but we must be mindful that such positions are often based on subjective reactions to negative feelings that eclipse a more critical or logical examination of a given theoretical model. In fact, when pomocentrics profess to question the establishment by attacking, let's say, absolute truth claims, they themselves make absolute pronouncements that reinforce absolutism rather than refute it, thus devolving into a philosophy of contradiction. As I have previously argued, we may see this time and again by many identified postmoderns who wish to replace traditional paradigms for their own theoretical framework, which by definition should not carry any more weight than the viewpoints of those they criticize due to their implicit relativist interpretations of nature and culture.

In their enthusiasm to jettison foundationalist and objectivist principles inherent to essentialism, pomocentrics fail to properly understand that essentialism does not necessarily annul uniqueness or difference, but instead accounts for it within the larger parameters that define human experience. Here we may observe a confusion between phenomenology and ontology, the former being privileged and emphasized, while the latter being displaced. But how can Being be displaced? Do we not exist? Or are we merely a figment of our imaginations—like the postmodern ego—a fiction, illusion, or social construction? While we may surely not agree about the nature of our existence and essential characteristics, it nevertheless becomes palpably absurd to imply, let alone deny, that we exist—that we share a common ontic ground and existential structure. No sane person truly believes this, so the implications of such arguments must be motivated by ignorance or other psychological factors, such as political identifications governed by a discourse of emotion and ideology.

Is there a shared common essence that motivates all human beings? If the answer to this question is no, then there can be no universals. I take for granted that different experiences shape our individual epistemologies that in turn inform our personal identities and collective identifications; and just as we are impacted by our families and society differently, we have different defenses and desires; therefore, we have different psychologies. But this does not negate the notion of universals. Despite the fact that particular aspects of intrapsychic life may not be duplicated or identical to others' subjective experience, or that certain groups who share a certain commonality based on thrownness, sex, gender, ethnicity, race, religion, economics, political identification, or embodiment cannot be adequately compared to others, we are more fundamentally conjoined in essence than in phenomenology. This is one reason why we as clinicians fundamentally observe universal patterns emanating from within each individual psyche regardless of historicity, gender, culture, or race. For example, what we commonly call "defense mechanisms" occur in all minds and have so since the beginning of human life. Although the content may vary from person to person, from time to time, geographic location, and from skin color to skin color, the form or pattern is universal. Denial is denial no matter what is being denied. This transcends particularization. In fact, defenses are *essential* to human existence, without which we would surely all be basket cases.

The same may be said for endogenous drives or biological (evolutionary) urges (*Triebe*), as well as the phenomena of transference and repetition. Although what is being transferred, reactivated, or dislocated from psychic territory originating in the patient's personal past onto the contingencies of the immediate analytic encounter will vary from person to person in particular content, thematic structure, and form, we would be hard pressed to find an analyst willing to deny these universal occurrences present in all patients. The same is true for countertransference enactments. Repetition is the desire, motive, or compulsion to re-experience an earlier event within the present, albeit under different contingencies and expressed valences. Just as the organic impetus informing the need to satiate hunger and thirst is a universal process unique to living species, defense, transference, and repetition are predicated on unconscious organizations that are purported to exist within us all.

Here, I have attempted to introduce in a variety of ways the incoherency of many postmodern claims while acknowledging the virtue of the postmodern message: namely, respect and value for difference. But with the overzealous commitment to celebrating difference and plurality comes an underappreciation for universal aspects of meaning and existence that conjoin us all. Here, contemporary psychoanalysis could profit from revisiting modernism characterized by the inherent holism that allows for the unification of difference within universality, a philosophical position that accounts for particularization within its broad metaphysical inquiry.

We cannot legitimately pass the false generalization that particularization cancels universality. Instead, particularization may be understood within the context of *subjective universality*—the notion that individual difference is an objective, collective experiential activity of mind expressed idiosyncratically yet shared by all. Self and subjectivity are objectively instantiated in culture and our social institutions through intersubjective exchange. Here, the universality of subjectivity as a collection of individualized, autonomous subjects conjoined through intersubjective social engagement allows for both difference and plurality within a dynamic complex totality of universality, unification, and generality. Singularity is individuated yet belongs to the whole. Unless one is a misanthrope, disturbed, traumatized, or deranged, all people deep down want to be happy, experience peace, to flourish or prosper, to beget or create, to have a family or be a part of what a family signifies—love, acceptance, empathy, validation, recognition—the very fabric of the relational platform. And here enters the wisdom of what relationality truly has to offer.

Enjoy your *Jouissance*: Self-disclosure and countertransference revisited

Relational psychoanalysis has become a world phenomenon; and I speculate that its success is largely due to the way practitioners relate to patients. Relationality has opened up a permissible space for comparative psychoanalysis by challenging fortified traditions ossified in dogma, such as orthodox conceptions of the classical frame, neutrality, abstinence, resistance, transference, and the admonition against analyst self-disclosure. Relational perspectives have had a profound impact on the way we have come to conceptualize the therapeutic encounter, and specifically the role of the analyst in technique and practice. Relational approaches advocate for a more natural, humane, and genuine manner of how the analyst engages the patient rather than cultivating a distant intellectual attitude or clinical methodology whereby the analyst is sometimes reputed to appear as a cold, staid, antiseptic, or emotionless machine. Relational analysts are more revelatory, interactive, and inclined to disclose accounts of their own experience in professional space (e.g., in session, publications, and conference presentations); enlist and solicit perceptions from the patient about their own subjective comportment; and generally, acknowledge how a patient's responsiveness and demeanor is triggered by the purported attitudes, sensibility, and behavior of the analyst. The direct and candid reflections on countertransference reactions, therapeutic impasse, the role of affect, intimacy, and the patient's experience of the analyst are revolutionary ideas that have redirected the compass of therapeutic progress away from the uniform goals of interpretation and insight to a proper holistic focus on psychoanalysis as process.

From the standpoint of redefining therapeutic intervention, analytic posturing, and technical priority, relational analysis is a breath of fresh air. Having questioned, disassembled, and revamped the classical take on neutrality, anonymity, and abstinence, analysts now behave in ways that are more personable, authentic, humane, and reciprocal rather than reserved, clinically detached, socially artificial, and stoically withholding. While it is indeed difficult to make generalizations about all relational clinicians, which is neither desirable nor possible, one gets the impression that within the consulting room there is generally more dialogue rather than monologue, less interpretation and more active attunement to the process within the dyad, more emphasis on affective experience over conceptual insight, and more interpersonal warmth conveyed by the analyst; thus, creating a more emotionally satisfying climate for both involved. In my opinion, relational and intersubjective viewpoints have convincingly overturned the dogmatic inculcation of Americanized classical training and encourage free thinking, experimentation, novelty, spontaneity, creativity, authentic self-expression, humor, and play. And here is what I believe is the relational position's greatest contribution—the way they practice. There is malleability in the treatment frame, selectivity in interventions that are tailored to the unique needs and qualities of each patient, and a proper burial of the prototypic solemn analyst who is fundamentally removed from relating as one human being to another in the service of a withholding, frustrating, and ungratifying methodology designed to provoke transference enactments, deprivation, and unnecessary feelings of rejection, shame, guilt, and rage.

Therapeutic excess and the limits of self-disclosure

Despite these noted strengths, relational analysis has generated a great deal of controversy with regard to the question and procedural role of analyst self-disclosure. On one hand, relational approaches break down barriers of difference by emphasizing dyadic reciprocal involvement, which naturally includes the analyst having more liberty to talk about his or her own internal experiences within the session. However, the question arises: Where do we draw the line? Of course, this is a question that may only be answered from within a well-defined frame of analytic sensibility, is contextually determined, and open to clinical judgment. But this question has led many critics of the relational turn to wonder about the level of what Jay Greenberg (2001) refers to as "psychoanalytic excess," or what Freud (1912) called "therapeutic ambition." Equally, we may be legitimately concerned about the undisciplined use of self-disclosure, countertransference enactments, uninhibited risk taking, and flagrant boundary crossings that have the potential to materialize within this evolving framework of analytic practice. Although I believe that most relational analysts are sound clinicians, it is incumbent upon us to flag potentially questionable or experimental practices in order to bring them into a frank and open discussion on exactly what constitutes a legitimate execution of analytic method (if there is such a thing). Recall that the earliest relational analysts within Freud's inner circle were borne out of extreme and excessive forms of experimentation: Jung, Rank, Ferenczi, and Groddeck displayed palpable sexual transgressions under the illusion of analytic treatment, and they were also advocates of mutual analysis (Rudnytsky, 2002), which is not unlike the current trend (with qualifications) to return to an emphasis on mutuality, reciprocity, and equality.

On the one hand, relational analysts are commendably brave to report case studies where their own internal processes and intimate experiences are discussed openly in professional space, which I find of great service to the community because it breaks down oppressive taboos surrounding restrictive attitudes on analytic disclosure, self-censorship, education and training, dishonesty among colleagues, and creates a clearing for acknowledging the value of the analyst's phenomenology in analytic work. On the other hand, we are introduced to material that evokes questions of potential misuse. Is there a tendency by relationalists to enjoy their self-disclosures too much, to the degree that we enter into a realm of technical *jouissance* or therapeutic excess that does more harm than good? There is always a danger with the overexpression of personal communications, countertransference disclosures, and the insistence on providing reciprocal revelations that may reveal more about the needs of the analyst rather than the patient's. Although relational analysts operate with degrees of variance and specificity with regard to the employment of self-disclosure, this description from Lewis Aron (1999) may serve as an example:

> I encourage patients to tell me anything that they have observed and insist that there must have been some basis in my behavior for their conclusions. I often ask patients to speculate or fantasize about what is going on inside of me, and *in particular I focus on what patients have noticed about my internal conflicts*… I assume that the patient may very well have noticed my anger, jealousy, excitement, or whatever before I recognize it in myself. (pp. 252–253, emphasis added)

This statement leaves the reader wondering who is the one being analyzed, thus raising the question of whether a relational approach could subtly be in the service of the analyst's narcissism. Having said that, for anyone who knew Lew Aron, he was far from being a narcissist. In fact, he was a very warm, genuine, intelligent, and caring human being. But my point is that his words could easily be misinterpreted and taken as a permissible stance to encourage our patients to focus on us rather than on their own internal processes. I admit that self and other—inner and outer—are never cleanly separated; however, this technical recommendation places an emphasis on the assumption of mutual internal conflict and a *direct encouragement* on the part of the analyst for the patient to explore such conflict in the analyst.

Presumably, Aron (1996) is conducting his practice under the guidance of mutuality, what he specifically says is "asymmetrical," or what I prefer to call proportional. The acceptance of mutuality within relational discourse is often unquestioned due to the systemic emphasis on dyadic reciprocal relations, dialogic exchange, and the value of the analyst's presence and participation in the therapeutic process. This is given and uncontested. But we may ask: What do we mean by mutual? Is everything mutual or are there independent forces, pressures, and operations at play that are defined in opposition to difference? When relational analysts employ the notion of mutuality, do they really mean equality, such as having the same relationship, or are they merely inferring that something is shared between them?

Equality implies that there is no difference between each subject in the dyad, that they are identical, and that they have the same value. This position seems to ignore the substantial individual differences that exist between the analyst and the analysand, not to mention the power differentials, role asymmetry, and purported purpose of forming a working relationship to begin with. Here mutuality merely means existing in relation to another subject who, despite harboring individual differences, still shares collective values and qualities that define us all as human beings, but they are far from being equal (*aequalis*). Individualities exist while concurrently participating in a collective shared universal. We all have competing needs, agendas, defenses, caprices, ideals, and wishes, and these clash with others. So, mutuality is merely a formal category of co-existence, not the qualitative implications it signifies. This is why I prefer to refer to analytic mutuality as defined through proportional exchange, whereby a patient, namely, one who suffers (*patiens*), seeks out my professional assistance as an identified authority and pays me a large fee to help. There is nothing equal about it: I'm not the one being analyzed nor paying for treatment.

In another work, Aron (2006) continues to encourage analysts to speak openly about their own inner conflicts or "double mindedness" (p. 358) to their patients, however, the context is entirely different. In the examples he gives, such as revealing some aspect of one's inner oppositions to a patient, allowing the patient to witness polarities at work in the analyst's mind, disclosing uncertainty, and spelling out differences that divide the analyst's thoughts, Aron is specifically directing the purpose of disclosure toward the patient within the therapeutic moment, and not merely revealing a private conflict about oneself. Here the focus is on the patient; hence, we may appreciate the spirit of what he means: self-disclosure in the context of the patient's self-experience is not the same as self-disclosure about a certain psychic artifact or personal experience the analyst feels compelled to confess in the session. Unlike Davies and Benjamin who often condone a "mode of feeling free to tell it like it is, to own up to feelings" to the patient (Benjamin, 2004, p. 744), here Aron is encouraging a proportional approach to self-disclosure focused on the question of optimal therapeutic efficacy. Although this may beg the question of therapeutic action, his point is that such self-disclosures by the analyst may free the dyad from impasses that threaten to keep the analysis mired in polarity, splitting, stasis, and fortified oppositions.

Intersubjectivity, dialectics, and the reification of the analytic "third"

Following the work of Benjamin, Ogden, Green, and others, Aron (2006) evokes the metaphor of the "Third." He likes this notion for its clinical utility. But what is it? What do we mean by a third? Is it merely a third perspective that is introduced in the analytic dyad, an observing ego so to speak introduced by the analyst as a reflective function? Or does it entail another mediating force or presence? Because the whole notion of intersubjectivity within relational psychoanalysis rests on the problematic of reifying the dyadic system to that of an extant independent phenomenon, we must be careful in the conclusions we draw. We must first acknowledge that intersubjectivity theory, as introduced by Benjamin and Stolorow independently, is nothing new. There is no novelty about it whatsoever. At the very least, this dates back to German Idealism, most notably Hegel. It involves the common observation that self and subjectivity exist in tandem with otherness, interpersonal complementarity, contrariness, difference, and division that are mutually implicative oppositions; in a word, dialectics. Benjamin (1988) annexed Hegel's treatment of intersubjectivity within the master–slave dialectic and introduced it to psychoanalytic audiences, but her account of Hegel's work is in fact very skewed and narrow in its application, for she misinterprets and misrepresents Hegel's (1807) project in the *Phenomenology of Spirit*. In particular, she overemphasizes Hegel's notion of being-for-self as a desire for omnipotence at the expense of undermining the importance of being-for-another, when both are of reciprocal importance in Hegel's notion of the coming into being of self-consciousness (Mills, 2010; also see Jurist, 2000, pp. 204–206).

What is clearly privileged in the relational platform over above the unique internal experiences and contingencies of the individual's intrapsychic configurations is the intersubjective field or dyadic system that interlocks, emerges, and becomes contextually organized as a distinct entity of its own. The primary focus here is not on the object, as in relatedness to others (object relations) or the objective (natural) world, nor on the subject, as in the individual's lived phenomenal experience; rather, the emphasis is on the system itself. The intersubjective system, field, territory, domain, realm, world, network, horizon, matrix—or whatever words we wish to use to characterize the indissoluble intersection and interactional enactment between two or more human beings—these terms evoke a spatial metaphor, hence they imply presence or being, the traditional subject matter of metaphysical inquiry. Following key propositions from the relational literature, the intersubjective system must exist for it is predicated on being, hence on actuality; therefore, we may assume it encompasses its own attributes, properties, and spatiotemporal dialectical processes. This can certainly be inferred from the way in which relational analysts use these terms even if they don't intend to imply this as such, thus making the system into an actively organized (not static or fixed) entity of its own. Ogden (1994) makes this point most explicitly: "The analytic process reflects the interplay of three subjectivities: that of the analyst, of the analysand, and of the analytic third" (p. 483). In fact, the intersubjective system is a process-oriented entity that derives from the interactional union of two concretely existing subjective entities, thus making it an emergent property of the multiple (often bidirectional) interactions that form the intersubjective field. This ontological commitment immediately introduces the problem of agency.

The problem of agency

How can a system acquire an agency of its own? How can the interpersonal field (i.e., the analytic third) become its own autonomous agent—a subject, no less? What happens to the agency of the individual subjects that constitute the system? How can a "third" agency materialize and have determinate choice and action over the separately existing human beings that constitute the field to begin with? It can't; so, we must return to Aron's (2006) suggestion that the "third" should be viewed as an intervening perspective introduced within the analytic dyad.

While he clearly offers disclaimers as to its conceptual simplicity in guiding therapeutic technique, we may ask: What does it accomplish? By telling patients about your inner conflicts about them and the treatment, Aron thinks this will break the impasse or the dialectical fixation that anchors each participant of the system in firm opposition. Maybe this is the case, or maybe it is merely an attempt to break up the stalemate and rigid bifurcation. While I am sympathetic to his case, I can't help but wonder: Where's the Hegelian *Aufhebung*? Where's the transcendent function? What gets the analysis to a higher stage of sublation and synthetic understanding? In actuality, there are two dialectics that are operative in the analytic dyad that stand in a double relation to each other, and this fundamental otherness functions in relation to its sublated Other. Here the Third becomes the sublation (the new moment) of this earlier doubling function. But unlike Aron (2006), I would never say "the third refers to something beyond the dyad" (p. 356), for it is always present and immanent within the dyad. I prefer to call it a new *spacing* within the treatment frame.

Spacings manifest through different contents, forms, and patterns, fall on a continuum of positive and negative valences with various qualitative intensities (Mills, 2010), and on an axis of progression, refinement, and elevation, or conversely, on a retrograde plane of negation, inversion, withdrawal, or declension. Yet, this change in the intersubjective system is facilitated by a mediation from one and/or both of the agents in the dyad, not a third entity, but rather a movement via the introduction of a new psychic function germane to the relationship that leads to higher integration, meaning, and mutual growth, or at least, that is what we hope. But we have no real way of knowing the direction this will take, the vistas that will emerge from analysts' confessions, or the emotional mine fields that may explode intrapsychically and interpersonally. So, therapist self-disclosure in the moment is really an experiment as to see where it leads the treatment dynamic. It is only by looking back at the developmental process can we come to judge whether self-disclosure introduces therapeutic currency.

When self-disclosure goes too far

One cannot help but wonder how the overtly self-disclosing analyst reconciles the tensions that inevitably occur when the patient's personality via the therapeutic process radically resists wanting to know anything personal about the analyst at all, let alone the analyst's "internal conflicts." Here, I have in mind patients with histories of developmental trauma, attachment disruptions, abuse, and/or personality disorders who are generally mistrustful of any kind of relationship. And narcissistic analysands will be the first to let you know that they are not paying you to talk about yourself, let alone demand mutual recognition. Of course, we as analysts want to be recognized and appreciated by our patients, not only because the desire for recognition is a basic human need, but because our work is laborious and we wish some gratitude. Despite how intrinsically rewarding our work can be, we often serve as a filter and container for a plethora of pain, hate, and rage with some emotional cost to ourselves; therefore, external validation is affirmative and rewarding. But we must be mindful that we need to be sensitive to the patient's unique needs and not foist or superimpose our own for the sake of our desires for gratification despite identifying with a certain therapeutic ideal. In saying this, I realize that our ideals sometimes tend to betray the reality or pragmatics of how we conduct ourselves in the consulting room, because we are human and every intervention is governed by contextual dynamics. Of course we want to be recognized by our patients, as we strive to recognize and validate them. When this happens naturally and unfolds organically from within the intimate parameters of the treatment process, it becomes an aesthetic supplement to our work, and moreover, to our way of being, which speaks of the depth of attachment therapeutic relatedness affords.

Some relationalists have forayed into what certainly looks like excess, at least out of context, including the disclosure of erotic feelings (Davies, 1994), lying to patients (Gerson, 1996), and even screaming while invading personal body space (Frederickson, 1990). Wilber (2003) confessed to a patient that he had had a sexual dream about her, and she reportedly became furious. In a highly controversial paper, Jody Messler Davies (1994) confessed her own sexual longing for a 27-year-old male graduate student, which in her words was "pushed along by this young man's adamant need to deny the reality that he could be the object of a woman's sexual desire" (p. 166). Torn between her own countertransference reactions and the need to be "honest," Davies tells us:

> I said to the patient one day, "But you know I have had sexual fantasies about you many times, sometimes when we're together and sometimes when I'm alone." The patient began to look anxious and physically agitated. I added,

> "We certainly will not act on those feelings, but you seem so intent on denying that a woman could feel that way, that your own mother might have felt that way, I couldn't think of a more direct way of letting you know that this simply isn't true." The patient became enraged beyond a point that I had ever seen him. I was perverse, not only an unethical therapist, but probably a sick and perverted mother as well. He thought he needed to press charges, professional charges, maybe even child abuse charges; how could I help him when my own sexuality was so entirely out of control. He was literally beside himself. Unaware of what he was saying, he could only mutter, "You make me sick, I'm going to be sick. God, I'm going to throw up." (p. 166)

Despite appearing incredibly exhibitionistic, to her credit, I admire her grit and honest revelation in reporting this vignette. If we cannot have honest disclosures in psychoanalytic writings and professional communications about what we actually say in sessions to our patients, then we cannot have honest professional discourse either.

But what happened to the patient? The patient ends up weeping while punching "his fist into his palm repeatedly." Davies' subsequent commentary on her intervention minimizes any "serious unresolved countertransference pressures" and instead argues that her intervention "represented one of the most therapeutic alternatives" (p. 167). Her argument is that therapy is a real relationship between two people and not merely some one-way internal relation that belongs solely to the intrapsychic life of the patient's mind, but rather is a "mutually constructed, intersubjective playground… and perpetual interaction between two actively engaged participants" (p. 168). While this is arguably the case, does it necessarily follow that her intervention was "one of the most therapeutic alternatives?" From her description of how the patient acted following her self-disclosure, it can be argued that it represented one of the least effective things to say. Davies continues to defend her position under the rubric of honesty. She concludes: "Within such a scenario, the analyst oftentimes *must* speak the dangerously charged words for the first time" (p. 168, emphasis added).

Must we? In the province where I live and work, if I, as a male therapist, disclosed that I have "sexual fantasies" for my female patient, not only could this be construed as sexual abuse, I could potentially be arrested.[6] With regards to the consequences of Davies' intervention, I am once again left wondering: Whatever happened to the patient? She does not tell us whether he stayed or eventually bolted from treatment (which is what I would predict). Could you possibly repair such a rupture after telling a patient about your lust? Is honesty for the sake of honesty a sufficient justification supporting this type of intervention? Furthermore, is it always necessary to be honest when making self-disclosures? In other words, do we want to be this truthful? And if so, what therapeutic benefit would this have?

Apparently, Davies has a penchant for confessing erotic desires to her patients. In another article (Davies, 1998), she admits that she was flirting with her male analysand after he called her on it in session. Regardless of context, the most salient question becomes: Why is she flirting in the first place?

Suffice it to say that these are some examples of therapeutic excess that alert our attention to the possibility of attribution of error in contemporary technique. Of course, there is a theoretical distinction between truth and honesty versus our choice to verbally disclose certain internal processes to an analysand. I admit that I am rather conservative about these matters, preferring to foster a safe climate for self-reflection, emotional release, and pathological containment, whereby the patient is not burdened by my "inner conflicts." But this does not mean that risqué or "dangerously charged words" ipso facto are not legitimate to say in certain circumstances. They may very well be—and necessarily so. The problem becomes defining a uniform or universal touchstone on which to make such choices. In fact, it is precisely the criteria of what is appropriate or inappropriate to say that is lacking general consensus, which is indissolubly laced to the context that influences the appropriateness of that decision in the first place. Indeed, intervention choice is contingent on such criteria, as criteria is contingent on context. And since we lack a clear guidepost on what criteria to follow under contingent circumstances, we may be eternally begging the question if we tarry on this path much longer. Here, I think the more important issue for debate becomes, not the particular verbalizations of what therapists say in session, but rather the question of permissibility itself.

Admittedly, I have been using Davies (as well as other relational authors) here in a self-serving fashion as examples to accentuate my concerns about therapeutic excess in relational discourse. If we were only to focus on the content of these aforementioned interventions without taking into account the context and the overall process of treatment, then these enactments could be deemed as unethical, if not outrageous. I myself would be guilty of this on many occasions, which many of my colleagues could claim are countertransference dramas at best. For example, I am not ashamed to admit that I had dropped my afternoon responsibilities to pick up a bipolar patient from his apartment who was suicidal, loaded up his dogs in my minivan, and drove him to the hospital after taking his dogs to a kennel and helping him shop for personal toiletries. Nor do I think it was unprofessional of me to visit a patient late in the evening in the ER after he attempted suicide, and then visited his wife and child that same night to debrief them and help contain their trauma. The patient particularly enjoyed my unannounced visit the next day when I brought him his favorite food of freshly cooked Polish kielbasa after he had been checked into the psychiatric ward. Despite my ancillary criticism of my colleagues, my main point here is to draw increasing attention to how relational analysts are bringing their own personalities into the consulting room, presumably under appropriate discretion guided by clinical intuition and experienced judgment, as well as having the courage to discuss their countertransference enactments in professional space.

It has been argued time and again that it is far too easy for someone outside the lived analytic encounter to become an armchair quarterback and call all the plays after the game. While certainly no intervention is beyond scrutiny or reproach, what strikes me about some of these therapeutic transactions is their humanness and authentic spontaneity despite seeming excessive. The hallmark of a relational approach to treatment is that it approximates the way real relationships are naturally formed in patients' external lives, including the rawness, tension, and negotiability of the lived encounter, with the exception that the process falls under analytic sensibility. This is why the relationalists demand malleability in the treatment frame rather than applying a rigid, orthodox, or authoritarian procedure because malleability is necessary in order to cater to the unique contingencies of each dyad; and this necessitates abolishing any illusory fixed notions of practice that can be formulaically applied to all situations.

I believe most analysts can buy into this premise, but regardless of its pragmatic value, it still begs the question of method. If every intervention is contextually based, then it is relative and subjectively determined, hence not open to universal applications. The question of uniform technique becomes an illegitimate question because context determines everything. The best we can aim for is to have an eclectic skill set (under the direction of clinical judgment, experience, self-reflectivity, and maybe even wisdom) to apply to whatever possible clinical realities we may encounter. But perhaps I am being too naive or idealistic in assuming that every analyst is capable of achieving this level of professional comportment. Here I am wondering how this revisionist relational methodology affects training, supervision, pedagogy, and practice. Hoffman (1994) tells us to "throw away the book," presumably once we have mastered it. Fair enough. But what if a neophyte were reading the relational literature and took such statement literally? What about reliability and treatment efficacy if there is no proper method to which we can claim allegiance? Could this not lead to an "anything goes" approach conducted by a bunch of loose cannons justifying interventions under the edict of relationality—a modern day "wild analysis"? Yet the same potential for abuse exists when applying any approach rigidly, whether it is a formal procedure, orienting principle, or general technical considerations; thus, the question of method will always remain an indeterminate question with some approaches being more justifiable than others.

Concluding remarks

I have been criticized by several relational analysts (Jacobs, 2006; Pizer, 2006; Stolorow, Atwood, & Orange, 2006; Altman, 2007; Davies, 2007; Hoffman, 2007) for reporting clinical events out of context. For the record, I am not making any ethical charge nor am I showing any malice or ill-will toward anyone in the relational field for simply taking their words seriously. I have critiqued people whom I find have something of value to say, even if my disagreements have generated bad feelings. My intent is to stimulate noteworthy attention and serious debate about these ideas and practices so our profession can continue to prosper and advance.

One point I want to convey in my adumbrated and excerpted examples of "excess" is the overdetermined motivations and multiple implications embedded within an intervention. Here, the audience will observe the dialectical tension between my praise for the technical liberation the relational tradition has introduced as well as the potential for ethical concern and admonishment. The main issue here becomes a serious inquiry into the ground, breadth, and impediments to psychoanalytic method. This is an important area in the relational field that needs continued discussion and debate. Here, the fate of advancing psychoanalysis rests on our ability to embrace critique rather than repudiate it.

Endnotes

1. For example, see Hartman's (2005) inaccurate assessment of the role and meaning of postmodernism in contemporary psychoanalysis.
2. These propositions problematize the whole contemporary psychoanalytic edifice. If nothing exists independent of language and the social matrix that sustains it (in essence, the relational platform), then not only is subjectivity causally determined by culture, subjectivity is dismantled altogether. When analysts use terms such as construction, hence invoking Foucault—whose entire philosophical project was to get rid of the subject and subjectivity—or even worse, deconstruction, thus exalting Derrida—the king of postmodernism, whose entire corpus is devoted to annihilating any metaphysical claims whatsoever, thus collapsing everything into undecidability, ambiguity, chaos, and chance—analysts open themselves up to misunderstanding and controversy, subsequently inviting criticism.
3. Mitchell's epistemological critique of metaphysical realism—that is, on the knowability of the object world—in favor of linguistic interpretive construction may very well be the hallmark of relational pomocentrism. Based upon his antiobjectivist dismissal of scientific observation and analytic neutrality, from this standpoint there is no such thing as a fact. Instead, all human experience is predicated on language and interpretation, and this specifically means conscious conceptual thought. Not only does this privilege consciousness over unconsciousness, it logically displaces the presumption that unconscious mentation precedes conscious thought, for language is a socially constructed enterprise. I have grave concerns with this conceptual move in contemporary circles because psychoanalysis loses its contribution to the human sciences, which places unconscious processes at the pinnacle of mental operations.
4. Schelling's (1800) *System of Transcendental Idealism* may be said to be the first systematic philosophy that dissolved the subject–object dichotomy by making pure subjectivity and absolute objectivity identical: mind and nature are one. It can be argued, however, that it was Hegel (1807, 1817) who was the first to succeed in unifying the dualism inherent in Kant's distinction between phenomenal experience and the noumenal realm of the natural world through a more rigorous form of systematic logic that meticulously shows how subjectivity and objectivity are dialectically related and mutually implicative. Relational psychoanalysis has left out one side of the equation, or at least has not adequately accounted for it. When relational analysts return to the emphasis on subjectivity by negating the objective, they foreclose the dialectical positionality that is inherently juxtaposed and reciprocally intertwined in experience (see Mills, 2002, for a review).
5. One persistent criticism of relational theorizing is that it does not do justice to the notion of personal agency and the separateness of the self (Frie, 2003). It may be argued that relational thinking dissolves the centrality of the self, extracts and dislocates the subject from subjectivity, decomposes personal identity, and ignores the unique

phenomenology and epistemological process of lived experience by collapsing every psychic event into a relational ontology, thus usurping the concretely existing human being while devolving the notion of contextualism into the abyss of abstraction.

6. In Section 4 of the *Regulated Health Professions Act*, 1991, under subsection 3, "Sexual abuse of a patient," it states: "In this Code, 'sexual abuse' of a patient by a member means, (a) sexual intercourse or other forms of physical sexual relations between the member and the patient, (b) touching, of a sexual nature, of the patient by the member, or (c) behaviour or remarks of a sexual nature by the member towards the patient. 1993, c. 37, s. 4." Last amendment: 2009. Notice that Davies' remarks would clearly fall under paragraph (c) of this clause under Ontario legislation.

References

Altman, N. (2007). A lapse in constructive dialogue: The journal's responsibility. *Psychoanalytic Psychology*, 24(2), 395–396.

Aron, L. (1996). *A Meeting of Minds.* Hillsdale, NJ: The Analytic Press.

Aron, L. (1999). The patient's experience of the analyst's subjectivity. In S. Mitchell, & L. Aron (Eds.), *Relational Psychoanalysis: The Emergence of a Tradition.* Hillsdale, NJ: Analytic Press, 1999, pp. 243–268.

Aron, L. (2006). Analytic Impasse and the Third: Clinical implications of intersubjectivity theory. *International Journal of Psycho-Analysis*, 87: 349–368.

Benjamin, J. (1988). *The Bonds of Love.* New York: Pantheon Books.

Benjamin, J. (2004). Escape from the Hall of Mirrors: Commentary on Paper by Jody Messler Davies. *Psychoanalytic Dialogues*, 14: 743–753.

Bromberg, P. (1998). *Standing in the Spaces: Essays on Clinical Process, Trauma, and Dissociation.* Hillsdale, NY: The Analytic Press.

Davies, J.M. (1994). Love in the afternoon: A relational reconsideration of desire and dread. *Psychoanalytic Dialogues*, 4, 153–170.

Davies, J.M. (1998). Between the disclosure and foreclosure of erotic transference-countertransference: Can psychoanalysis find a place for adult sexuality? *Psychoanalytic Dialogues*, 8: 747–766.

Davies, J.M. (2007). Response to Jon Mills: An open letter to the members of Division 39. *Psychoanalytic Psychology*, 24(2): 397–400.

Frederickson, J. (1990). Hate in the countertransference as an empathic position. *Contemporary Psychoanalysis*, 26, 479–495.

Fosshage, J.L. (2003). Contextualizing self psychology and relational psychoanalysis: Bi-directional influence and proposed syntheses. *Contemporary Psychoanalysis*, 39(3), 411–448.

Freud, S. (1912). Recommendations to physicians practicing psycho-analysis. In: *The Standard Edition*, Vol. XII. London: Hogarth Press, pp. 109–120.

Frie, R. (Ed.) (2003). *Understanding Experience: Psychotherapy and Postmodernism.* London: Brunner-Routledge.

Gerson, S. (1996). Neutrality, resistance, and self-disclosure in an intersubjective psychoanalysis. *Psychoanalytic Dialogues*, 6, 623–645.

Govrin, A. (2006). The dilemma of contemporary psychoanalysis: Toward a "Knowing" post-postmodernism. *Journal of the American Psychoanalytic Association*, 54: 507–535.

Greenberg, J. (1991). *Oedipus and Beyond: A Clinical Theory*. Cambridge: Harvard University Press.

Greenberg, J. (2001). The analyst's participation: A new look. *Journal of the American Psychoanalytic Association*, 49(2), 359–381.

Greenberg, J. & Mitchell, S. (1983). *Object Relations in Psychoanalytic Theory*. Cambridge, MA: Harvard University Press.

Hartman, S. (2005). Book Review of Roger Frie's, *Understanding Experience: Psychotherapy and Postmodernism. Contemporary Psychoanalysis*, 41(3): 535–544.

Hegel, G.F.W. (1807). *Phenomenology of Spirit*, trans. A.V. Miller. Oxford: Oxford University Press, 1977.

Hegel, G.F.W. (1817). *The Encyclopaedia Logic*, tr. T.F. Geraets, W.A. Suchting, & H.S. Harris, Indianapolis: Hackett Publishing Co, 1991.

Hoffman, I.Z. (1994). Dialectical thinking and therapeutic action in the psychoanalytic process. *Psychoanalytic Quarterly*, 63, 187–218.

Hoffman, I.Z. (1998). *Ritual and Sponteneity in the Psychoanalytic Process: A Dialectical-Constructivist View*. Hillsdale, NJ: Analytic Press.

Hoffman, I.Z. (2007). Reply to Jon Mills (2006): An open letter to the members of division 39. *Psychoanalytic Psychology*, 24(2), 401–405.

Jacobs, M.S. (2006). Assertions of therapeutic excess: A reply to Mills (2005). *Psychoanalytic Psychology*, 23(1), 189–192.

Jurist, E. (2000). *Beyond Hegel and Nietzsche: Philosophy, Culture, and Agency*. Cambridge, MA: MIT Press.

Lichtenberg, J.D., Lachmann, F.M., & Fosshage, J. (2002). *A Spirit of Inquiry: Communication in Psychoanalysis*. Hillsdale, NJ: The Analytic Press.

Mills, J. (2002). *The Unconscious Abyss: Hegel's Anticipation of Psychoanalysis*. Albany: SUNY Press.

Mills, J. (2010). *Origins: On the Genesis of Psychic Reality*. Montreal: McGill-Queens University Press.

Mills, J. (2012). *Conundrums: A Critique of Contemporary Psychoanalysis*. New York: Routledge.

Mitchell, S.A. (1988). *Relational Concepts in Psychoanalysis: An Integration*. Cambridge, MA: Harvard University Press.

Mitchell, S.A. (1992). True selves, false serves, and the ambiguity of authenticity. In N.J. Skolnick, & S.C. Warshaw (Eds.), *Relational Perspectives in Psychoanalysis*. Hillsdale, NJ: Analytic Press, pp. 1–20.

Mitchell, S.A. (1993). *Hope and Dread in Psychoanalysis*. New York: Basic Books.

Ogden, T.H. (1994). The analytic third: Working with intersubjective clinical facts. *International Journal of Psycho-Analysis*, 75, 3–19.

Pizer, S. (2006). "Neither Fish nor Flesh": Commentary on Jon Mills (2005). *Psychoanalytic Psychology*, 23(1), 193–196.

Regulated Health Professions Act (1991), Ministry of Ontario; Section 4 (Subsection 3), Sexual Abuse of a Patient. Last Amended, 2009.

Rudnytsky, P.L. (2002). *Reading Psychoanalysis*. Ithaca, NY: Cornell University Press.

Schelling, F.W.J. (1800). System des transzendentalen Idealismus. Peter Heath (Trans). In *System of Transcendental Idealism*. Charlottesville: University Press of Virginia, 1978.

Seligman, S. (2003). The developmental perspective in relational psychoanalysis. *Contemporary Psychoanalysis*, 39(3), 477–508.

Stern, D.B. (1997). *Unformulated experience: From dissociation to imagination in psychoanalysis*. Hillsdale, NJ: Analytic Press.

Stolorow, R.D. (1998). Clarifying the intersubjective perspective: A Reply to George Frank. *Psychoanalytic Psychology*, 15(3), 424–427.

Stolorow, R.D., & Atwood, G., & Orange, D.M. (2006). Contextualizing is not nullifying: Reply to Mills (2005). *Psychoanalytic Psychology*, 23(1), 184–188.

Wilber, W. (2003). Hope, Play and Emergent Unconscious experience. *Paper presentation at 23rd Annual Spring Meeting of Division of Psychoanalysis (39)*, American Psychological Association, April, Minneapolis, MN.

10 Straw men, stereotypes and constructive dialogue

A response to Mills' criticism of the relational approach

Chana Ullman

Abstract: This discussion of Mills' presentation first takes issue with his divisive discourse which pushes differences to the extreme and erects straw men in order to vehemently attack them. I then present an alternate view of postmodern influences on relational psychoanalysis and respond to Mills' criticism of self-disclosure, specifically as related to the work of Jody Davies.

It is not without hesitation that I accepted the invitation to participate in this panel. The title of this conference itself, "The Relational Approach Responds to its Critics" is problematic from the start. It places the relational approach in the role of the defendant, challenging us to justify our position, as if arguing our case with a plea—"not guilty." I asked myself how it is that (to the best of my knowledge) we have never had a conference entitled "The Kleinian, or Freudian Approach Responds to its Critics," as we have today with respect to the relational approach.

I believe (part of) the answer is obvious—It is an important assumption of the relational approach that questions, constant reflection, and comparative dialogue are essential for the advancement of theory and practice of psychoanalysis. For example, *Psychoanalytic Dialogues*, the first relational journal, which became the most widely read and cited journal in psychoanalysis this year, was founded on the principles of critical dialogue, with each paper published accompanied by evaluative discussions of its main ideas. Similarly, from a relational perspective, the psychoanalytic process itself hinges on the capacity of the analyst not only to point out to patients their defensive manoeuvers, self-destructiveness, and strengths, but also on our willingness as analysts to examine our own participation and contributions to failures, stalemates, or even harm. Reexamining our theoretical claims, staying in the "depressive position" vis a vis our own convictions, and being open to alternative formulations is where the relational approach started, and I believe it is this openness which accounts for its growth. As such, the relational approach invites critical dialogue as a part of a continual creative and innovative process.

However, in reading Mills' works critiquing the relational approach, I found myself thinking about the fine line between constructive intellectual exchange and assigning blame through the exploitation of the other's perceived faults.

Despite points of agreement with Mills, I found myself objecting to the method of discourse itself, wishing for a rendering of ideas that does not rely on presenting colleagues in the worst possible light, on divisive rhetoric pushing differences to their extreme, and on creating straw men that are then vehemently destroyed. This is the kind of debate that can easily deteriorate into destructive finger-pointing, and that we do not need this in our professional life. In a paper entitled "A Plea for Constructive Dialogue" (2003). Altman and Davies suggest that productive and worthwhile dialogue must involve presenting the others' point of view in the best possible light. They ask: "Why is it that our theoretical exchanges are as colorful and as interesting as overboiled vegetables?" (p. 147).

Relational analysts find ourselves responding to the same tired stereotypes: portrayed as narcissistic, impulsive, more interested in our own subjectivity than the patients' world and needs, and as radical relativists guided by postmodern ideology rather than professional knowledge and ethics. The caricatures are familiar to all of us. This is about as truthful as the stereotype of the Freudian analyst as an unresponsive, cold and rigid, superior authoritarian. Perpetuating the same tired stereotypes, we never engage in the really interesting questions. Having said that, and in the little space allotted to this dialogue and discussion—I wish to focus on two points that emanate from Mills' criticism and try to reformulate them into the more important questions I believe we need to ask in contemporary psychoanalysis, relational or not.

My first point concerns the equation, explicit and implicit, of relational theory with radical postmodernism. There is much that I agree with in Mills' criticism of postmodernism; indeed, some relational writings have swung too far in that direction. The relational perspective is influenced by postmodernism, and in that respect it is similar to most contemporary disciplines in the social and liberal arts. Psychoanalysis becomes frozen, isolated, dead if we do not let our culture and zeitgeist infuse our concepts and our practice. In this same way Freud was influenced deeply by the science and culture of his time. Postmodernism's contribution is invaluable in shaking the monolithic hegemony of one dominant voice in culture and in psychoanalysis. Hegemony breeds stagnation; postmodernism is indispensable in freeing us from the simplistic assumption that there is only one person in our office who can see reality in an objective, rational way and that there is one truth waiting to be revealed, uncovered by the analyst's knowledge.

This liberating influence that is at the foundations of the relational approach, is, however, a far cry from the claims that equate relational theory with radical postmodernism. The influence of postmodernism does not automatically imply an extreme extension into relativism nor does it mean that there is no reality or "natural" constraint. Attributing this drastic view to the relational approach is a straw man argument. There is a reality outside of our constructions; but social reality and the reality inside the treatment room is always ambiguous, subject to a myriad although not unlimited number of interpretations. The fact that contemporary psychoanalysis is not "one" but many (that psychoanalysts can be Freudian, Klienian, Kohutian, Winnicottian, Lacanian, etc.) already means that alternative constructions of the mind are possible and that the intrapsychic is not readily discernible except via the theoretical constructions and the intersubjective mutual exchange between patient and analyst. Mutuality does not mean equality (this is another straw man), it means constant mutual influence, impacting both partners in dialogue with one another.

I see the relational approach as one that proposes universals with which one can agree or disagree, but certainly not one that advocates relativism. The relational approach is founded on several "naturals" or universals. Let me focus on one: that the drives are subsumed by the primacy of relationships. A fundamental claim of relational psychoanalysis is that psychic change rests in the encounter of two minds; an encounter in which we try to hold and understand not only the intrapsychic, but the inextricably linked choreography of two sets of unconscious experiences. This is very much in keeping with what we have come to understand from the most contemporary research on early parent/child interaction and the centrality of dyadic experience to the neurobiological developments essential to psychic functioning. In this respect, relational theory is in fact more closely linked to positivistic claims emanating from research on attachment, trauma, developmental psychopathology, etc. than any other psychoanalytic approach. So, here is a question that we should all consider—how do we reconcile the scientific knowledge that comes from empirical research and other sources (medical, cultural); and how do we use it in this most intimate subjective encounter in which we are flawed observers as well as participants? How do we combine or allow the movement between what we understand as universals and what is specific and unique to the intersubjective meeting of minds?

My second point has to do with the issue of self-disclosure. Specifically, with respect to Davies' famous papers, (e.g., 1994) so often used as the red flag raised to discredit relational psychoanalysis again and again, as if the disclosure of erotic countertransference is the hallmark of the relational approach.

Picking out these charged examples of heightened moments in extraordinary circumstances obfuscates the day-to-day work of relational psychoanalysis. Relational analysts do a lot between these colorful moments of enactment and self-disclosure. Framing the question as a matter of technique, as whether to disclose or not to disclose, obscures the more fundamental issues raised in Davies' by now classical papers (Davies, 1994, 1998, 2015). Davies challenges us to examine the inevitably seductive nature of the psychoanalytic encounter. Her writings (as well as others—e.g., Benjamin 1991, 1995) theoretically challenge the oedipal complex, reformulating it as an oedipal complexity, enriching our understanding of the developmental vicissitudes and implications of love, desire and hate between child and parent. She (as well as others) draws our attention to the distinction between specific intentional analytic interventions and the kind of unconscious analytic participation that goes on continuously and exists as an ongoing leitmotif harmonious or discordant with our more thoughtful and rational choices. To boil this down to the topic of self-disclosure is a grave oversimplification and does great disservice to the complexity of thought and ground-breaking nature of these ideas.

At the end of Freud's (1915) "Transference Love," Freud writes about the general reaction to his paper and the common perception of the "dangers of the psychoanalytic method." Psychoanalysts, like chemists, work with explosives, he says, but it would never occur to us to forbid chemists their work because of the risks involved. We cannot give up a psychoanalysis which dares to explore the most explosive human emotions, and Davies invites us to do just that—explore the erotic in the psychoanalytic relationship including the countertransference, as the proverbial elephant in the analytic room. She dares us to own, it seems to me, the meanings of Adam Philips' (2008) provocative statement: "Psychoanalysis is what two people can talk about when they agree not to have sex" (p. 6). She breaks new ground, and is attacked by the analytic community for all the new problems that emerge in the treatment room and beyond (Hoffman, 1998); but the problems are there for all of us to struggle with. The more interesting question I wish to ask is this: Is there a space that is neither one of exploitation nor one of denial of what is clearly going on in the relationship? This question addresses how to recognize that we are creating the experience even as we are studying it.

Relational theory grew out of the criticism of existing psychoanalytic models and offered new ways of looking at and approaching these issues. There are never new solutions that do not also create new problems (Hoffman, 1998), but it is the readiness to question, the readiness to live with the inherently enigmatic and with diverse answers, that ensures the viability of psychoanalysis now and for future generations.

References

Altman, N., Davies, J.M. (2003). A Plea for Constructive Dialogue. *Journal of the American Psychoanalytic Association*, 51S, 145–161.

Benjamin, J. (1991). Father and Daughter: Identification with Difference—A Contribution to Gender Heterodoxy. *Psychoanalytic Dialogues*, 1, 277–299.

Benjamin, J. (1995). What Angel Would Hear Me?: The Erotics of Transference. *Psychoanalytic Inquiry*, 14, 535–557.

Davies, J.M. (1994). Love in the Afternoon: A Relational Reconsideration of Desire and Dread in the Countertransference. *Psychoanalytic Dialogues*, 4, 153–170.

Davies, J.M. (1998). Between the Disclosure and Foreclosure of Erotic Transference-Countertransference: Can Psychoanalysis Find a Place for Adult Sexuality? *Psychoanalytic Dialogues*, 8, 747–766.

Davies, J.M. (2015). From Oedipus Complex to Oedipal Complexity: Reconfiguring the (pardon the expression) Negative Oedipus Complex and Disowned Erotics of Disowned Sexualities. *Psychoanalytic Dialogues*, 25(3), 265–283.

Freud, S. (1915). Observations on Transference-Love (Further Recommendations on the Technique of Psycho-Analysis III). In *The Standard Edition of the Complete Psychological Works of Sigmund Freud,* 24 vols. Trans. and gen. ed. James Strachey, in collaboration with Anna Freud, assisted by Alix Strachey and Alan Tyson. London: Hogarth Press, pp. 157–171.

Hoffman, S. (1998) Poetic Transformations of Erotic Experience: Commentary on Paper by Jody Messler Davies. *Psychoanalytic Dialogues*, 8(5), 791–804.

Philips, A., & Bersani L. (2008). *Intimacies*. Chicago: University of Chicago Press.

11 On multiple epistemologies in theory and practice

A response to Jon Mills' critique of the postmodern turn in relational psychoanalysis

Shlomit Yadlin-Gadot

Abstract: Mills' critique of relational psychoanalysis is pivotal in reintroducing issues of truth into psychoanalytic theory, but does not allow us the full benefit of the many insightful criticisms of traditional psychoanalytic claims. A way forward may be found by admitting multiple epistemologies into analytic discourse and unveiling the domains within which each epistemology may allow us to determine whether a statement or a belief is true or false.

I wish to address Jon Mills' critique of the postmodern turn in relational psychoanalysis, first by extolling its immense importance: it forces us to rethink and reformulate our ideas about relational psychoanalysis and its theory's basic tenets; it encourages us to formulate technique and methodology. I will begin by discussing issues of epistemology, objectivity and truth in psychoanalysis, and end in a related fashion by touching upon our motivations for constructing theories, and our ways of validating them.

As a brief introduction to my address, I wish to define six paradigmatic notions of truth (Yadlin-Gadot 2016). *Correspondent truth* compares a statement to perception of the external world; *coherent truth* is established by the compatibility among different statements; *subjective truth* is established in relation to experience and emotion; *intersubjective truth* equates objectivity with consensuality; *ideal truth* is established by the correspondence between abstract eternal entities and their phenomenological expressions; *pragmatic truth* refers to the compatibility between a statement and its future implications.[1]

Grappling with the difficult issues of objectivity and truth didn't begin with the relational turn, but rather with the earliest days of psychoanalytic theory. Freud strove to establish psychoanalysis on the basis of scientific truth, simultaneously anchoring its standing among the sciences and supplying a rationale for clinical technique. When he stated in 1937 that "an assured conviction of the truth of the construction… achieves the same therapeutic result as a recaptured memory," Freud acknowledged the import of two additional types of truths: coherent and pragmatic truths. The former manifests in the patient's acceptance of a narrated construction, the latter in its therapeutic effects. While remaining a staunch believer in the externally validated correspondence theory of truth, Freud acknowledged the functioning and relevance of these other truths on the level of experiencing *and* on the level of validation of theory.

Following Freud, psychoanalytic "Truth" splintered into a multiplicity of truths: subjective, ideal, intersubjective, coherent, and pragmatic truths appeared, respectively, in the work of Donald Winnicott, Heinz Kohut, Stephen Mitchell, Roy Schafer, and Donald Spence. Some saw this as a setback in psychoanalytic theory's ability to attain scientific standing. Others focused on the potency and potential of these developments in creating more diverse guidelines for the practice of psychotherapy.

These developments regarding "truth" were encountered inside the consultation room, and apprehended as relevant for understanding and processing the internal experience of our patients. This did not necessarily entail the *denial* of realistic truth. When Kohut or Winnicott championed subjective truths, they were not denying objective realities, but questioning their relevant positioning in the processes and service of therapeutic progress. Schafer (1992), advocating the potency of narratives, namely, of coherent truth, was not denying the epistemology of realism. Rather, he highlighted and emphasized the centrality of the coherence theory of truth in psychic structure and particularly in the analytic process. So, actually, long before the relational turn, psychoanalysis was developing theory and practice in the light of different perspectives on truth.

When discussing "truth" in the multiple form (i.e., truths), we shift from traditional metaphysics, from the simplicity and clarity of the true-false, subjective-objective divide. But I think that this still leaves us well within the confines of traditional epistemological discussion, albeit, in a multiple mode. The realm of multiple truths still leaves us barred from Kant's "thing-in-itself." Our consciousness remains standing between what we *know* and what truly *is—the* independent reality "out there" around us. We acknowledge its existence, but know it only in a mediated fashion. We mold and remold our realities, in light and by means of different epistemologies. In the words of philosopher and psychoanalyst Gemma Corradi Fiumara (1992):

> … speaking of reality… we are not referring to the world in itself… but rather to the sort of reality which the individual laboriously carves out… as a construct negotiated within the limits of what may be thought and done within his symbolic horizon… Before we decide to inhabit a specific epistemology… we may have gone through several epistemological migrations. (pp. 3, 8)

My basic contention is that we do not decide in which epistemology to dwell. *Rather, our basic psychological needs determine our multiple existence within several definable epistemologies.*

The truths governing our lives are realistic, corresponding to what we perceive as facts. They are also subjective, cohering with what we feel. We plan and live in accordance with intersubjective truths, be they of mythological, cultural, or parental decrees, often not even aware they are rooted in interpersonal agreements. We consider and act upon our ideal truths, as grounded in our principles and ethics. Similarly, foreseeing practical implications of our decisions, we define our pragmatic truths. All serve as mental guidelines, all are experienced as truths. All may be traced to recurring philosophical arguments.

Viewed from this perspective, the relational turn may be grasped as incorporating a particular epistemology into the sphere of psychoanalytic theoretical thinking. Its intersubjective epistemology is an essential, pivotal one in the multiple epistemologies of the mind, one through which the individual finds and forms the reality common to him and his social, human environment. As I understand it, the co-construction of reality in the treatment room as described by relational theorists, roughly repeats what we believe occurs in early developmental stages, when a child co-constructs his reality with, and guided by, his parents. This basic tenet of early development is repeated in maturity, in certain dimensions of lived experience, and negotiated consciously and unconsciously with significant others.

So, to reiterate, when accepting that psychoanalysis dwells in the realm of multiple truths, we acknowledge a few essential premises of the psychoanalytic field. First, we stand outside the strict metaphysics of "one truth." Second, we retain the *need for truths as organizing principles*, as Archimedean points for conscious constructions of reality. Third, we acknowledge the reality exterior to us, but realize that it is grasped in a mediated manner. And fourth, we presume that our construals of this reality are determined by psychological needs that lend themselves to observation and inquiry.

Accepting the fact that the human psyche dwells in parallel realities and moves among different epistemologies is not the same as saying that "everything is relative" or that "anything goes." As Mills so well described, the eagerness to escape the despotism of the metaphysical has run us into the illnesses of postmodernism. But in addressing this, we must not necessarily fall back on the simplicity of the binary of true and false. Rigorous epistemological inquiry reveals that, beyond metaphysical certainty and without falling into relativism, the human psyche constitutes several realities by means of several definable epistemological routes. Careful observation may show that it's possible to follow the needs motivating these routes, the logic of their construction and the grammar governing them.

Seen in this manner, the point would be to apprehend the rich insights of relational theorists, showing the constitution, logic and workings of an intersubjective epistemology, noting its singular characteristics—such as, heavy reliance on language and the experience of permeable personal boundaries. *This doesn't necessarily indicate the negation or denial of other crucial epistemologies and truths in the psychoanalytic field or in the consulting room.* On the contrary, taking a bird's-eye view of psychoanalytic theory and practice, we may notice that different schools create a heterogeneous arc which parallels the epistemic multiplicity of the mind.

"Truth" in the consulting room

In the vignette, Mills relates on his work with a patient who was eager for justice, he illustrates the workings of several truths. He underlines the realistic one, but in my mind, was working with several others as well—Mills approached his patient with a pragmatic truth detailing the consequences of his fantasy had he acted upon it. I believe this touched upon the patient's ideal truths as well: does he truly think of himself as a murderer? Mills highlighted these truths in contradiction to the intersubjective truth that was ruling his mind at the time, one that was comprised only of murderers and victims. I believe he could not have done this work had he not acknowledged his patient's basic subjective truth, that he had been terribly, unforgivably injured and wronged.

In the room, we walk with our patients through their different epistemologies, formulating some, and almost always also processing those that are yet unformulated. We acknowledge the simultaneity of the realities they create, respecting their derivative truths. We needn't force these truths to converge or to mesh in the dynamics of a synthetic dialectic. We could, rather, detail and depict the various truths, locating tensions between them, as well as their conscious, unconscious or dissociated positions within the psyche. This methodological approach might elaborate and refine our understanding of selfhood and agency rather than relinquishing either as construct or concept.

In this approach, epistemic analytic authority is not given up, but reconceptualized as what enables a therapist to do good epistemological work, identifying the languages of truth that govern his/her as well as his/her patients' psychic processes, and their responses to them, attempting to engage their various dialects in a dialogue that appreciates and upholds their differences and singularities. At its best, this dialogue holds the potential to unravel dynamics of dissociation, denial, and repressive authoritarianism, creating a space in which the experience of possibility and reflective deliberate choice replaces restriction and inevitability.

We construe our realities, and it stands to reason that we do this in certain universal ways, which we may be piecing together in different areas of psychoanalytic theory. I've tried to offer a way of thinking about this epistemological multiplicity. The test of this way of thinking will be, *in part,* in its correspondence to reality. But that might not suffice. If theorizing does not have the value of a pragmatic truth, or enable us to work more creatively than before; if it will not lend more coherence to its applied field; if it does not create a common intersubjective truth; and if it does not add a touch of the ideal—wholeness or beauty; well, then it might be realistic, but it might not be good enough.

Endnote

1. Each of the specified truths are embedded in certain epistemic premises. Thus, the correspondent truth reflects a realistic epistemology which allows the comparison of statements and facts. The ideal truth is embedded in an objective-idealistic epistemology that posits the existence of ideal, mind-independent forms. Alongside

these two essentialist truths, subjective idealistic epistemology is home to the subjective and intersubjective truths. Coherent truth exists in both objective and subjective idealistic epistemologies. The pragmatic truth exists within the experiential realm and the confines of perceived external reality. For a detailed discussion of these issues, see Yadlin-Gadot (2016, 2017a, b).

References

Freud, S. (1937). Constructions in analysis. *Standard Edition*, vol. 23, 255–271.

Fiumara, G.C. (1992). *The Symbolic Function*. Oxford: Blackwell.

Schafer, R. (1992). *Retelling a Life: Narration and Dialogue in Psychoanalysis*. New York: Basic Books.

Yadlin-Gadot, S. (2016). *Truth Matters: Theory and Practice in Psychoanalysis*. Leiden: Brill.

Yadlin-Gadot, S. (2017a). (Ef)facing truth: Between philosophy and psychoanalysis. *Journal of Theoretical and Philosophical Psychology*, 37(1), 1–20.

Yadlin-Gadot, S. (2017b). Truth axes and the transformation of self. *Psychoanalytic Review*, 104(2), 163–201.

12 Relational psychoanalysis and the concepts of truth and meaning

Response to Jon Mills

Boaz Shalgi

Abstract: This response looks at Professor Mills' paper through the concepts of truth and meaning. It argues that the meaning of every experience, including, of course, experience in the psychoanalytic encounter, is created, and should be looked upon, through three dimensions: objectivity, subjectivity, and intersubjectivity, with no one of them having precedence over the others. It claims that looking at the patient's and therapist's experiences through these dimensions enables us to move from observing structures to observing processes, and from relating to an eternally repeated past to relating to a co-created "present moment of the past."

Out of the many, many points in Professor Mills' illuminating papers that could be more carefully discussed, I would like to use my brief discussion to look again at what seems to me to be the foundation of all of Professor Mills' arguments, that is the concepts of truth and meaning. To be able to present my argument, I would like to suggest that any comprehensive theory regarding the nature of human existence and experience must include three dimensions: subjectivity, intersubjectivity, and objectivity (Davidson, 2001), and that every moment of our life, including, of course, every moment in the therapeutic session, can be looked upon, and consists of these three dimensions. As Professor Mills mentioned German Idealism and Phenomenology, which means, first and foremost, Hegel's phenomenological system, it seems to me important to mention that in my own work (e.g., Shalgi, 2012) I have found in this very phenomenology, (i.e., Hegel's Phenomenology of Mind), a system that holds these three dimensions together, and, more importantly, does so without giving precedence to any one of them. Coming back to the treatment room, this means that when a patient is talking to me about his mother: (A) He has a mother, a specific woman who was the only person to give birth to him; should she enter the room, he would recognize her while I would not—the objective dimension; (B) That he has a specific, unique and particular way of experiencing his mother, that belongs to him and to no one else, based on a lifetime spent in relation to her—the subjective dimension; and (C) While he talks about her with me, now, considering who he is and who I am, considering who his mother is and who my mother is, considering both of our internal objects and the specific ways in which they encounter and co-create each other, his mother is being created again—the intersubjective dimension—which is no less true to who she is.

So, as I already mentioned, Professor Mill's critique of relational psychoanalysis is, to my mind, first and foremost a critique of the concept of truth which lies at its core. Professor Mills warns us time and again of the hazards and pitfalls which are entwined in an intersubjective concept of truth. While I strongly reject Professor Mills' equation of intersubjectivity with postmodernism, I wholeheartedly join and support his claim that if we were to adopt a view that sees the truth of what happens in analysis as only being co-created—now and again, moment by moment—by the specific singular encounter of any particular dyad, we lose the ground on which therapy can take place. Putting it very simply, we may say that if we let the truth of the feelings, thoughts, fantasies, and sensations of our patients be determined only by the mere intersubjective creation of the moment, we might forget the patients have a past, a history, and have subjective dynamics that dominate their inner worlds, which, for example, have brought them to therapy.

Thus, we might find ourselves in a world of Borges or Lewis Carroll in which one cannot hold onto meanings, perceptions, and ideas that exist beyond a fleeting kaleidoscopic moment. Indeed, listening to Professor Mills' critique might make us long for the old, reassuring, and comforting concepts of modernism. One can hardly avoid the compelling power of the modern concept of truth which seems strong and unquestionable: there is a truth there, waiting to be discovered. An objective observer can look carefully and discover the truth that exists, more apparent or concealed, within the object of his scrutiny. Yet, if this compelling concept has been proven problematic in the physical sciences, it has been proven disastrous in the human sciences, and, most of all, in regard to this method called psychoanalysis which has as its higher purpose the struggle for psychic change.

The grounds of this misfortune lie at the heart of the objectivist perspective. When one operates from this perspective, one tries to see things as they are, and not as they become. The blessing relational psychoanalysis brought to the therapeutic endeavor is the opportunity to look not at structures, but at processes. When one looks at structures, one tries to discover and describe them, and by doing so one finds himself, perhaps unnoticeably, preserving what he sees and ignoring the interminable dimension of process, change, and becoming which are immanent to what is going on, and makes it (e.g., a transference, a repetition) not only a replica of the past, but a particular and unique event that is taking place at that moment and within this context.

Let us look, for example, at an angry patient. He is angry, perhaps, because I touched an unresolved oedipal chord, and that filled him with guilt and anxiety he can only experience and express as anger; or he is angry because in the last session I, as a self-object, failed to recognize a basic need, a hidden part of his most sensitive and vulnerable self; or he is angry because he has learned to hate the link, and my interpretation, trying to hold feelings together, makes him fearful. So now he is angry, and I, as an observer, and in accordance with my psychoanalytic beliefs and education, try to locate the seeds of the anger, perhaps helping him to see those seeds, acknowledge them, and treat them compassionately. The patient may see that it could help him, but here is the thing: the patient is not angry. He is angry with me. And when he is angry with me, whatever the objective reason of that anger, and whatever the subjective psychological dynamics that produce the anger, he is not angry as he is always angry: he is angry with me. Since I am who I am, his anger is not only being discovered, but is just as well being created anew between who he is and who I am. That anger is not a replica of the past. It is, in Thomas Ogden's (1994) words, "the present moment of the past" (p. 61), a newly created past, a newly created anger. If I am to help the patient not just understand his anger, but also emerge into new ways of experiencing it, I must relate to this intersubjective creation of the anger.

This is why, the problem with Dr. Mills' arguments is not that he criticizes the precedence of intersubjectivity, but that he endorses the precedence of objectivity. Mills is right—the patient is objectively angry, and, yes, none of us would attempt to fly out of this building by flapping our arms. Yet, if man could not imagine doing so (being that dream unrealistically), Dr. Mills would not be able to fly here today and talk with us, he would not be able to fly into this building. Of course, objective reality exists. I don't think anyone really defies that. Yet, we should be wary of giving it precedence over the subjective or intersubjective dimensions of human existence. The psychoanalyst and philosopher Marcia Cavell wrote that "There is talk now of the way in which analyst and patient 'co-construct reality'. Each of us constructs *a picture* of reality. Reality is what keeps pulling us back to the drawing board." (1998, p. 465). This is so true: Objective reality is what holds us to the drawing board; but, objective reality would be meaningless unless the subjective and intersubjective dimensions could picture it again and again, each time with new and fresh meaning. Objective reality as such, the objective reality of our patients, would be a hollow ghostly replica of itself unless subjective reality, and intersubjective reality infused it with life.

References

Davidson, D. (2001). *Subjective, Intersubjective, Objective*. Oxford: Clarendon Press.

Ogden, T.H. (1994). *Subjects of Analysis*. London: Karnac Books.

Shalgi, B. (2012). The cat ate our tongues – but we got it back: Benjamin's journey from domination to surrender. *Studies in Gender and Sexuality*, 13(4), 277–294.

13 Projective identification and relatedness

A Kleinian perspective

Merav Roth

Abstract: This paper offers a Kleinian view of the relational understandings described in Mills' paper, regarding two central issues: The exploration of the analyst's subjectivity by the patient, and the use of self-disclosure. It is suggested that from a Kleinian perspective it is less advisable to "invite" the patient to explore the analyst's subjectivity, or to use self-disclosure as a curative procedure, since major analytic work focuses on the primitive parts of the personality, that is, the working through of deep anxieties, massive projective identification and a deep confusion between self and object. When working with these primitive parts of the personality, the transference relations are suffused with projections, and the patient is therefore unable to address the other's subjectivity. Furthermore, in these areas of object-relations the patient seldom uses symbolic language, but instead suffers from the dominance of symbolic equations, which enforce the delusion of sameness between internal and external objects. Inviting the patient to explore the analyst's subjectivity, or exposing the patient to otherness through self-disclosure thus serve as communications to the more adult, saner parts of the patient's personality, while the more psychotic, confused parts which bring about most of his sufferings remain neglected.

This paper offers a Kleinian glimpse into the important and complex ideas raised by Mills (2017). I focus my comments on the Kleinian understanding of the nature of *projective identification* and discuss its implications concerning two issues:

1. The exploration of the analyst's subjectivity by the patient.
2. The use of self-disclosure.

Relational aspects of Kleinian theory

Melanie Klein was one of the first to lay the foundations for the understanding of the psychoanalytic encounter as a relational experience. As Greenberg and Mitchell wrote: "In Klein's system drive regulation has been replaced by a complex web of relations with others, real and imaginary" (1983, p. 150). Klein emphasized the idea that in unconscious phantasy *there is no experience occurring outside the context of the relation to the object* (Klein, 1937, pp. 306–307). The crying baby does not think, "My stomach is aching." Rather he has a phantasy which might sound something like: "My object causes me stomach pain."

A second crucial step towards understanding the relational aspect of psychoanalysis was taken, when Klein discovered *projective identification* (1946). Thanks to Bion's (1967) contribution regarding the communicational aspects of projective identification; and thanks to the important developments made by other contemporary Kleinians such as Joseph (1987), Rosenfeld (1971), Sodre (2015), and others, Kleinian theory and technique further developed the concept of the analytic encounter as a relational experience, with a great deal of writing about the clinical implications of this conceptualization. An emphasis has subsequently been placed on the importance of containment and psychic metabolization of the patient's projections *within the analyst's mind,* as a means for getting a clearer understanding of the most primitive, confused and threatening parts of the patient's personality. The analyst is also simultaneously, unconsciously invited *not* to understand, and instead is pressured to merge with these primitive elements and mechanisms through projective identification and enactment. This is how the *total situation of the transference* enables the analyst to fully grasp the revived internal relations of the patient from within (Joseph, 1985).

From a Kleinian perspective, the working through of these massive attacks on linking (Bion, 1959), the blurring of identities, and the psychotic anxieties which lie behind them can lead to emotional growth in two ways: (1) Through the analyst's experiences of the patient's internal experience and projected material. This includes an understanding of primitive modes of relatedness, that is unconscious phantasies, anxieties, and psychic pain. The analyst uses this understanding to enable the patient to gradually gain *insight,* and with it the ability to tolerate and negotiate larger parts of his internal and external reality (Segal, 1962; Joseph, 1987); and (2) The patient also *internalizes the containing function* of the analyst, which was termed the alpha function by Bion. In other words, the patient internalizes the analyst's capacity to tolerate, metabolize, think, integrate, and transform within himself, instead of reacting, reprojecting, manically repairing, and so on.

Projective identification: A primitive meeting of minds

Klein believed that the mind is multidialectical, constantly moving between self and other, the life and death instincts, love and hate, projection and internalization, phantasy and reality, and between the paranoid-schizoid and depressive positions. In Kleinian practice, emphasis is laid on the working through—in the total situation of the transference—of the more primitive, even psychotic parts of the personality. It is believed that these are the parts which cause most of the patient's sufferings and distort (as part of their aim) his reality testing.

Projective identification is understood not only as a normal communicational mechanism, but also as a primitive defense used massively by the more disturbed parts of the personality. When used defensively, it can be accompanied by other mechanisms characteristic of the paranoid-schizoid position such as splitting, denial and an omnipotent effort to control the object from within. All these subjugate the self as well as the other (Ogden, 1994), and distort the ways these perceptions are internally perceived and externally manifested in relationships. The patient is afraid that his needs will not be met and is envious of the other who is perceived by him as someone who "has it all." In order to lessen the pain and anxiety of this experience he tries to gain false control over his internal objects, and exerts interpersonal pressure on the analyst to identify with his projections. The analyst's identifications with the patient's projections do not lead him to accusations of the patient, as it is sometimes wrongly understood, but to deeply empathic understandings concerning the patient's anxiety and pain connected to his separateness from the object.

When the patient is using massive projective identification, it is assumed that he is struggling with "disidentification" (Sodre, 2015, p. 44), trying to rid himself of unbearable experiences by projecting them into the other, or—on the contrary—trying to repair the object by investing him with his own good parts (Klein, 1946). In both cases the patient is suffering from confusion between self and object, thus causing great difficulties in genuinely experiencing the other. The patient's transference relation is colored by these massive projections, so that he is not able to identify "who's who" (Sodre, 2015). He is therefore unable, in this state, to meet the other's subjectivity, which remains buried beneath the screen of his projections. At this phase of the analysis we should not force the patient to prematurely experience the subjectivity of the analyst, because as Betty Joseph (1985) suggested *we try not to put our efforts into the saner, more adult parts of the personality, while neglecting the working through of the parts which most need our help.*

Symbolic equation

Furthermore, in these areas of object relations the patient does not often use symbolic language, but instead suffers from the dominance of symbolic equations, which enforce the delusion of sameness between internal and external objects (Klein, 1930; Segal, 1950). It is especially this ability—to explore, rather than project—that is impaired and less accessible to the patient. Instead, he is trapped in vicious cycles of anxiety and primitive defense mechanisms; this is exactly where he needs our help.

So, if we go back to the possibility of exploring the subjectivity of the analyst in relational technique, which is so beautifully described in the writings of many clinicians and thinkers whom I deeply appreciate, (such as Lew Aron and Thomas Ogden, for example), we see that *from a Kleinian perspective the relational aspect of the analytic relationship is utilized in a very different way than it is in relational psychoanalysis: the analyst is invited to feel all that is projected onto and into him as vividly as possible.* The analyst's intimate exploration of these projections from within serve as the royal road toward understanding the patient's internal object-relations, the roots of his pains, his confusions and internal turbulence, as well as his relation to external reality. A thorough working-through is needed before the patient can reinternalize more metabolized parts of the self and of the object, thus increasing his ability to discriminate between inside and outside, self and other, and to perceive more clearly the analyst's subjectivity, which can only then be explored.

Furthermore, the Kleinian premise contends (and incites a lot of easily understandable grudges for it) that *the analyst does hold more accurate judgments* of what is happening in the relational encounter, and that *he is better equipped to deal with universal sorrows and anxieties,* simply because he previously underwent a long psychoanalysis. Perhaps more evidently, the analyst is inclined to be less regressed than the patient because he is not the one on the couch. There is therefore from this perspective, serious asymmetry between transference and countertransference intensities and distortional influences.

I wish to stress that I, too, try to encourage my patient to explore the ways in which he experiences me. Only it is not a clear insight into my internal world which I assume he will find at the moment of his regression, but the confusing blend of my presence and his anxieties, unconscious phantasies, and projections. This is "the other" I wish to help him explore in the transference relationship to me. It is this exploration, along with the constant, unflinching interpretation of it that will eventually help the patient gain better access to his internal struggles, to reality and to the other.

The saner, stronger parts of the personality of the patient and his good internal objects (including the internalized good object of the containing analyst), are all active in the efforts to gradually abandon the dominance of distortional relations for the sake of real intimacy, trust and reparation, gained by the resolution of the depressive position. From a Kleinian point of view, it is only then that there is much more room for the mutual "meeting of minds" (Aron, 1996) that is the royal road towards health in relational psychoanalysis.

Self-disclosure

As early as 1912, Freud warned analysts against bringing their "own individuality freely into their discussion" (1912, pp. 117–118). Indeed, the relational corpus itself also contains repeated warnings against the too-free use of self-disclosure and against the radical interpretations and applications of the postmodern turn, as raised by Mills (2017).

Relational writers also remind us that self-disclosure is to some degree always a part of our communication. I agree. Nevertheless, *self-disclosure is much less applicable as an initiated tool in the Kleinian method of psychoanalysis* (but for different reasons then those described by Mills). Although I speak with my patients about my part in the transference relationship, I don't tend to share my internal reactions with my patient, *because I don't want to lessen the intensity of the transference and projections by exposing my countertransference.* On the contrary, I try to follow Betty Joseph's recommendation (1985) to keep the transference heat as high as possible for as long as it takes to be able to thoroughly work it through.

The actual differences in the Kleinian and relational uses of self-disclosure might be quite subtle and even sound quite similar. If, for instance, a patient feels that she has made me angry, I might say: "So, now that I am angry you can be relieved that I am totally awake, and will not desert you." In this interpretation, I do not deny her perception of me, but I am also not interested in focusing further on my subjectivity. Rather, I prefer to illuminate her urge to project her anger into me as a defense against the anxiety of being left alone, deserted by a dead or distracted object.

To give my example a combined Kleinian-Relational formulation, one could say that from a Kleinian point of view, it is not the true self of the analyst nor the subjectivity of "the other" that is explored, but *the false perceptions of the analyst's subjectivity that are loaded with the patient's projections, and the underlying anxieties and unconscious phantasies accompanying them.* Ultimately, the aim is to enable the patient to reclaim the lost parts of himself that were located in the analyst through projective identification, including the ability for insight and for "out-sight."

Last, I could not agree more with Lew Aron's (1996) statement that "the important thing about each and every intervention, including self-disclosure, is not whether it promotes autonomy or relation, but whether it opens or blocks analytic interrogation" (in Hebrew, p. 267). I am certain that in both methods—relational and Kleinian—patients are helped enormously, as long as their analysts use their tools in a genuine and responsible way.

References

Aron, L. (1996). *A Meeting of Minds: Mutuality in Psychoanalysis.* New-York: The Analytic press.

Bion, W. (1967). *Second Thoughts.* London: Heinemann.

Bion, W.R. (1959). Attacks on Linking. *International Journal of Psychoanalysis*, 40, 308–315.

Freud, S. (1912). Recommendations on analytic technique. In J. Strachey (Ed. and trans.), *The Standard Edition of the Complete Psychological Works of Sigmund Freud.* Vol. XII, London: The Hogarth Press, 1957, pp. 159–215.

Joseph, B. (1985). Transference: The total situation. *International Journal of Psychoanalysis*, 66, 447–454.

Joseph, B. (1987). Projective identification – Some clinical aspects. In J. Sandler (Ed.), *Projection, Identification, Projective Identification.* London: Karnac Books, pp. 65–76.

Klein, M. (1930). The importance of symbol-formation in the development of the ego. In *Love, Guilt and Reparation and Other Works 1921–1945.* London, UK: Vintage, pp. 219–232.

Klein, M. (1937). Love, guilt and reparation. In *Love, Guilt and Reparation and Other Works 1921–1945.* London: Vintage, pp. 306–343.

Klein, M. (1946). Notes on some schizoid mechanisms. In *Envy and Gratitude and Other Works 1946–1963.* London: Vintage, pp. 1–24.

Mills, J. (2017). Challenging relational psychoanalysis: A critique of postmodernism and analyst self-disclosure. *Psychoanalytic Perspectives*, 14(3), 313–335.

Ogden, T.H. (1994). The analytic third: Working with intersubjective clinical facts. *International Journal of Psychoanalysis*, 75, 3–19.

Rosenfeld, H. (1971). Contribution to the psychopathology of psychotic States – The importance of projective identification in the ego structure and the object relations of the psychotic patient. In E. Spillius, & E. O'Shaughnessy (Eds.), *Projective Identification, The Fate of a Concept*. New York: Routledge, 2012, pp. 76–97.

Segal, H. (1950). Some aspects of the analysis of a schizophrenic. *International Journal of Psychoanalysis*, 31, 268–278.

Segal, H. (1962). The curative factors in psycho-analysis. *International Journal of Psychoanalysis*, 43, 212–217.

Sodre, I. (2015). *Imaginary Existences*. New York: Routledge.

14 Psychoanalysis and postmodernism

A response to Dr. Jon Mills' "Challenging relational psychoanalysis: A critique of postmodernism and analyst self-disclosure"

Liran Razinsky

Abstract: Jon Mills' "Challenging Relational Psychoanalysis: A Critique of Postmodernism and Analyst Self-Disclosure" criticizes relational psychoanalysis for basing itself on postmodern thought. My paper offers a critique of Mills' critique. I start with noting that Mills supplies only vague, imprecise, and overgeneralized paraphrases of postmodern notions and does not directly address textual examples of postmodern philosophy. Some of the elements Mills finds faulty in postmodernism and, by proxy, in relational psychoanalysis are elements that are rather central to psychoanalytic thought itself. In the second part of my paper, I address the closing off of psychoanalysis from the humanities and argue that psychoanalysis should renew its links with the humanities and seek dialog with them. I end by urging psychoanalysis to explore and reestablish its affinity not only with the humanities in general but with the critical ethos of the humanities, an ethos that questions given identities and destabilizes structures, not unlike what analysts do in their clinics.

Jon Mills has presented us with a very rich and intriguing paper. Although I have reservations, I appreciate the way the paper brings up basic questions about psychoanalysis. Reading Mills, I wonder what it is about postmodernism as applied in relational psychoanalysis that makes him so angry. The "faults" of postmodernism are brought up, one after the other, with arguments against the postmodern position piling up. Some of the arguments are more challenging; others, it has to be said, are really too naïve and banal to be taken seriously. Is there really a need in 2017 to address provocative claims already dealt with in the 1980s, such as "Are there no objective facts? Would anyone care to defy the laws of gravity by attempting to fly off the roof of this building by flapping their arms?"

One thing that remains unclear, however, is what exactly stands behind the term "postmodernism" in Mills' argument. His attack on postmodernism seems to some extent an attack on a boogeyman that he himself created. First, if we speak about relational analysts, Mills does acknowledge that they are, generally speaking, good, responsible therapists. Does he feel that the problems he raises really do bias their judgment? And if not, what is all the vehement discussion really aimed at? Second, and more generally, I ask myself, what is the extreme form of postmodernism that Mills has so much trouble with? I acknowledge that the presence of postmodern and/or relativistic ideas in the North American academy is much more profound than elsewhere, and I assume that occasionally postmodern positions do reach absurd expressions. But are we to judge a theoretical movement by its less sound expressions or by its core ideas?

I would be less concerned if Mills went into some detail, telling us which philosophers he is criticizing and which ideas he wishes to disentangle, referring to something we can grasp hold of, be it a text or a citation. He settles instead for very vague paraphrases of postmodern notions that he raises himself and then attacks. I am really not sure that it is helpful to make one's argument against a caricature of postmodernism. Postmodernism is, in its better moments, a complex position. Postmodernism and especially post-structuralism associated with the French thinkers Mills seems not to like, is not a flat claim that there are no resemblances or shared elements among people. French poststructuralism focuses on the way our structures and tendencies are shaped and brought about through historical contexts and ideologies. It holds that the ways in which we understand ourselves, and our ideas about what the human being is, are themselves the expression of dominant discourses and are historically conditioned.

I have no wish to be a defender of postmodernism, but do we need to be reminded that if there was a need to surpass and transcend modernity, it was because there were some problems with the latter? If we widen the argument to the Enlightenment, its critique was not an arbitrary theoretical maneuver: It was necessitated by theories and ideas that could no longer be held; it was called for by injustice and oppression against minority groups in the name of Enlightenment. It was required also because of the disastrous outcomes of what many see as the direct result of modernity: World War II, the Holocaust, and the atomic bomb. Critics like Adorno, Arendt, and Zigmunt Bauman have seen such catastrophic events not as opposed to the Enlightenment and modernity but rather as realizing it in a profound sense.

Mills' paper attacks relational psychoanalysis through its adaptation of postmodern ideas, and yet what he really seems to take issue with are the original postmodern ideas themselves. I find it troublesome that, rather than addressing ideas directly, Mills attacks those who use them. He offers no analysis, let alone reference, to any of the French philosophers responsible for these ideas. One would expect that if the problem is with Foucault and Lyotard, Derrida, Deleuze and Baudrillard, that Mills' text would try to address these authors directly, which he does not do. Instead, Mills criticizes the relational analysts who employ these ideas; he focuses less on the adaptation and use of these ideas and more on the metalevel itself. Forgive the military metaphor, but Mills' problem is with the generals, but he addresses only the soldiers. In trying to discern what really bothers Mills (2017), I take my lead from a footnote, where he does mention two names:

> When analysts use terms such as construction, hence invoking Foucault … or even worse, deconstruction, thus exalting Derrida—the king of postmodernism, whose entire corpus is devoted to annihilating any metaphysical claims whatsoever, thus collapsing everything into undecidability, ambiguity, chaos, and chance—analysts open themselves up to misunderstanding and controversy, subsequently inviting criticism.

Leaving aside Foucault, I would like to talk a bit about Derrida, "the king of postmodernism." Let us leave the soldiers and the generals and bring in the king himself. Is Derrida's delicate deconstruction of Western metaphysics irresponsible? Is it malicious? I believe, rather, that the very slow analytic work in Derrida, done through meticulous close reading of canonical texts, testifies exactly to the contrary. He does not dismiss things, but rather works through them, uncovering with great patience the false propositions on which they lie, and their internal contradictions. He shows classic Western beliefs and positions to be untenable.

Let us briefly consider Derrida's position on subjectivity (the issue of subjectivity being at the center of Mills' paper). Derrida does not refute subjectivity. He is an author whose prose and philosophy are deeply personal; more than any other philosopher, an author who wrote autobiographical texts, an author whose goal is exactly to show how abstract, impersonal, theoretical systems and ideas tend to be interwoven with the person who communicates them. Derrida's critique of the subject does not mean there is no internal world or subjectivity, but that the notion that the subject can be an origin, a foundation, and a source of certainty, is untenable. Derrida shows that the idea of a moment, even if metaphorical, of self-presence, of a kind of closed-circuit when one hears oneself speak, where one can be like a Cartesian cogito, is an illusion. He shows that one is always at some distance from oneself, that the self is layered and is not monolithic. Moreover, the most profound texts of Derrida on the subject draw directly on his analysis of Freud.[1]

Postmodernism and its ancestors

Mills (2017) claims, and in his book *Conundrums* (2012) this claim rings even more strongly, that postmodernism is irreconcilable with the whole of Western philosophical tradition: "Because postmodern perspectives are firmly established in antithesis to the entire history of Greek and European ontology, perspectives widely adopted by many contemporary analysts today, relational psychoanalysis has no tenable metaphysic …" (2017). Mills' argument is that because, according to him, postmodernism goes against the Western philosophical tradition, it is dangerous to follow. Following it would disconnect relational psychoanalysis from the entire history of the West. Well, we may ask him whether, for example, in that Western tradition, we are entitled to include the sophists with their attack on the concept of truth? The Hellenistic skeptics like Sextus Empiricus? May we list the sixteenth-century philosopher and essayist Michel de Montaigne and his essay "On the Inconsistency of Our Actions," in which he claims that a unified self is not something one can find? Rather, I cite Montaigne: "We do not go; we are carried away, like floating objects, now gently, now violently, according as the water is angry or calm" (1958, p. 240). There is no self, Montaigne asserted. "We change like that animal which takes the color of the place you set it on" (p. 240); "We float between different states of mind; we will nothing freely, nothing absolutely, nothing constantly" (p. 240). "We are all patchwork," he wrote, "and so shapeless and diverse in composition that each bit, each moment, plays its own game" (p. 244). And Montaigne added, "I have nothing to say about myself absolutely, simply, and solidly, without confusion and without mixture" (p. 242).

Does Mills see, as part of that cherished Western tradition that postmodern perspectives are so antithetical to, the canonical philosopher David Hume, refuting the existence of any stable identity, or the idea of the self as an underlying essence for our actions, and claiming instead that our self is nothing but "a bundle of perceptions"? (Hume, 2007, p. 421) How about Nietzsche and his critique of the notion of I? And we have not even started with the twentieth century: One name that stands out and that could be added to this little list, an author often seen a precursor of postmodernism, is Sigmund Freud, who also wanted to deal a blow to Enlightenment notions of rationality and moral progress, and to the idea of transparency of the self to itself, very much like postmodernism.

Psychoanalysis and the humanities

Mills' attack on postmodernism and the relational school can serve to raise a crucial point concerning the nature of psychoanalysis, namely, its relation to critique. It is significant and refreshing that he is discussing psychoanalytic practices and theories from a philosopher's point of view, examining them as theories, looking at them as part of the humanities. In itself that is already noteworthy and, regretfully, uncommon. I am very concerned by tendencies in the psychoanalytic world to hide or close itself off from the humanities, to avoid intellectual discourse, to treat every intellectual discussion as intellectualization, as distanced from "what really matters," as it were. Where psychology departments have gone in their avoidance of the humanities and their turn to empirical science, is well familiar. But clinical dynamic departments, psychoanalytic institutions and psychoanalytic discourse are also taking their distance from the humanities and this is lamentable. Suffice it to remind the reader that today most academic courses on psychoanalysis take place in the arts and the humanities departments (Redmond & Shulman, 2008) for us to see that this relation with the humanities might prove vital for psychoanalysis. Hardly existent anymore in the medicine and psychology departments where it once used to flourish, psychoanalysis risks losing its last foothold in academia. It is in the interest of psychoanalysis not to enclose itself in its institutes and societies. In that sense, the Program for Hermeneutics and Cultural Studies at Bar Ilan University, where this symposium took place, as well as a few similar programs around the world, are important as they attempt to bridge this gap of psychoanalytic theory and the humanities.

Psychoanalysis is not open enough to a dialogue with the humanities (a much fuller presentation of my thoughts on this can be found in my 2016 "On the Need for Openness to the Humanities in Psychoanalysis," a contribution to a special issue of *Psychoanalytic Psychology* on "Psychoanalysis and the Humanities in Crisis" [Razinsky, 2016]). When analytic practitioners think of this type of dialogue they often have in mind an application of psychoanalytic notions to literature or history. I would like to stress the need for openness for the reverse: the influence of the humanities on psychoanalysis. It is time for psychoanalysis to renew its links with the humanities, to seek to be influenced by and to be in dialogue with thought coming from outside. I say "renew," for Freud himself, in formulating his ideas, was always in dialogue with ideas coming from philosophy, literature, and other fields of knowledge.

Psychoanalytic educational contexts rarely include philosophy, literary studies, history, or anthropology in their curricula. More broadly, clinical psychology as a whole suffers from a similar lack: Academic clinical programs in psychology, whether they have a psychodynamic aspect or not, tend to be narrow and set bounds within their disciplines with regard to how the human being is to be understood.

Beyond the larger question of the openness of psychoanalysis to the humanities, there is the question of its openness specifically to the contributions of the humanities to psychoanalytic thought. I wish to argue for the importance of more acceptance of humanities-informed readings of psychoanalysis, as a theory and field of knowledge about human beings. Mills has given us a good example of such reading. Such acceptance clearly involves the question of who can write on psychoanalysis, who can interpret it and develop it. It also involves, indirectly, the issue of the sources of authority on psychoanalytic texts. As things stand today, both conceptually and in the practice of publications in journals, and so on, psychoanalysis closes itself off from the possibility of being read, augmented, or challenged by readings that come from the humanities.

A larger question at stake of course is that of who is entitled to study psychoanalysis and contribute to it. This is the issue of the source of authority of analytic theory: Is clinical practice the sole way of advancing the theory? Among other things, I believe that refinding this relation and affinity with the humanities is important with regard to some recent trends occurring around psychoanalysis: The turn to neuroscience and to general psychology, and the constant evaluation of psychoanalytic therapy in outcome studies. Both trends risk uprooting psychoanalysis from its essence, for psychoanalysis is rooted in meaning. The dialogue with the humanities, the sciences of meaning, would help psychoanalysis reconnect with its core. Renewing the link with the humanities, the fields of knowledge whose center is meaning, would allow psychoanalysis to remain close to its essence rather than fading away.

Within psychoanalysis, one of the characteristics of the relational school is that much more than other schools (except the Lacanians), it is open to influences from the humanities. Mitchell himself was a reader of philosophy, and of course other names such as Aron, Benjamin, and Stolorow could be mentioned here. Although what I like about Mills' work is exactly that he brings philosophical discourse into psychoanalysis, and although such integration is exactly the feature I like best about relational psychoanalysis, I am slightly perplexed by the fact that this dialogue with philosophy is exactly what Mills wishes to refute in relational thought. This is because he accuses relational psychoanalysts of integrating philosophical thought of a certain kind. It is not philosophy in itself that troubles Mills; were they more modernist, adopting notions of progress, rationality, and the self, metatheory, and so on, Mills, so it seems, would be content. Rather what troubles him is a philosophy of a special kind that he believes should be kept out of psychoanalysis: that of postmodernism.

I would urge psychoanalysis to explore its affinity not only with the humanities in general but much more specifically with what I call the critical humanities or the critical ethos of the humanities—an ethos that sets itself the tasks of criticizing existing power structures and questioning given identities. This critical ethos has always been part of the humanities. Indeed, Socrates was put to death by his fellow Athenians for his philosophical critique. This can of course be more strongly identified in nineteenth-century thinkers such as Marx or Nietzsche, in the Frankfurt School and starting from the 1960's in French thought. They embody this critical ethos. I wish to stress that among these thinkers is Freud himself. And indeed, in a more general manner, the critical ethos is very close to psychoanalysis. This critical ethos in the humanities aims toward destabilizing structures, exploring hidden power relations and putting solid identities in question. The critical ethos, and within it, postmodernism, is deconstructing the overencroachment of metanarratives and ideologies in our lives, protesting the illusion that arbitrary notions imposed on us are natural, and therefore eternal. It is a movement of liberation. And yet, this ethos often tends to encounter resistance.

Similarly, psychoanalysis calls into question much that is taken for granted in society. More important, in the treatment room, psychoanalysis is a practice that challenges the patient's existing identities, roles, reactions, and patterns and explores his or her hidden structures; it seeks to deautomatize and denaturalize the givens of one's mind and behavior. And, not surprisingly, psychoanalysis too, like the critical humanities, is met with resistance—in treatment, to be sure, but also on a cultural level. It is met with resistance from those whom it seeks to help see clearly.

This is one reason to be careful when criticizing psychoanalytic stances for their affinity to postmodernism—it really might play into the hands of the resistance to psychoanalysis. Rejecting the relational school specifically because it questions notions of truth and identity seems to me too awfully close to rejecting psychoanalysis per se, for psychoanalysis questions precisely these notions. It is exactly this critical ethos of the humanities that I would like to see psychoanalysis dialoging with more intensively.

Mills (2017) writes at the beginning of his text that "[a]mong [the] postmodern assumptions" that he opposes "are the abnegation of the Enlightenment modern notions of rationality, objectivity, epistemic certainty, truth, universal absolutes, individuality and free will, and positivistic science, just to name a few." I wish to encourage psychoanalysis to explore its affinities with the critical ethos of the humanities. I believe it is helpful, in guise of conclusion, to recall that the undermining of Enlightenment modern notions of rationality, objectivity, positivistic science, epistemic certainty, and free will are the heart of Freud's Copernican revolution in the discovery of the unconscious.

Endnote

1. Suffice it to mention here "Freud and the scene of writing" (Derrida, 1978), a text in which, tracing the textual metaphors of Freud, Derrida shows the psyche's internal difference and the absence of an original central point. For a reading of Freud that underlines similar elements see Weber (1982, 1997).

References

de Montaigne, M. (1958). Of the inconsistency of our actions. In *The Complete Essays of Montaigne* (D. M. Ferme, Trans). Stanford, CA: Stanford University Press, pp. 239–244.

Derrida, J. (1978). Freud and the scene of writing. In *Writing and Difference* (A. Bass, Trans.). Chicago, IL: University of Chicago Press, pp. 196–231.

Hume, D. (2007). In D.F. Norton, & M.J. Norton (Eds.), *A Treatise of Human Nature*. Oxford, UK: Oxford University Press.

Mills, J. (2012). *Conundrums: A Critique of Contemporary Psychoanalysis*. New York: Routledge.

Mills, J. (2017). Challenging relational psychoanalysis: A critique of postmodernism and analyst self-disclosure. *Psychoanalytic Perspectives*, 14(3), 313–335.

Razinsky, L. (2016). On the need for openness to the humanities in psychoanalysis. *Psychoanalytic Psychology*, 33(1), S56–S74. doi: 10.1037/pap0000064

Redmond, J., & Shulman, M. (2008). Access to psychoanalytic ideas in American undergraduate institutions. *Journal of the American Psychoanalytic Association*, 56, 391–408. doi: 10.1177/0003065108318639

Weber, S. (1982). *The Legend of Freud*. Minneapolis, MN: University of Minnesota Press.

Weber, S. (1997). Wartime. In H. de Vries, & S. Weber (Eds.), *Violence, Identity, and Self-Determination*. Stanford, CA: Stanford University Press, pp. 80–105.

15 Relational psychoanalysis out of context

Response to Jon Mills[1]

Steven Kuchuck and Rachel Sopher

Abstract: The authors close the panel by mapping out and responding to Jon Mills' critique of Relational psychoanalysis, and provide a historical background within which to contextualize the framework for the debate. Specifically, they take up the flaws inherent in judging a theory based on an objectivist perspective and address indeterminate, decontextualized, and selective understandings of the constantly evolving theory and practice of contemporary relational and Relational psychoanalysis.

There is much to appreciate in Jon Mills' writing. His knowledge of philosophy and psychoanalysis, and his critical, analytical approach to evaluating theory, serve him well in this 2017 essay and previous writings on this and other subjects (2002, 2005, 2012). Although we were not part of the presentation in Israel that served as the basis for this publication, we would like to take this opportunity to close the panel by mapping out and responding to his critique, as well as providing a historical background within which to contextualize the framework for this debate.

It seems important to first locate ourselves theoretically in order to establish a frame of reference for our comments on Dr. Mills' critique. We both have training and interest in classical theory, which later expanded to include what has sometimes been referred to as the "small r" relational interpersonalist theories of Harry Stack Sullivan, the British object relations theorists, the self-psychology theories influenced by Heinz Kohut including intersubjectivity theory, and particularly Relational psychoanalysis (see below for a definition of Relational psychoanalysis as it differs from small r relational theory) as introduced by Stephen Mitchell and his colleagues. Relational psychoanalysis has become a theoretical home, offering a broader amalgam of psychoanalytic theories that attend to both the intrapsychic and the interpersonal aspects of psychoanalytic process and the dialectical movement between them. Our response to Mills emerges from this theoretical and professional background. We will approach this brief commentary by recapitulating the author's main arguments and responding to them individually as they arise.

Indeterminate theoretical differences: Relational psychoanalysis out of context

Many of the criticisms that Mills launches against relational psychoanalysis are the very same ones that Jay Greenberg and Stephen Mitchell (1983) sought to correct for in differentiating between object relations theory—what they saw as an intrapsychic theory—and interpersonal psychoanalysis, which deemphasized the internal world. Greenberg and Mitchell (1983) first coined the term relational (small r) as a way of identifying a common theme among a diverse group of theories that had not previously been considered connected or unified in any way. Each of the schools that appeared under the new umbrella of relational (which are primarily—as Mills mentions—interpersonal, object relations, self-psychology, intersubjectivity theory) emphasized a person's embeddedness in the social context (rather than the isolated individual) as the primary unit of study. But it wasn't until his first solo authored book (1988) that Mitchell began using the term Relational to *also* refer to a newly developing perspective—in some ways overlapping with but also distinct from the earlier theories that he and Greenberg had included under the heading of relational psychoanalysis. Mitchell's new thinking arose from a melding of Fairbairn's object relations theory with interpersonal psychoanalysis, feminist, queer, gender, and other social theories and is now sometimes referred to as the New York School or North American Relational psychoanalysis. This new and expanded perspective also became referred to as "big R" Relational psychoanalysis in order to distinguish it from Mitchell's original use of the term relational. Mills collapses the complexity of history and specificity of terminology by keeping definitions vague and indeterminate, moving in and out of discussions of small r and big R relational models, usually without noting which of the two frameworks he is evaluating in his arguments.

Further complicating the field that Mills critiques, there is no singular "school" of big R Relational psychoanalysis. For that reason, the approach to psychoanalysis that Mitchell first identified in 1988 has often been referred to as a perspective rather than a theory. Although there are a number of universal characteristics including dialectical movement between intrapsychic and interpersonal, acknowledgment of intersubjectivity and the inevitable impact of the analyst's subjectivity, multiplicity, and many other variables (Aron, 1996; Harris, 2011), each Relational analyst defines and practices the perspective in his or her own particular way. Given the numerous stances that Mills collapses and decontextualizes, and his further conflation of relational and Relational psychoanalysis, it becomes difficult to fully track and respond to his work. Thus, the same critique he levels at Relational Psychoanalysis for its lack of specificity in terminology may be true of Mills' own arguments. But the difficulty doesn't end there.

There is an additional problem with terminology. Although Mills correctly notes that different theorists utilize independently derived definitions for the terms thirdness and intersubjectivity (i.e., Benjamin, and Stolorow, Atwood & Orange, Aron, Ogden), he uses the words freely without noting how he is defining the terms or whose definition he is addressing. At some points, he even seems to be using the *term* intersubjectivity (by which we believe he means what is called intersubjectivity theory or intersubjective systems theory, which assumes that no two people can be seen as separate, disembedded objects or subjects) and the *phenomenon* of intersubjectivity, generally speaking; the study of experience that does not focus on either subject or object exclusively and takes into account both conscious and unconscious experience, interchangeably.

The anxiety of influence: Theoretical growth as a process

Mills refers to Benjamin's and Stolorow's work on intersubjectivity as problematic in that "There is no novelty about it whatsoever," then immediately contradicts this claim, stating that Benjamin "misinterprets" and "misrepresents" Hegel in her treatment of the master–slave dynamic. Mills contends that in extending Hegel's theory Benjamin appropriates philosophy, utilizing it for her own ends, twisting its meaning and stretching its applicability to fit the frame of psychoanalytic theory. But if true, this, in direct contradistinction to Mills' assertion, is in actuality a part of the generative process of creative thought and one of the key ways theories develop through generations. As Bloom wrote, "poets make history by misreading one another, so as to clear imaginative space for themselves" (p. 15, in Feiner, 1977). If we were to relate to Hegel only in his original form and intent, it would become a solipsistic, dead project without applicability to present thought or usefulness to contemporary psychoanalytic process. Indeed, the most generative revolutions in psychoanalytic theory have proceeded in this manner, by keeping, "a firm connection with the classical base but to swerve, as need be, to keep our own perceptive identities… Each new conceptual scheme embraces the phenomena explained by its predecessors and adds to them" (p. 15, Feiner, 1977). Relational psychoanalysis has not broken with the history of psychoanalysis, nor detracted from the importance of the Classical school, but rather, added to the richness and complexity of psychoanalytic discourse. It has revolutionized psychoanalysis while remaining well within the psychoanalytic tradition, and in continual constructive and mutually enhancing dialogue with other theoretical schools. It is a mistake to assess a constantly evolving perspective as if it were set in stone and judge it based on this reified view. The relational and Relational movements have grown and continue to develop through a lively process of scholarship and dialogue that continues to evolve over time.

Mills' arguments about the apparent slippages in the application of postmodern ideas to relational psychoanalysis do at times hold true; but perhaps it is worth sacrificing the purity of original ideas in static form, if that results in the expansion of both philosophy and psychoanalysis in innovative new directions. He takes issue with the lack of depth in the dialogue around philosophy in contemporary psychoanalytic scholarship, but out of the dialogue of differences which postmodernism opened up through its emphasis on perspective comes much creativity, space for freedom of thought, development of ideas, and cross-germination with other theories. Indeed, one of the sequelae of the postmodern movement has been the self-reflexive knowledge that we choose our theories for deeply personal and often unconsciously determined reasons (Stolorow & Atwood, 1979; Kuchuck, 2014). Putting one's theoretical leanings into context makes them more meaningful in their subjective truth rather than more suspect, as an objectivist might believe.

The critique that relational psychoanalysis has nothing theoretically new to add allows critics of the newer theories to justify maintaining the status quo and gives support to the theoretical, political, and institutional powerbase, to diminish the important contributions of the relational schools. This stance rationalizes not having to learn new theory or deal with the threatening, possibly disorienting experiences of changing how one might think about theory, prior personal and professional treatments, and current ways of practicing. Freud (1905/1960) told the following joke: A. borrowed a copper kettle from B. and after he had returned it was sued by B. because the kettle now had a big hole in it which made it unusable. A.'s defense was: "First, I never borrowed a kettle from B. at all; secondly, the kettle had a hole in it already when I got it from him; and thirdly, I gave him back the kettle undamaged." (p. 62). Each one of these defenses is valid in itself, but taken together they exclude one another. In our view, the mainstream response to innovation in psychoanalysis is structured very much along the lines of this joke. First, what you are saying is wrong or partial. Second, we have already known it and have always maintained this to be the case; third, whatever is good in what you are saying we have now learned from you and incorporated, but with the advantage of putting it into its proper place within the whole comprehensive theory of psychoanalysis, while you have merely substituted the part for the whole.[2]

Objective truth, constructivism, and the drives

Mills notes that "the relational school has constructed a false dichotomy between drive theory and relational theory…" Although initially founded on the premise that object seeking rather than drive discharge is what motivates us and therefore needs to be central to any relational theory, and while this is still a significant component of the relational zeitgeist, Greenberg (1993) later suggested that relationalists (including Relational analysts) consider retaining some form of a drive theory model. Other relationalists have since adapted that view as well, and from the very beginning, Mitchell was clear that his new vision of psychoanalysis was not to be hegemony.

Further, there is much less of a dichotomy between these metapsychologies than Mills seems to recognize. He goes on to note that Mitchell's rejection of the drives is equal to wholesale renunciation of our embodied selves. This seems a gross oversimplification of Mitchell's understanding of essentialism as related to the body and development of identity. In a discussion of this split with regards to gender he wrote:

> Is there a universal grammar of gender and sexuality? This is a question for which there can never be a final answer; yet it is crucial that we keep

> asking the question. Any answer is bound to be temporary—any bit of biologizing will always be deconstructable, eventually found to express the culture in which it is generated; *any bit of constructivism will always have to be reanchored to the body and human biology to keep it grounded and emotionally relevant* (Mitchell, 1996, p. 56, italics added)

Why does Mills focus on the first half of Mitchell's dialectic describing deconstruction of the drives and disregard the latter's acknowledgment of the importance of biology? Mitchell's is a more balanced view of the drives and what is universally human than Mills gives the relational movement credit for. This is just one example in which he selectively chooses the authors and quotations he critiques for the purposes of argument, without crediting a wider survey of relational psychoanalytic thought, which is more subtle and nuanced than he acknowledges. Mitchell does not throw out the drives, but rather, understands their importance without giving them precedence over other factors in the process of human meaning-making. Relational psychoanalysis did not throw out the drives, but rather humanized them by placing them in the context of relationship (Altman & Davies, 2003). We need not assume that our primary motivations are for the gratification of bodily based drives in order to argue that our bodies are central to our sense of self, relatedness with others, and the world around us. In addition, there has been much discussion concerned with how to understand, make room for, and acknowledge some of these body-based realities. In fact, there is a large and growing Relational literature on embodiment (Knoblauch, 1996; Sletvold, 2014; *Psychoanalytic Perspectives* special issue: The Analyst's Body in the Consulting Room (2016, issue 13.2)).

Intersubjectivity and psychoanalytic depth

Mills equates the change of focus from drive to relationship with a lack of depth and diminished focus on unconscious process. But one doesn't have to abandon notions of intersubjectivity or go back to Freud to achieve depth of inquiry and experience. More critically, why would an enhanced focus on the relational aspects of the analytic interaction necessarily be contrasted with exploring the unconscious? Certainly, there are unconscious dynamics operating with regard to the here-and-now that might be explored without referring back to the past or to other objects. When we explore a patient's unconscious perceptions of us, let alone fantasies about our subjectivity, there is much about these perceptions that is out of awareness, some of which is preconscious but much of which is dynamically unconscious, maintained out of awareness by unconscious defenses which themselves need exploration. Why, then, would more awareness of and attention to the here-and-now necessarily imply any disregard for or de-emphasis of unconscious material?

In his discussion of conscious versus unconscious work, Mills may be accurately describing some early versions of interpersonal psychoanalysis (as mentioned above, here again is yet another category error—the conflation of interpersonal psychoanalysis and other schools of relational and/or Relational psychoanalysis), for example, Merton Gill's (1979) ideas about the necessity of focusing exclusively on the here-and-now. This is an inaccurate interpretation of both contemporary interpersonal theory and relational/Relational psychoanalysis, though probably not an uncommon misperception of what relationalists do.

It is difficult to imagine that many relational psychoanalysts work only with here-and-now, secondary process material, or that it's even possible to practice any form of psychotherapy or psychoanalysis that doesn't involve some amount of unconscious to unconscious communication.[3] This is a perplexing split that is difficult to understand; conscious and unconscious aspects of mind are not separate entities, but a continuum of experience (Bion, 1962; Searles, 1990; Ogden, 2007). Many or more likely all of us in the relational world move between attending to the here-and-now, which is usually both conscious and unconscious, making genetic interpretations, and engaging in deeper unconscious to unconscious communications. In fact, there is most often a movement back and forth between intersubjective and intrapsychic foci over the course of the analytic hour, with the analyst's fixed attention to one over the other often a meaningful phenomenon worthy of analysis.

Mills raises similar concerns about multiplicity, asking how it is possible to adhere to a theory of multiple selves without introducing a "plurality of contradictory essences," which is "philosophically problematic on ontological grounds." Multiplicity does in fact assume contradiction. As we know even anecdotally, different aspects of oneself are by nature often in opposition to one another. By example, think about the fact that on certain days and under particular circumstances, the very same person might feel shy, outgoing, eager for social contact, or longing for solitude. The examples of differing and often contradictory self-states are likely endless. Indeed, we agree with Mills that by definition, multiplicity does assume just such a plurality. At least in practice though, this concept does not present a (philosophical or other) problem. Multiplicity does not negate what Mills describes as "essence" nor does it exclude the idea of self.

The self does not become "anesthetized" as Mills would have it, or lose its ontological importance but rather, various self-states move in and out of foreground and background, constituting a flow of different aspects of the internal world, all identified with and embodying a unique sense of self. Self-states are not necessarily caused by the relational encounter as much as they may be stirred and assume lesser or greater dominance in the here-and-now. One goal of a Relational analysis is to increase a patient's understanding of and access to various self-states and, as Philip Bromberg writes, to help patients develop the capacity to remember and be aware of a multitude of other self-states even while inhabiting one specific set of such states; what Bromberg calls "standing in the spaces" (1996).

Objectivity and subjectivity: A false binary?

For Mills, relational/Relational psychoanalysis privileges intersubjectivity over both subjectivity and objectivity; he believes that these perspectives favor conscious experience over the primacy of the unconscious. Most contemporary analysts do challenge a positivistic notion of objectivity; the ability of the analyst to be the holder of absolute, objective truth. But other than perhaps Stolorow and his colleagues (intersubjectivity/intersubjective theorists—relational but not Relational) who note that all dynamic formulations must assume intersubjectivity because there is no such thing as a separate, disembedded object or subject, Mills' assertion does not hold. Relational analysts move dialectically between exploring the patient's and analyst's subjectivity and mutual, intersubjective impact. Indeed, "...relational analysts, in speaking of a 'two-person psychology,' have never intended to deny that there are two distinct individuals with their own minds...and...inner worlds...Rather, the purpose of a 'two-person psychology' is to recognize the emergence of what Ogden calls 'the intersubjective analytic third.' These emergent properties of the dyad exist in dialectical relation to the individual subjectivities of the patient and the analyst" (Mitchell & Aron, 1999, p. xv). Thus, the intersubjective aspect does not subsume the subjectivities of patient and analyst, but exists as a point of analysis in tension with these factors. This emergent intersubjective third enhances the analyst's understanding of the patient's unsymbolized dynamics as they manifest in the analytic couple, leading to a deepening relationship and psychoanalytic growth.

This perceived privileging of the intersubjective has led Mills to the belief that "the most widely shared claim in the relational tradition is the assault on the analyst's epistemological authority to objective knowledge" quoting Stolorow (1998) who stated, "...there are no neutral or objective analysts...(p. 425)." Mills is correct that Relational (and some small r) analysts do adhere to a newer model of clinical technique and attitude in which the all-knowing, "neutral" "objective" analyst is now replaced with a creative, interactive, human who is willing to recognize his or her part in the psychoanalytic process. It's not just that relationalists simply believe analysts need to gratify patients by being warmer, more "human," and less remote. The fact is, a major change brought about by both relational (including but not limited to intersubjective theorists) and Relational thinking is that we no longer believe patients and analysts have isolated minds. The relational move beyond the "neutral" emerges from a significant rethinking of Freud's metapsychology, and drive theory/metapsychology has been reevaluated based on newer thinking about patients' minds as intersubjective rather than isolated. In fact, the concept of the relationally constituted self is a byproduct of scientific research done in recent years by infant research and attachment studies (Stern, D. N. 1985; BCPSG, 1998; Beebe & Lachmann, 2002; Fonagy, Gergely, Jurist & Target, 2002). How does this empirically derived data square with Mills' views about objective truth?

Additionally, Mills argues that in their rethinking of the analyst's access to objective truth relational analysts mistake mutuality for equality, and strive for each of these in ways that are harmful to patients. We are not aware of relational/Relational writing that suggests this, but can point the reader to Lewis Aron's frequently cited writing about the importance of mutuality in a two-person psychology, and the necessary differentiation between mutuality and symmetry.

In his seminal text on relational psychoanalysis, Aron (1996) writes that the analyst–patient relationship is mutual but asymmetrical. This stands in direct contrast to what strikes us as Mills' possible misunderstanding of the role of the analyst's power in relational thinking and practice. Ogden similarly argues for an asymmetric construction of the analytic third that respects the subjective experiences of both parties, stating that "the relationship of the roles of analyst and analysand structures the analytic interaction in a way that strongly privileges the exploration of the unconscious internal object world of the analysand" (p. 883).

An interesting contradiction arises in that Mills both asserts that the Relational analyst gives up his power and authority in the psychoanalytic relationship, while simultaneously robbing the patient of his agency. This internal inconsistency in his argument arises when he mistakenly asserts that "the whole notion of intersubjectivity within relational psychoanalysis rests on the problematic of reifying the dyadic system to that of an extant independent phenomenon" (this issue). The ascendancy of the intersubjective, he argues, takes over the entire psychoanalytic project, becoming the most important aspect of the therapeutic process, over and above the subjective experiences of both participants. The agency of the patient is thus, he claims, subsumed by the importance of the co-created dynamics of the relationship. Though careful thought about the intersubjective aspect of the dyad is important to the contemporary psychoanalytic process, asserting that it is the only and most important aspect of relational work is an extreme view that does not pertain to most theorists and practitioners of Relational psychoanalysis.

Self-disclosure

As for the author's concerns about misuse and overuse of self-disclosure, we don't know of a single relational/Relational analyst who would disagree with the necessity of vigilance in this area. Deliberate self-disclosure is seen as an option to be engaged in only selectively and with great caution—not an imperative. In addition, inadvertent disclosure, whether conscious or unconscious is a ubiquitous phenomenon that is important to acknowledge and track to the best of one's ability (Aron, 1996; Kuchuck, 2009; Barsness, 2018).

Mills specifically calls our attention to Aron's (1991) cue to invite the patient to explore the analyst's subjectivity, warning that this draws attention away from the patient and on to the analyst, potentially intruding on her experience. This "therapeutic excess" as Mills describes it might then lead to disclosures in the service of the analyst's narcissism. It is interesting that Mills does not disagree with Aron per se, but rather with a potential misunderstanding of Aron's words that would give undue license to the analyst to breach his responsibilities towards the patient. Further, Aron clearly states in this same paper that there might be "long intervals, when focusing on perceptions of the analyst is intrusive and disruptive," (p. 42) and thus contraindicated. This exploration of the analyst's subjectivity was not meant to be a prescription but a tool to be used with caution and sensitivity to the patient's needs.

Mills makes numerous thoughtful critiques about excesses and disclosures which inspire us to more rigorously examine our core assumptions. But his assessment of Davies' (1998) *singular* case example is taken out of context; boiling this sophisticated case down to a "penchant for confessing erotic desires to her patients" seems somewhat misleading and even if not intended as such, a statement that could be interpreted as a personal attack. As to "why is she flirting in the first place?" our answer would be because she is "more simply human than otherwise" (Sullivan, 1953) and therefore not exempt from transference-countertransference enactments.

As Relational analysts, our challenge is not to strive for the impossible—banishment of our subjectivity (most of which is unconscious), or achievement of neutrality and/or "perfect" clinical technique and behavior—whatever those might be (Kuchuck, 2014). Rather, as much as possible, we see our mission as making space for and reclaiming the most objectionable and shame-filled parts of ourselves and each other, which if avoided only lead to dissociation, secret-keeping, and potential for acting out (Kuchuck, in press). Davies' work addresses the dangers of locating the illness solely inside of the patient (Racker, 1957; Searles, 1978), as we may tend to extrude the bad, awkward, and more shameful parts of ourselves into the Other. Her examples can be thought of as unique illustrations, or potential ways the analyst might take ownership of the difficult feelings that may arise in the analytic relationship, demystifying troubling interactions and when available for conscious use, examining these within a relational context. Other analysts might choose to address transference-countertransference enactments in a more indirect manner, but this is a matter of clinical discretion, to be considered carefully for usefulness, and based on the comfort levels and dynamics of both patient and analyst (Black, 2003).

Wild psychoanalysis

It might be arguable that relational psychoanalysis has overcorrected for the positivistic Classical stance, swinging too far into relativism and lack of rigor. But this is a part of the internal dialogue which the movement itself continues to self-reflexively address. Despite this possibility, Mills' claims of the wild relational psychoanalyst who practices, "undisciplined use of self-disclosure, countertransference enactments, uninhibited risk taking, and flagrant boundary crossings that have the potential to materialize within this evolving framework of analytic practice" is an extreme mischaracterization at best. This is a "slippery slope" argument that takes the most drastic extrapolation of a theory as its paradigmatic example of r/Relational psychoanalysis gone awry. Mills' concerns seem to imply a lack of trust of the individual clinician and her sanity, her care for the patient, and her ability to contain her possible narcissistic excess.

Mills observes that relational analysts advocate for flexibility in the therapeutic frame in order to cater to the unique needs of each dyad. We agree, and would go so far as to remind the reader that Thomas Ogden suggests "it is the analyst's responsibility to reinvent psychoanalysis for each patient and continue to reinvent it throughout the course of the analysis" (p. 861, 2004). Mills doesn't seem to dispute this assertion and even quotes Irwin Hoffman's (1994) contention that we must "throw away the book" (p. 188), making what most relationalists would agree is a valid claim:

> The best we can aim for is to have an eclectic skill set (under the direction of clinical judgment, experience, self-reflectivity, and wisdom) to apply to whatever possible clinical realities we may encounter… But what if a neophyte was reading the relational literature and took (Hoffman's) statement literally? What about reliability and treatment efficacy if there is no proper method to which we can claim allegiance? Could this not lead to an "anything goes" approach conducted by a bunch of loose-cannons justifying interventions under the rubric of relationality? (Mills, 2005)

We would answer that indeed, this could and does happen whenever someone—of any theoretical background—is undertrained or otherwise enacting unconscious dynamics. Indeed, this problem arises in each theoretical school: earlier versions of such irresponsible behavior were practiced by our classical ancestors and colleagues and called "wild analysis" (Schafer, 1985). Perhaps Mills agrees with us on this because he seems to contradict himself or at least removes the specificity of his concern from the confines of relational theory when he adds, "Yet the same potential for abuse exists when applying any approach rigidly… thus the question of method will always remain an indeterminate question…" (2017). On this we can agree, as is also the case when Mills credits the relational perspective for advancing numerous treatment techniques and necessary changes in older, more rigid, and inhibiting analytic attitudes.

Moving forward

We will close as we began, by expressing genuine appreciation for the opportunity to respond to Mills' thoughtful, erudite essay. This is just the latest iteration of an ongoing dialogue that can help to clarify and expand the depth of our understandings of the often complex and overlapping meanings of relational theories and perspectives. We thank Jon Mills for moving the conversation forward and the panelists for responding with such incisive and thoughtful discussions.

Endnotes

1. Parts of this essay are based on an unpublished manuscript by Lewis Aron and Steven Kuchuck. We are grateful for Aron's permission to include that material here.
2. We are grateful to Lewis Aron for bringing this joke and its relevance here to our attention.

3. Because this is such a pervasive misunderstanding of relational psychoanalysis, perhaps there is work to be done in further defining ways of maintaining this dialectic, and more explicit relational psychoanalytic scholarship needed around elucidating the movement between the intrapsychic and intersubjective in psychoanalytic process.

References

Altman, N., Davies, J.M. (2003). A plea for constructive dialogue. *Journal of the American Psychoanalytic Association*, 51S, 145–161.

Aron, L. (1991). The patient's experience of the analyst's subjectivity. *Psychoanalytic Dialogues*, 1, 29–51.

Aron, L. (1996). *A Meeting of Minds: Mutuality in Psychoanalysis*. New York: Routledge.

Barsness, R. (2018). *Core Competencies of Relational Psychoanalysis: A Guide to Practice, Study, and Research*. New York: Routledge.

Beebe, B., & Lachmann, F. (2002). *Infant Research and Adult Treatment: Co-constructing Interactions*. Hillsdale, NJ: Analytic Press.

Bion, W. (1962). *Learning from Experience*. London: Heinemann.

Black, M.J. (2003). Enactment: Analytic musings on energy, language, and personal growth. *Psychoanalytic Dialogues*, 13, 633–655.

Boston Change Process Study Group. (1998). Non-interpretative mechanisms in psychoanalytic therapy: The "something more" than interpretation. *International Journal of Psychoanalysis*, 79, 903–921.

Bromberg, P. (1996). Standing in the spaces: The multiplicity of self and the psychoanalytic relationship. *Contemporary Psychoanalysis*, 32, 509–535.

Davies, J.M. (1998). Between the disclosure and foreclosure of erotic transference-countertransference: Can psychoanalysis find a place for adult sexuality? *Psychoanalytic Dialogues*, 8(6): 747–766.

Feiner, A.H. (1977). Countertransference and the anxiety of influence. *Contemporary Psychoanalysis*, 13, 1–15.

Fonagy, P., Gergely, G., Jurist, E., & Target, M. (Eds.). (2002). *Affect Regulation, Mentalization, and the Development of the Self.* New York: Other Press.

Freud, S. (1960). Jokes and their relation to the unconscious. In J. Strachey (Ed. and Trans.), *The standard edition of the complete psychological works of Sigmund Freud*, Vol. 8. London: Hogarth Press, pp. 9–236, (Original work published 1905).

Gill, M. (1979). The analysis of the transference. *Journal of the American Psychoanalytic Association*, 27, 263–288.

Greenberg, J. (1993). *Oedipus and Beyond: A Clinical Theory*. Cambridge, MA: Harvard University Press.

Greenberg, J., & Mitchell, S. (1983). *Object Relations in Psychoanalytic Theory*. Cambridge, MA: Harvard University Press.

Harris, A.E. (2011). The relational tradition: Landscape and canon. *Journal of the American Psychoanalytic Association*, 59, 701–735.

Hoffman, I. (1994). Dialectical thinking and therapeutic action in psychoanalytic process. *Psychoanalytic Quarterly*, 63, 187–218.

Katz, A., & Kelly, J. (Guest Eds.) (2016). Special issue: The analyst's body in the consulting room. *Psychoanalytic Perspectives*, 13(2).

Knoblauch, S. (1996). The play and interplay of passionate experience: Multiple organizations of desire. *Gender & Psychoanalysis*, 1, 323–344.

Kuchuck, S. (2009). Do ask, do tell?: Narcissistic need as a determinant of analyst self-disclosure. *The Psychoanalytic Review*, 96, 1007–1024.

Kuchuck, S. (2014). *Clinical Implications of the Psychoanalyst's Life Experience: When the Personal Becomes Professional*. New York: Routledge.

Kuchuck, S. (in press). *The Clinical Impact of the Psychotherapist's Subjectivity*. New York: Routledge.

Mills, J. (2002). *The Unconscious Abyss: Hegel's Anticipation of Psychoanalysis*. Albany, NY: SUNY Press.

Mills, J. (2005). A Critique of relational psychoanalysis. *Psychoanalytic Psychology*, 22(2), 155–188.

Mills, J. (2012). *Conundrums: A Critique of Contemporary Psychoanalysis*. New York: Routledge.

Mills, J. (2017). Challenging relational psychoanalysis: A critique of postmodernism and analyst self-disclosure. *Psychoanalytic Perspectives* 14 (3): 313–335.

Mitchell, S. (1988). *Relational Concepts in Psychoanalysis*. Cambridge, MA: Harvard University Press.

Mitchell, S., & Aron, L. (1999). *Relational Psychoanalysis: The Emergence of a Tradition*. Hillsdale, NJ: The Analytic Press.

Mitchell, S.A. (1996). Gender and sexual orientation in the age of postmodernism: The plight of the perplexed clinician. *Gender and Psychoanalysis*, 1:45–73.

Ogden, T.H. (2004). This art of psychoanalysis: Dreaming undreamt dreams and interrupted cries. *International Journal of Psychoanalysis*, 85, 857–877.

Ogden, T.H. (2007). Reading Harold Searles. *International Journal of Psychoanalysis*, 88, 353–369.

Racker, H. (1957). The Meanings and uses of countertransference. *Psychoanalytic Quarterly*, 26, 303–357.

Schafer, R. (1985). Wild analysis. *Journal of American Psychoanalytic Association*, 33(2), 275–299.

Searles H. (1990). Unconscious identification. In L.B. Boyer, & P. Giovacchini (Eds.), *Master Clinicians: On Treating the Regressed Patient*. New York, NY: Aronson, pp. 211–226.

Searles, H.F. (1978). A Dialogue on psychoanalysis. *Modern Psychoanalysis*, 3:3–11.

Sletvold, J. (2014). *The Embodied Analyst: From Freud and Reich to Relationality*. New York: Routledge.

Stern, D.N. (1985). *The Interpersonal World of the Infant*. New York: Basic Books.

Stolorow, R. (1998). Clarifying the intersubjective perspective: A reply to George Frank. *Psychoanalytic Psychology*, 15:424–427.

Stolorow, R.D., & Atwood, G.E. (1979). *Faces in a Cloud: Subjectivity in Personality Theory*. Northvale, N.J.: Aronson.

Sullivan, H.S. (1953). *The Interpersonal Theory of Psychiatry*. New York: W. W. Norton.

16 Challenging relational psychoanalysis

A reply to my critics

Jon Mills

Abstract: I reply to my critics' counter-critique of my lectures delivered at the 2015 Israeli symposium, *Challenging the Relational Approach: A Conference with Dr. Jon Mills*, held at Bar-Ilan University. Points of consilience are advanced in this important dialogue between my critique of relational psychoanalysis and contemporary perspectives that are advancing the value and future identity of the relational movement. I advocate for the need to develop a more robust philosophical foundation to relational theory that can be engaged through the investigation of truth and ontology.

There is nothing more exciting than a clash of ideas, except for, perhaps, sex. But as psychoanalysis shows, libidinal activity suffuses the very fabric of intellectual passion. I am honored that the Israeli contingent of IARPP and Bar-Ilan University had invited me for an international conference to challenge my critique of relational psychoanalysis. Even though I walked into the Lion's Den, I made many new friends despite the erudite, intellectually sophisticated, and philosophically shrewd arguments levelled against me by these kindred academics and clinicians. This event was truly in the spirit of what relationality practically and symbolically embodies, namely, a reaching out through the genuine desire to engage, hence an auspicious harbinger for the future of psychoanalytic dialogue.

I am sincerely grateful to my hosts and the Editors of *Psychoanalytic Perspectives* in their support of publishing these conference proceedings because it speaks to the openness of constructive discourse in advancing the field, whereas other groups and venues in this community are often closed to critique, the anathema of any intellectual discipline. And after all, is this not what psychoanalysis amounts to—an intellectual discipline capable of self-critique? Tribal or guild mentality is the death of any specialty (also see Barsness, 2018, p. 321). I am very pleased that the relational school has moved beyond its earlier insular, albeit revolutionary coalition (Govrin, 2017), to now stand as the world's most innovative contemporary psychoanalytic movement.

Due to space restrictions, I will offer a brief reply to each panelist's criticism of me and then address the substance of the Editors' analysis of my essay. As the then current president of IARPP, it is predictable that Chana Ullman would be less than flattering. But to characterize the detailed arguments in my paper (Mills, 2017) as merely being informal fallacies of logic, that is, "divisive rhetoric pushing differences to their extreme, and on creating straw men that are then vehemently destroyed" (Ullman, 2017, p. 337), is inane. She did not respond to the essence of my arguments, and hence only offered non sequiturs and ad hominem harangues. Speaking of extreme differences and straw men, let us take this one example:

> postmodernism is indispensable in freeing us from the simplistic assumption that there is only one person in our office who can see reality in an objective, rational way and that there is one truth waiting to be revealed, uncovered by the analyst's knowledge. (p. 337)

Here, Ullman is creating an extreme view of differences, a manufactured theoretical straw man, only to burn it. Freud nor did classical psychoanalysis ever espouse such a view because it would be preposterous. In fact, it was Freud (1900, pp. 613, 615), following Kant, who believed that we could never know reality in itself—the *Ding-an-sich* is occluded. Ullman would do better to pay attention to the work of Shlomit Yadlin-Gadot (2016), whose analysis of the complexities and epistemologies of truth are much more robust, nonbinary, and nuanced. As a complex topic, Yadlin-Gadot's (2017) novel introduction of a truth axis in psychoanalysis deserves our serious engagement, although we may wish to differentiate "our basic psychological needs" from our "epistemologies" (p. 343), not to mention the ontological parameters that make truth and epistemology possible.

Boaz Shalgi (2017) also engages the themes of truth, objectivity, subjectivity, and intersubjectivity in a most coherent and sensible manner, and reminds us that we inhabit these domains all at once. We are in simpatico when it comes to viewing the psychic world and the clinical encounter as process, especially in relation to his appreciation of Hegel's philosophy, although we interpret him differently (see Mills, 2002). The one problematic Shalgi faces, however, is making the claim that within these dimensions, "no one of them [has] precedence over the other" (p. 346). Not only does this open us up to the specter of relativism and the sanitization of Being, it suggests there is no ontological ground (even as a process of becoming) that conditions the coming into being of truth, objectivity, subjectivity, and intersubjectivity. The question becomes not whether all spheres of reality are operative at once, but rather, Are they derived from earlier ontological conditions?

This brings us to the question of metaphysics, what Liran Razinsky (2017) is railing against when he attempts to champion postmodern thinking by chiding me for not critiquing the "original postmodern ideas themselves" rather than relational authors' "who use them" (p. 357), as if this would have been remotely possible given the time limitations, let alone relevant, given that the conference venue was on relational psychoanalysis. To suggest I should have critiqued the key figures in 20th century continental philosophy instead of relational theorists who have adopted many postmodern ideas and their philosophical implications seems rather supercilious, if not ridiculous. But Razinsky is correct that I take objection to the arbitrarily culled and undisciplined use of concepts void of theoretical coherence and systematic articulation. Although I have no objection to philosophy in general, it is the logic, scope, quality, and sophistication of arguments that matter. Razinsky is mistaken in saying that I believe postmodernism "should be kept out of psychoanalysis" (p. 361), rather I would advocate for a more developed, systematic, and theoretically cohesive body of ideas which may contribute to an overall relational philosophy. This is conceptual work that lies ahead for the relational community to undertake.

I agree with Razinsky that psychoanalysis should embrace the humanities as there is much fertile ground for a mutual simpatico; but I must once again correct his wholesale mischaracterization of me as "rejecting the relational school" (p. 362), when I have only critiqued certain theoretical aspects negatively while highlighting its positive dimensions, particularly in terms of clinical praxis. And given that I have openly referred to myself as a "relational practitioner" for decades (Mills, 2005a,b; Mills, 2012), this misperception needs to be rectified for the record. But the one thing Razinsky does not address in his criticism of me is the historical contrast between the Western tradition of metaphysics and the relatively new postmodern analysis in the history of ideas. The essence of my critique of pomocentrism is that it does not sufficiently offer its own ontology, and depending upon what theorist one consults, it may even negate the notion of a science or logic of Being. To illustrate this problem in postmodern negation, I would like to draw attention to Razinsky's own confessed motives behind theorization: we should "be careful when criticizing psychoanalytic stances for their affinity to postmodernism—it really might play into the hands of the resistance to psychoanalysis" (p. 362). In other words, don't reject postmodernism because it could lead to political suicide. Hardly an argument interested in the greater metaphysical principles governing the ground, scope, and meaning of ontology, truth, and the philosophy of culture.

The one main theme that emerges from the panelists' critique of my critique is the implication for the Relational perspective's notion of and critique of truth. But what do we mean by truth? It is a word—a semiotic—that cannot be taken for granted, which is the very thing under debate. With the exception of Yadlin-Gadot's thoughtful analysis, the term "truth" being used here seems to imply an objectivist epistemology tied to scientific realism based on empirical facts, when this is the very thing in question that postmodern theories wish to challenge and denounce. By setting up a false binary between subject and object, self and world, truth and falsity, the concept loses its original signification and connection to archaic ontology. It was the pre-Socratics who alerted us to this most important concept, what they called *aletheia* (ἀλήθεια), where truth is defined as a process of disclosedness or unconcealedness. Here, the notion of truth as disclosure or unconcealment cannot be properly discussed outside of a conceptual discourse on the presencing of Being, what I have addressed elsewhere as a distinct psychoanalytic contribution to truth conditioned on unconscious processes reappropriated from Heidegger's project of fundamental ontology (Mills, 2014). Here, the notions of truth and being are inseparably connected, and hence any significance to the postmodern emphasis on language, culture, the socio-symbolic order, identity politics, the displacement of metaphysics, and so forth, must reconcile the ontological parameters in which consciousness and society arise. It is on this account that I have offered my own dialectical metaphysics based on unconscious process that conditions the coming into being of subjectivity and intersubjectivity within the objective energetic world of matter and our physical embodiment (Mills, 2010).

Steve Kuchuck and Rachel Sopher (2017) provide a very thorough and detailed review essay of my critique, of which I can only address certain portions due to page constraints. I find their distinction between "small r" and "big R" relational models useful, as it shows the differentiation and progression of the movement since Mitchell and Greenberg's inaugural work, but it also problematizes the issues when there may be a cross-fertilization and confluence of small and big R models, especially when they claim "there is no singular 'school' of big R Relational psychoanalysis" (p. 365). So, here those identified with the movement are either relegated to factions or are identified as independents within a coterie. Even more problematic is the claim that "each Relational analyst defines and practices the perspective in his or her own particular way" (p. 365), which on one level maybe said to generically apply to any practitioner based on the nature of their training and group identifications, but this also highlights the individuality, even possible radical subjectivity, employed by the analyst, which opens us up to potential charges of relativism. If we cannot define, let alone agree upon, a common classification system and their differential elements, the very thing that is most contestable, then we have difficulty finding any shared common ground among those identified with the movement other than professed plurality and personal preference for particular theories and clinical attitudes. So even if I am "conflating" fine distinctions established by the movement's founders, if they cannot agree upon what sets their differences apart from the historical specificity of terminology they employ, then this appears to be begging the question of what constitutes relationality in the first place. I think these self-definitional propositions need to be set out more clearly so I and others are not confused by the presupposed meaning of terms, which are always under hermeneutic mediation.

There are many laid accusations that I equivocate, distort, collapse distinctions, and oversimplify what relational authors actually say in vast bodies of works, including revisionist extensions and emendations to earlier, previously published positions that are out of date. Fair enough. It is hard to be aware of, let alone read, everyone in the field. I have certainly offered more extended engagement and arguments in my book *Conundrums* (2012) than I could have addressed in such precision at a symposium, including a more detailed critique of the concepts of intersubjectivity and drive theory. My criticisms of Benjamin and Stolorow that Kuchuck and Sopher draw attention to are more about scholarly accuracy than in applying various philosophical concepts toward advancing relational perspectives, as well as with Mitchell, who later acknowledged the locus of the drives and embodiment within relational processes. But you can't claim that everything is relational (Mitchell, 1988, pp. 2, 4, 54; Greenberg, 1991, p. vii, 69–70) and then backtrack and retract such earlier theoretical commitments without suffering some philosophical embarrassment. These overarching absolute statements are equally problematic with some of the great metaphysical systems in Western thought, so I suppose the relational founders are in good company.

The one criticism I must insist on against relational propaganda is the fabricated difference of a one-person versus two-person psychology. When Relationalists claim that "we no longer believe that patients and analysts have isolated minds" (Kuchuck & Sopher, 2017, p. 371), they have to know this is an invented binary designed to create an appearance of incredulity in order to depart from (and disparage) classical psychoanalysis, when Freud never said any such thing in all of his *Gesammelte Werke*. I would invite anyone to point me out any direct quote where Freud says we have an isolated (solipsistic-monadic) mind; and I would be humbled to stand corrected. As I have argued at length (Mills, 2012, pp. 90–96), the one-person isolated mind allegation is a *myth* designed to exaggerate differences that philosophically do not exist between traditional and contemporary adherents. In fact, it would be impossible in Freud's system to espouse such a view, as I have shown (Mills, 2012, pp. 75–90), because this would negate the object-seeking activity of the ego-drives (*Ichtriebe*), the nature of attachment and identification, Freud's relational theory of mind, the social dimension to classical theory, and the interpersonal nature of therapeutic technique. Even in his notion of primacy narcissism, before the differentiation and developmental growth of the ego occurs, Freud (1914, pp. 75–77, 100) is clear that the infant and mother are one and the same, an undifferentiated matrix where self and world are a unity. In his later works, he echoes this earlier sentiment when he declares that "originally the ego includes everything, later it separates off an external world from itself" (Freud, 1930, p. 68). So, here in its original psychic form, symbiosis "includes everything." There is nothing solipsistic, let alone isolated, about the mind when the external objective world of reality is already incorporated in the infant's interiority as an ontic (hence relational) encounter with its ontological thrownness, whether this be conceived of as biological, environmental, cultural, or due to the brute materiality of nature that imposes itself on us, or otherwise.

Of course, my views on the admonition of excessive self-disclosure are not new to relational critiques (Maroda, 2010; Loewenthal & Samuels, 2014; Roth, 2017), and I am pleased to see that Kuchuck and Sopher are in agreement with the need to be vigilant in this regard, despite appearing overly qualifying (if not apologetic) for other analysts' behavior. But I am also in agreement with their overall concern that we should not judge others without knowing the full context of what actually transpires in the session. And for the record, despite my unease, as we have all been there, I do not place any prescriptive approach on how one *ought* to navigate clinical praxis, let alone malign or "attack" someone's character for acting on their most well-intentioned clinical judgements. It is for this reason I believe the relational approach cuts across many therapeutic landscapes and is attractive as a general therapeutic sensibility that can apply to many different mental health therapists working in a variety of diverse clinical environments. Traditional psychoanalysis cannot claim to boast such efficacy.

The overall tenor of many of the criticisms levelled against me is in reaction to a false dichotomy between objective and subjective epistemologies that are believed to be operative. It appears that because I adopt the belief in an objective world, this discounts a subjective world full of rich content, minutia, context, and continuity, and that only an objective view of reality is the correct one. This is not the case. These are divisions invented by rival disciplines, such as observational, experimental, and computational science, mathematics, and deductive logic, which uphold reason and evidence as the gold standards of "truth," whereas subjectivity, phenomenology, and psychological experience of all types—from affect, intuition, perception, the idiosyncrasy of thought, and the life of feeling, are inferior models that explain and interpret reality. This makes it seem like there is a metaphysical battle taking place between subjectivist and objectivist camps (Kuchuck & Sopher's statements such as, what "an objectivist might believe" [p. 367], and "Most contemporary analysts do challenge a positivist notion of objectivity" [p. 370] do not help); when in actuality, both domains are always operative and dialectically, mutually implicative for either phenomenon to exist. What is important here is finding theoretical rehabilitation where such bifurcations are contextualized and unified within an overarching relational philosophy that does not negate the natural sciences, propositional logic, or the phenomenology of the lived experience, even though we may conclude we emphasize and value some aspects over others.

I wish to end on a note of conciliatory optimism. The one corrective I am most appreciative of in reading the panelists' and editors' comments is the reassurance that small r and big R Relational psychoanalysis has not abandoned the primacy of the unconscious, and has instead proclaimed to have embraced it and have incorporated its significance in both theory and practice. This is very reassuring, as my earlier readings of relational authors seemed to have neglected its importance and value, as my book details. This equanimity reaffirms the one thing that unifies psychoanalytic theory throughout every school by reinstating the omnipresence of unconscious process. The overall appreciation I have is there is acknowledgment that the unconscious is still very much alive in relational discourse and that by bringing the unconscious back to the foreground deepens relational theory. As a sidebar, Merton Gill was my supervisor, and that his then interpersonal approach to here-and-now transference monitoring and interpretation was not merely focused on conscious transactions; rather, it was deeply attuned to unconscious communications within the here-and-now relational dynamics of the treatment.

I also stand corrected on my misperception that the concept of "essence" and the notion of the "self" has not been anesthetized in relational theory, but rather has been rejuvenated as the movement takes on theoretical augmentation and refinement. I am encouraged by seeing this willingness to engage in self-critique, because it means that the relational movement will only move forward, especially given that it has attained international prominence. I also encourage healthy internal debate, as this tends to spur on novel developments in theory and praxis that often take on unexpected new directions. In the end, we all want a vibrant professional and intellectual discipline that contributes to the human sciences, society, and the humanities.

References

Barsness, R.E. (Ed). (2018). *Core Competencies of Relational Psychoanalysis*. London: Routledge.

Freud, S. (1900). *The Interpretation of Dreams. Standard Edition*, Vol. 5, London: Hogarth Press.

Freud, S. (1914). *On Narcissism: An Introduction. Standard Edition*, Vol. 14, 67–104.

Freud, S. (1930). *Civilization and its Discontents. Standard Edition*, Vol. 21, London: Hogarth Press.

Govrin, A. (2017). Introduction to The Relational Approach and its Critics: A Conference with Dr. Jon Mills. *Psychoanalytic Perspectives*, 14, 309–312.

Greenberg, J. (1991). *Oedipus and Beyond: A Clinical Theory*. Cambridge: Harvard University Press.

Kuchuck, S., & Sopher, R. (2017). Relational Psychoanalysis out of Context: Response to Jon Mills. *Psychoanalytic Perspectives*, 14, 364–376.

Loewenthal, D., & Samuels, A. (Eds.). (2014). *Relational Psychotherapy, Psychoanalysis and Counselling*. London: Routledge.

Maroda, K. (2010). *Psychodynamic Techniques*. New York: Guilford.

Mills, J. (2002). *The Unconscious Abyss: Hegel's Anticipation of Psychoanalysis*. Albany: SUNY Press.

Mills, J. (2005a). A Critique of Relational Psychoanalysis. *Psychoanalytic Psychology*, 22(2), 155–188.

Mills, J. (2005b). *Treating Attachment Pathology*. Northvale, NJ: Jason Aronson.

Mills, J. (2010). *Origins: On the Genesis of Psychic Reality*. Montreal: McGill-Queens University Press.

Mills, J. (2012). *Conundrums: A Critique of Contemporary Psychoanalysis*. New York: Routledge.

Mills, J. (2014). Truth. *Journal of the American Psychoanalytic Association*, 62(2), 267–293.

Mills, J. (2017). Challenging Relational Psychoanalysis: A Critique of Postmodernism and Analyst Self-Disclosure. *Psychoanalytic Perspectives*, 14: 313–335.

Mitchell, S.A. (1988). *Relational Concepts in Psychoanalysis: An Integration*. Cambridge, MA: Harvard University Press.

Razinsky, L. (2017). Psychoanalysis and Postmodernism: A Response to Dr. Jon Mills's "Challenging Relational Psychoanalysis: A Critique of Postmodernism and Analyst Self-Disclosure." *Psychoanalytic Perspectives*, 14: 356–363.

Roth, M. (2017). Projective identification and Relatedness: A Kleinian Perspective. *Psychoanalytic Perspectives*, 14: 350–355.

Shalgi, B. (2017). Relational Psychoanalysis and the Concepts of Truth and Meaning: Response to Jon Mills. *Psychoanalytic Perspectives*, 14: 346–349.

Ullman, C. (2017). Straw Men, Stereotypes, and Constructive Dialogue: A Response to Mills's Criticism of the Relational Approach. *Psychoanalytic Perspectives*, 14: 336–340.

Yadlin-Gadot, S. (2016). *Truth Matters: Theory and Practice in Psychoanalysis*. Leiden: Brill/Rodopi.

Yadlin-Gadot, S. (2017). On Multiple Epistemologies in Theory and Practice: A Response to Jon Mills's "Challenging Relational Psychoanalysis: A Critique of Postmodernism and Analyst Self-Disclosure". *Psychoanalytic Perspectives*, 14, 341–345.

Index